THE CONSULTANT'S BIG BOOK SERIES

THE CONSULTANT'S BIG BOOK OF ORGANIZATION DEVELOPMENT TOOLS

50 Reproducible, Customizable Interventions to Help Solve Your Clients' Problems

Other books in "The Consultant's Big Book" series

- Silberman, *The Consultant's Big Book of Reproducible Surveys and Questionnaires* (0071408827)
- Silberman, *The Consultant's Toolkit* (0071362614)

THE CONSULTANT'S BIG BOOK SERIES

THE CONSULTANT'S BIG BOOK OF ORGANIZATION DEVELOPMENT TOOLS

50 Reproducible, Customizable Interventions to Help Solve Your Clients' Problems

Edited by Mel Silberman, Ph.D.

McGraw-Hill

New York   Chicago San Francisco   Lisbon London
Madrid   Mexico City   Milan New Delhi San Juan
Seoul Singapore Sydney   Toronto

CONTENTS

PART IV: ORGANIZATION DEVELOPMENT   201

PREFACE

The Consultant's Big Book of Organization Development Tools has been compiled with the goal of providing incredible value for the consultant who wants to use structured interventions as a vital part of his or her consultation approach.

For over 30 years, I have been a consultant who seeks to help others improve their current effectiveness and to facilitate change. I can't tell you how many times I wished that I could have at my fingertips a variety of organizational development tools, designed by expert consultants, that I could freely use to meet the needs of my clients. To expect such resources would have been unthinkable at a time when they were limited to proprietary use or would cost the user a small fortune.

Times have changed. Many consultants view other consultants as their partners, not their competitors. Fortunately, I know a lot of them. And I have invited a talented and willing group of consultants to offer their tools to guide your efforts and, if you wish, to give to your clients.

The Consultant's Big Book of Organization Development Tools is a collection of 50 intervention activities you can use to help solve individual, team, and organizational performance problems. These intervention activities are organized in five areas: *Leadership Development; Employee Development; Team Development; Organizational Development;* and *Strategic Planning and Change Management.*

The section on *Leadership Development* focuses on developing the attitudes and skills needed by those in key management positions within an organization. With these tools, you can help them do a better job as coaches, motivators, and facilitators of performance improvement.

The section on *Employee Development* concentrates on ways to improve how the people who carry out the day-to-day functions of the organization are trained and supported back on the job. With these tools, you can cultivate new insights into how your client brings out the best in its people and optimally manages their daily performance.

The section on *Team Development* centers on the developmental tools needed by the project teams and staff groups that drive the success of today's team-based organizations. With these tools, you can promote team cohesion, creativity, and conflict resolution.

The section on *Organizational Development* emphasizes the processes that help the entire organization function as a coherent, energized system. With these tools, you can help your client organization recognize its current level of success and identify new initiatives that will bring it to greater heights.

The section on *Strategic Planning and Change Management* tackles the problem of how organizations move from "business as usual" to "business as unusual." With these tools, you can help your client to clarify its vision and carefully strategize how it can be achieved.

You can use the tools in this book with your clients in a variety of settings:

✔ Meetings and retreats,

✔ One-to-one coaching or consultation, and

✔ Training sessions.

These tools are especially designed to facilitate nonthreatening discussion of the difficult "soft issues" involving organizational politics, interdepartmental communication, conflict among leaders, and so forth that are often the cause of serious business problems. Most of the tools consist of structured activities that enable your client to explore problems that have previously been unattended. The activities, by themselves, are not meant to solve problems directly. Rather they serve as the catalyst for a rich conversation about the concerns that block an organization from becoming more productive and effective.

All of the activities featured here are highly participatory. They are designed with the belief that learning and change best occur through experience and reflection. As opposed to preaching or lecturing, experiential activities place people directly within a concrete situation. Typically, participants are asked to solve a problem, complete an assignment, or communicate information.

Often, the task can be quite challenging. Sometimes, it can also be a great deal of fun. The bottom line, however, is that participants become active partners in the learning of new concepts or in the development of new ideas.

The experiences contained in the activities you are about to read can also be of two kinds: simulated and real-world. Although some may find them to be artificial, well-designed simulations can provide an effective analogy to real-world experiences. They also have the advantage of being time-saving shortcuts to longer, drawn-out activities. Sometimes, of course, there is no substitute for real-world experience. Activities that engage clients in actual, ongoing work can serve as a powerful mechanism for change.

Experience, by itself, is not always "the best teacher." Reflecting on the experience, however, can yield wisdom and insight. You will find that the activities in this book contain helpful guidelines for reflection. Expect a generous selection of questions to process or debrief the actual activities.

All of the activities have been written for ease of use. A concise overview of each activity is provided. You will be guided, step-by-step, through the activity instructions. All of the necessary participant materials are included. Any materials you need to prepare in advance have been kept to a minimum. Special equipment or physical arrangements are seldom needed.

Best of all, the activities are designed so that you can easily modify or customize them to your specific requirements. Also, time allocations are readily adaptable. Furthermore, many of the activities are "frame exercises"—generic activities that can be used for many topics or subject matter areas. You will find it easy to plug in the content relevant to your client's circumstances.

As you conduct any of these activities, bear in mind that experiential activity is especially successful if you do a good job as facilitator. Here are some common mistakes people make facilitating experiential activities:

1. *Motivation:* Participants aren't invited to buy into the activity themselves or sold the benefits of joining in. Participants don't know what to expect during the exercise.

2. *Directions:* Instructions are lengthy and unclear. Participants cannot visualize what the facilitator expects from them.

3. *Group Process:* Subgroups are not composed effectively. Group formats are not changed to fit the requirements of each activity. Subgroups are left idle.

4. *Energy:* Activities move too slowly. Participants are sedentary. Activities are long or demanding when they need to be short or relaxed. Participants do not find the activity challenging.

5. *Processing:* Participants are confused or overwhelmed by the questions posed to them. There is a poor fit between the facilitator's questions and the goals of the activity. The facilitator shares his or her opinions before first hearing the participants' views.

To avoid these pitfalls, follow these steps:

I. Introduce the activity.
   1. Explain your objectives.
   2. Sell the benefits.
   3. Convey enthusiasm.
   4. Connect the activity to previous activities.
   5. Share personal feelings and express confidence in participants.

II. Help participants know what they are expected to do.
   1. Speak slowly.
   2. Use visual backup.
   3. Define important terms.
   4. Demonstrate the activity.

III. Manage the group process.
   1. Form groups in a variety of ways.
   2. Vary the number of people in any activity based upon that exercise's specific requirements.

3. Divide participants into teams before giving further directions.

4. Give instructions separately to groups in a multipart activity.

5. Keep people busy.

6. Inform the subgroups about time frames.

IV. Keep participants involved.

1. Keep the activity moving.

2. Challenge the participants.

3. Reinforce participants for their involvement in the activity.

4. Build physical movement into the activity.

V. Get participants to reflect on the activity's implications.

1. Ask relevant questions.

2. Carefully structure the first debriefing experiences.

3. Observe how participants are reacting to the group debriefing.

4. Assist a subgroup that is having trouble processing an activity.

5. Hold your own reactions until after hearing from participants.

The tools in this collection include downloadable, customizable handouts that you can reproduce and use with clients. Enjoy them.

Mel Silberman
Princeton, New Jersey

1

LEADERSHIP DEVELOPMENT

1

COMMUNICATING CLEARLY AND EFFECTIVELY

Richard Whelan and Robert Merritt

Overview   This "one-way communication" activity is designed to help participants learn about the many roadblocks inherent in the communication process. Through a simple and entertaining exercise in "giving directions," participants will experience various interferences to being able to effectively give and receive messages.

Suggested Time   45 minutes

Materials Needed
- ✔ Easel
- ✔ Flip chart pad
- ✔ Markers
- ✔ Forms A, B, C, D

Procedure

1. Ask who in the group see themselves as effective communicators. Choose two of the participants who have raised their hands. Of these two, ask which one likes to talk. This is the person who will be the "speaker" and the other will be the "listener."

2. The listener will be given a marker and asked to go to the easel that is in the front of the room. The listener will stand at the easel, back to the rest of the group.

3. The speaker will be instructed to take the templates (Forms A, B, C, D) and stand in the center of the room, back to the listener so that what is drawn will not be seen by the speaker. (The remaining participants can sit or stand anywhere they choose, as long as they are facing the listener.)

Contact Information: Richard Whelan and Robert Merritt, Associated Consultants for Training and Education, PO Box 5312, Deptford, NJ 08096, 609-227-4273.

4. Tell the speaker to describe what is drawn on one or more of the templates to the listener so that it can be drawn on the flip chart paper. **Privately,** give the speaker the following instructions:

   ✔ In describing the figure to be drawn, if there is a geometric figure on it, like a triangle or square, it cannot be called a triangle or square. Another description, such as a half-diamond or box, must be used. A circle could be described as "a 360-degree line that ends at its starting point." (We had one experience in which this activity was done with a group of professional football players and one, in describing a triangle, said, "Imagine the top of a goal post where the two end poles fell in to each other.")

   ✔ The speaker cannot look at what is being drawn or ask any questions about what or how the listener is doing; just proceed until the speaker feels all four figures (or whichever of the four have been chosen) have been described.

   ✔ The speaker may show the templates to the remainder of the participants before describing them to the listener. (You might also decide to provide copies for the remainder of the participants.)

   Tell the listener not to ask any questions or say anything until the exercise is completed.

5. The other participants in the room may react in any manner they choose as long as they are not giving help or suggestions to the listener.

6. At the conclusion of the drawing(s), the speaker looks at the completed drawing(s) and shows the listener what they were supposed to look like.

7. The facilitator can ask the following questions of the listener and the speaker as part of the processing of the activity and their learning from it:

   ✔ How did you do in your role?
   ✔ How did you feel while you were in your role?
   ✔ How successful were you?
   ✔ What was difficult about the activity?
   ✔ What would have made the task easier?

8. After the speaker and listener have had a chance to respond to the questions, solicit audience reaction to the process, obtaining their observations and learning.

9. Ask all the participants these questions:
   - ✔ What helps you to be clearer in your communication with others?
   - ✔ What helps you to listen accurately and retain what has been said to you?

Variation

A modification in the design can be used, such as:

- ✔ For the first template, follow the instructions as described above.
- ✔ For the second, allow the speaker to ask questions while still facing away from the listener.
- ✔ For the third, allow only the listener to ask questions while facing the easel.
- ✔ For the fourth template, allow the speaker to actually view what is being drawn as a way of modifying any future instructions, without making changes to previous instructions or trying to correct any "mistakes" the listener may have made in drawing.

As part of the processing questions, ask what differences, if any, these changes had on the successful completion of the task.

As part of this variation, questions can also be asked after each one of the drawings, such as:

- ✔ How was this different from the previous method?
- ✔ What situations in real life mimic this type of communication?
- ✔ How can you compensate for this type of limitation?

FIGURE 1: FORM A

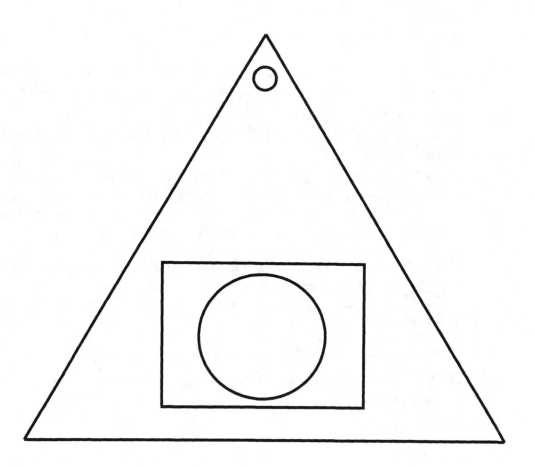

FIGURE 2: FORM B

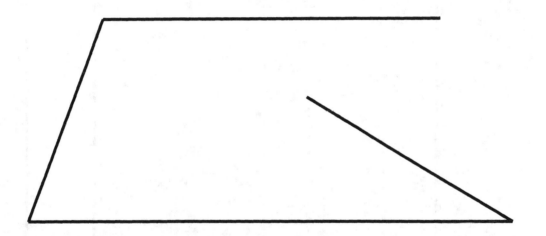

FIGURE 3: FORM C

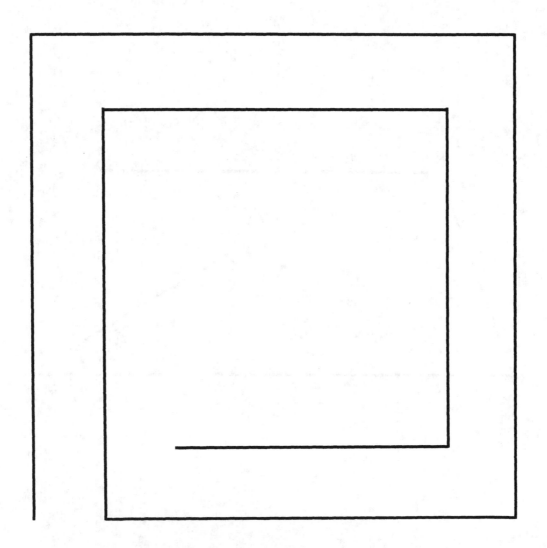

FIGURE 4: FORM D

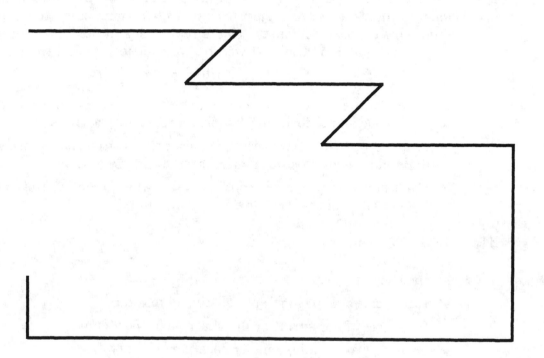

2

MANAGING TIME EFFECTIVELY

Steve Sugar and Bob Preziosi

Overview   Time scheduling is never done in a vacuum. Even the most meticulously planned days are subject to changes to accommodate the unforeseen. This exercise demonstrates the real time and flexibility that are required in planning the next workday and some personal time.

Using this exercise, a facilitator can:

✔ Demonstrate the day-to-day demands that require participants to be flexible and to focus on the most important priorities.

✔ Demonstrate the need to establish a set of priorities along with your daily plan to guide participants through their workday.

✔ Identify ways that people can be flexible when handling the changing demands of the workday.

Suggested Time   75 to 120 minutes

Materials Needed   ✔ Overhead projector

✔ Newsprint or flip chart and felt-tipped markers

✔ One piece of newsprint or flip chart paper per team

✔ Form A (Case Study), one for each participant

✔ Form B (Schedule), one for each participant

✔ Form C (Day Log), two for each participant

✔ Form D (Messages), one for each participant

✔ Set of telephone messages, one for each team

Contact Information: Steve Sugar, The Game Group, 10320 Kettledrum Court, Ellicott City, MD 21042, 410-418-4930, info@thegamegroup.com, www.thegamegroup.com.

Bob Preziosi, School of Business and Entrepreneurship, Nova Southeastern University, 3301 College Avenue, Fort Lauderdale, FL 33314, 954-262-5111, preziosi@sbe.nova.edu.

✔ Masking tape

✔ Whistle, bell, or other noise-making device

✔ Stopwatch or timekeeping device

Procedure 1. Distribute one set of Forms A, B, C, and D to each participant.

Round 1: Individual Assignments

2. Define the task for round 1: "This is a planning exercise. It is the last half-hour of your Tuesday workday. You are planning for Wednesday, your next workday. You have 15 minutes to review Form A: Case Study and Form B: Schedule, then prepare your Day Log on Form C for the next day."

3. Begin play for round 1

4. After 15 minutes, stop the exercise.

5. Have participants form teams of 3 to 5. Give each team one blank Day Log (Form C).

Round 2: Team Assignments

6. Define the task for round 2: "It is still the night before your next workday. Each team must prepare one Day Log that represents input from the entire team. You have 25 minutes to prepare a new log. At the end of the allotted time, one member of your team will present your log to the rest of the participants."

7. Begin round 2.

8. After 3 minutes, stop play and announce: "It is now Wednesday morning. Continue scheduling your day." (*Note:* Changing the time from Tuesday evening to Wednesday morning allows you to use telephone message interventions.)

9. Eight minutes into the exercise, distribute one copy of telephone message 1 to each team.

To:　　　Time Management Team

From:　　Dr. Berringer

Message: The staff meeting has been rescheduled for 2 p.m.

10. Thirteen minutes into the exercise, distribute one copy of telephone message 2 to each team.

To:	Time Management Team
From:	Spouse
Message:	Car broke down. Had to put car in repair shop. Please pick me up on the way home.

(*Note:* Driving to spouse's office causes a 15-minute detour.)

11. After another 5 minutes, hand out one copy of telephone message 3 to each team.

To:	Time Management Team
From:	Property Management Office
Message:	There has been a water leak in the cafeteria. The cafeteria will be closed until next Monday.

12. After 25 minutes, call time to end round 2.

Round 3: Team Presentations

13. Define the task for round 3: "Each team must present its plan for the next day to the rest of the group. Select a team member to make a 3-minute presentation and prepare a sheet of newsprint or flip chart paper with your team's plan on it. You have 15 minutes."

14. Distribute one sheet of newsprint or flip chart paper, strips of masking tape, and several felt-tipped markers to each team.

15. After 15 minutes, call time.

16. Have each team present its plan to the group. Time limit for each presentation is 3 minutes.

17. Debrief the exercise using the suggested questions.

Debriefing Questions This is the time to help players reflect on their experiences during the exercise and ask them what they learned from the experience and how they can apply it.

What did you experience?

- How did you feel when you first received the information?
- What was the hardest part of getting started? What made it easy?
- What happened when your team first met?
- What was helpful or not helpful in your team meetings? Why?
- Who played what roles in helping the team complete the Day Log (i.e., information provider, negotiator, etc.)?

What learning took place?

- What one major concept or idea did you learn?
- What did you learn from your individual work?
- What did you learn from your team work?
- Did you hear things you've heard before but have not started doing yet? Why?

What applications can be made to real life and the workplace?

- From your experiences here, what behaviors would you take back to your own personal scheduling? Your interactions at the office? Your interactions at home?
- What are the challenges in planning and sticking to a daily routine back on the job? How can you make those challenges work positively for you?
- What are your best suggestions for balancing your own work needs with the needs of others?

Variations

1. Expand the times for each round and for team presentations.
2. Create your own telephone messages to substitute for the ones used in the exercise. Add additional telephone messages, as needed.
3. Change days to match the actual day of workshop. For a Thursday workshop you could change the scenario to Wednesday evening and Thursday morning.
4. Have each team record its Day Log on a piece of newsprint or flip chart paper. Allow all teams to review all other teams' Day Logs. Then have each team hold another meeting to revise its Day Log, as necessary.
5. Use this exercise with a cyber team, using computerized scheduling and e-mail messages.
6. Eliminate the personal items in the evening.

CASE STUDY: FORM A

It is Tuesday afternoon and you are now planning your next workday.

You work at Stone Container Corporation (SCC) as a Project Manager. The work site is 20 to 25 minutes from your home (only 15 minutes in early traffic). Your normal workday is from 8:30 a.m. to 5 p.m. Your normal routine has you awaken at 6 a.m., do 30 minutes of exercises, shower, dress, read the morning paper, have coffee at home, and get to work around 8:20 a.m. You usually check in at your desk and then catch a quick breakfast in the cafeteria.

> (*Personal note:* Your best biorhythm times are from 8:30 to 11:30 a.m. and from 3:30 to 6 p.m. Your worst biorhythm time is from 1 to 3 p.m.)

You have several important tasks waiting for your attention on Wednesday. The most important (A1) is the Rosensweig Mineral Easement (RME) project due on Dr. Berringer's desk by 10 a.m. on Thursday. It is heavy work that requires clear thinking, good planning, and attention to detail. You will need at least one hour of solid, uninterrupted time. You may need another 30 minutes of busy work to coordinate the details of the project. A review of the work may require another 30 minutes before you submit the project to Dr. Berringer.

You have a batch of phone calls to attend to. Most of the calls can be handled by your assistant, Kim Kostoroski. But the Rosensweig Mineral Easement (RME) may require your attention for 30 minutes of uninterrupted telephone time to map out a strategy for your resource plan.

Your office is a little too convenient to pedestrian traffic. The Conference Center has booked rooms for meetings all day, starting at 9:30 a.m. The Conference Center is available from 8 a.m.

14

SCHEDULE: FORM B

Remembering that minor crises are always surfacing, this is how your schedule looks for tomorrow.

8:00-9:45 Informal meeting with Marie Dillon (extension 472). You are helping Marie write a Project Proposal. Although it is Marie's proposal, you promised your help. The proposal is due next week but Marie needs time to line up clerical support. Marie always gets into the office before 8 a.m.

10:00-11:35 Staff meeting scheduled for conference room B. You have a resource presentation prepared (overheads and handouts are in your desk). You need 15 minutes to brush up on your presentation. You will be allowed to leave after you have finished the presentation. You are scheduled to present from 10:30 to 10:45.

12:00-1:00 Lunch meeting in the cafeteria with Jason David (extension 603) of Production Management. Jason wants to get your feedback on a new product line.

1:30-2:30 Client meeting with Matthew Glyder (475-6047) of Marina Services. Matt's company, a marginal customer, is interested in the new roller container line, a small profit-making item that can lead to sales of other products. Your meeting is scheduled for conference room A.

3:15-4:00 Informal meeting with Bert Randolph (337-9001) of Sports 'R Fun, a client who can always be counted on for a medium-size order. Bert's meetings are always a great deal of fun but usually run past their scheduled closure. Your meeting is scheduled for conference room A.

5:30 Pick up kids (spouse will go directly home to prepare dinner).

6:30 Finish up dinner.

7:15 Attend school play: Wizard of Oz. Your daughter Clarisse plays the Wicked Witch of the East. Your son Michael plays a Munchkin.

DAY LOG: FORM C

Things to Do Today

Date

Item	Priority	Time Needed	Done		Scheduled Events	
			☐		7:00	
			☐		7:15	
			☐		7:30	
			☐		7:45	
			☐		8:00	
			☐		8:15	
			☐		8:30	
			☐		8:45	
			☐		9:00	
			☐		9:15	
			☐		9:30	
			☐		9:45	
			☐		10:00	
			☐		10:15	
			☐		10:30	
			☐		10:45	
			☐		11:00	
			☐		11:15	
			☐		11:30	
			☐		11:45	
			☐		12:00	
			☐		12:15	
			☐		12:30	
			☐		12:45	
			☐		1:00	
			☐		1:15	
			☐		1:30	
			☐		1:45	
			☐		2:00	
			☐		2:15	
			☐		2:30	
			☐		2:45	
			☐		3:00	
			☐		3:15	
			☐		3:30	
					3:45	
					4:00	
					4:15	
Notes					4:30	
					4:45	
					5:00	
					5:15	
					5:30	
					5:45	
					6:00	
					EVENING	

© Time Management Center

Nightingale-Conant reorder no. 880-1

Printed in U.S.A.

16

MESSAGES: FORM D

To _Time Management Team_ ☑ URGENT
Date_____ Time _8:15_ Ⓐ.M P.M.

WHILE YOU WERE OUT

From _Dr. Berringer_
of _Special Projects_
Phone _____
⎯⎯ Area Code ⎯⎯ Number ⎯⎯ Ext.
Fax _____
⎯⎯ Area Code ⎯⎯ Number

Telephoned	☒	Please call	
Came to see you		Wants to see you	
Returned your call		Will call again	

Message _The staff meeting has been rescheduled for 2 p.m._

Signed _SES_

Perfect print®

To _Time Management Team_ ☑ URGENT
Date_____ Time _8:20_ Ⓐ.M P.M.

WHILE YOU WERE OUT

From _Spouse_
of _____
Phone _____
⎯⎯ Area Code ⎯⎯ Number ⎯⎯ Ext.
Fax _____
⎯⎯ Area Code ⎯⎯ Number

Telephoned	☒	Please call	
Came to see you		Wants to see you	
Returned your call		Will call again	

Message _Car broke down. Had to put car in repair shop. Please pick up on way home._

(Note: Driving to Spouse's office causes 15-minute detour.)

Signed _SES_

Perfect print®

To _Time Management Team_ ☑ URGENT
Date_____ Time _8:25_ Ⓐ.M P.M.

WHILE YOU WERE OUT

From _Property Management Office_
of _____
Phone _____
⎯⎯ Area Code ⎯⎯ Number ⎯⎯ Ext.
Fax _____
⎯⎯ Area Code ⎯⎯ Number

Telephoned	☒	Please call	
Came to see you		Wants to see you	
Returned your call		Will call again	

Message _There has been a water leak in the cafeteria. The cafeteria will be closed until next Monday._

Signed _SES_

Perfect print®

To _____ ☐ URGENT
Date_____ Time _____ A.M. P.M.

WHILE YOU WERE OUT

From _____
of _____
Phone _____
⎯⎯ Area Code ⎯⎯ Number ⎯⎯ Ext.
Fax _____
⎯⎯ Area Code ⎯⎯ Number

Telephoned		Please call	
Came to see you		Wants to see you	
Returned your call		Will call again	

Message _____

Signed _____

Perfect print®

3
DEVELOPING COACHING SKILLS

Andrew Kimball

Overview Conventional wisdom and most coaching courses recommend balancing positive and negative feedback in order to improve performance. Yet recipients of this "balanced feedback" often wind up feeling totally demotivated after a well-intended performance conversation. This exercise provides a direct experience of a more successful approach to coaching. Using the tools presented in this simulation, coaches learn how to tell the most difficult truths in a way that leaves coachees looking forward to being coached again.

Suggested Time 90 minutes (see also Variations, Abbreviated)

Activities	Minutes
Positioning	5
Round 1: Negative Feedback (with debriefing)	15
Round 2: Positive Feedback (with debriefing)	15
Round 3: Negative Ideas (with debriefing)	15
Round 4: Positive Ideas (with debriefing)	15
Round 5: Choose two of the above (with debriefing)	25
Total Time	**90**

Materials Needed For each two teams of 4 to 6 people:

✔ 3 unique, fun "bombs" to be hidden around the room (Note: To make the game more playful and to appeal to the kinesthetic and auditory modalities, use fun objects that make noise, such as a dinosaur that squeaks when squeezed or a bicycle horn.)

✔ 2 flip charts set up as score pads (see illustration).

✔ 1 flip chart set up to scribe notes

✔ 1 whistle or other device to signal the end of each round

Contact Info: Andrew Kimball, QB International, 824 E. Street, San Rafael, CA 94901, 415-457-1919, akimball@qube.com, www.qube.com.

- ✔ 4 blindfolds
- ✔ 1 stopwatch
- ✔ 4 sets of color-coordinated Direction Cards
- ✔ 1 pack of colored index cards
- ✔ Prizes for the winners (Be creative! How about a new BMW—a toy one, that is?)
- ✔ Forms A, B, C, D

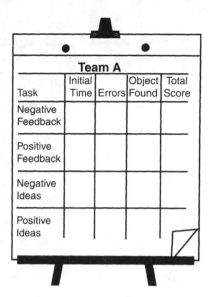

Team A				
Task	Initial Time	Errors	Object Found	Total Score
Negative Feedback				
Positive Feedback				
Negative Ideas				
Positive Ideas				

Procedure *Note:* You may play this game with as many as 30 teams. For every pair of teams, use a complete set of materials and designate a separate Bomb Zone.

Round 1: Negative Feedback

Setup

1. Divide participants into 2 teams. Explain that a terrorist organization has called in a bomb threat to your building. The bombs are due to go off in 5 minutes. Two rival bomb squads, Team A and Team B, have been called in. However, there is one problem. Today was the day when all the city's demolition experts went to the eye doctor to have their eyes dilated and examined. As a result, all the demolition experts are currently wearing blindfolds. They will be teamed up with expert guides who will act as their eyes. To make the situation even more explosive, the mayor is planning to cut the bomb squad's budget in half at the end of the month. Only the best team will survive the budget cuts.

2. Ask for a volunteer from each team to play the blindfolded demolition expert.

   Note: Some people have an aversion to being blindfolded. Once in a while an entire team refuses to be blindfolded. If no one on a team wishes to be blindfolded, ask for two volunteers from the opposite team. Trade one of the volunteers to the opposite team in exchange for one of their players. Announce that there has been an intersquad transfer.

3. Ask for a volunteer from each team to play the expert guide.

4. Explain that the rest of the team members will play the role of bomb squad efficiency experts.

5. Show the players the three bombs (noise-making objects). Explain that after the guides blindfold the demolition experts, you will place the three bombs around the room (or bomb zone).

6. Explain the role of the demolition experts:

   a. Designate two starting lines on opposite sides of the room. Try to ensure that both starting lines are equidistant from where you plan to hide the three bombs.

   b. Explain that the blindfolded demolition experts will have up to 5 minutes to find all three bombs and defuse them by ringing, squeaking, or holding them.

   c. Because each bomb may be found by more than one team, the demolition experts should be sure to return the bombs to where they found them once they have been defused. After the team has found and defused all three bombs, they must return to the starting line.

7. Explain the role of the guide:

   a. All demolition experts will have guides to help them move about the bomb zone. The guides and the demolition experts will act as teams.

   b. Guides may provide information to the demolition experts only in the form designated by their Direction Cards.

   c. Pass out the Negative Feedback Direction Cards (Form A) to everyone.

   d. Explain that in this first round, guides may not give any positive feedback or make any recommendations to the demolition experts. Guides may only give negative feedback about what the demolition experts have already done.

   e. Define negative feedback as negative judgments about past actions.

   f. Review the examples on the Negative Feedback Direction Cards (Form A).

   g. Elicit three or four other examples of negative feedback from the group.

8. Explain the role of the bomb squad efficiency experts:

   a. Team members who are not guides or demolition experts will be bomb squad efficiency experts.

   b. Each bomb squad efficiency expert should carry a pencil and an index card or pad of paper.

   c. Bomb squad efficiency experts are responsible for observing the opposing team's demolition expert and guide and keeping track of their errors, including:

   - From the opposing guide: illegal directions.
   - From the opposing demolition experts: illegal bumps, brushes, or touches of objects other than the bomb.

   d. Each time they observe an error, the bomb squad efficiency experts should call, "Fault!" and briefly explain the error to the opposing team's guide. Then they should record the error on the index card or paper.

   e. Remind them that at the end of each round, the Game Director will add the bomb squad efficiency experts' fault points to the opposing team's score, so it is critical that bomb squad efficiency experts be accurate.

   f. Scoring:

   - The team with the *fewest points* at the end of the four rounds is the winner.
   - Teams will earn *1 point for each second it takes to find the three bombs* and return to the starting line.

   Example:

   If a demolition expert finds all three bombs and returns to the starting line in 2 minutes and 15 seconds, the team will score: 2 minutes × 60 seconds plus 15 seconds = 135 points.

   If the 5-minute time limit runs out before the bombs are found, the team will receive 5 × 60 seconds = 300 points.

   50 penalty points will be added to a team's score every time the guide uses illegal directions.

   Example:

   In Round 1, if the guide slips up and says, "Turn left" (a recommendation) or says, "Good, keep going in that direction" (positive feedback), the team will be penalized 50 points for each occurrence.

- *10 penalty points* will be added to a team's score every time a demolition expert bumps into, brushes against, or in any way touches an object that is not a bomb.

Example:

If a demolition expert bumps into three chairs and brushes against one of the bomb squad efficiency experts, the team will have added to its final score $4 \times 10 = 40$ penalty points.

- *100 bonus points* will be subtracted from the team's score for defusing all three bombs.

Practice

1. Ask the guides to blindfold the demolition experts.
2. When demolition experts are blindfolded, ask a bomb squad efficiency expert from the opposing team to examine the blindfolds to ensure that the demolition experts cannot see anything.
3. Give the guides 1 minute to practice giving negative feedback commands, with bomb squad efficiency experts watching for faults.
4. Be sure to correct any mistakes that the bomb squad efficiency experts miss.

Play

1. Have the guides move the demolition experts to their respective starting lines.
2. Silently, and with great show, walk the bombs to their "hiding" spots, using hand motions to direct the attention of the guides to their locations.
3. Check one last time for questions.
4. Check to make sure everyone is ready.
5. Blow the whistle to begin play.
6. Keep track of time and call out each minute as it passes.
7. Count down the last 10 seconds.
8. When 5 minutes have passed, stop the clock and blow the whistle.
9. Ask the bomb squad efficiency experts to record the times, faults, and objects on the flip chart scorepads.

How do you feel? (*to the demolition experts*)
What were you feeling during this round?

How do you feel? (*to the guides*)
What were you feeling during this round?

What happened? (*to the efficiency experts*)
What did you notice going on?
What happened next?
What happened after that?

What values were evident? (*to the group*)
If we start with the assumption that our values drive our behaviors, what values may have been driving the behavior of the demolition experts?
What values drove the other behaviors you observed?

What did you learn? (*to the group*)
As you reflect on what you observed and what the demolition experts have told us about their feelings and their choices, what general principles might you come up with to explain what you observed? (Elicit several responses.)
What else?

How does this relate to the real world? (*to the group*)
Assume for a moment that this game is a metaphor for something you experience every day in each of your jobs. What do you experience in your jobs that is governed by the same principles we discussed?

Round 2: Positive Feedback

Setup

1. Reset the clock for 5 minutes.

2. Explain that all roles will stay the same except the role of the guide.

3. Ask for a new guide from each team. Thank the old guides.

4. Explain the role of the guide:

   a. The new guides and the demolition experts will continue to act as teams.

   b. Pass out the Positive Feedback Direction Cards (Form B) to everyone.

c. Explain that in the second round, guides may not give any negative feedback or make any recommendations to the demolition experts. Guides may only give positive feedback about what the demolition experts have already done.

d. Define positive feedback as positive judgments about past events.

e. Review the examples on the Positive Feedback Direction Cards (Form B).

f. Elicit three or four other examples of positive feedback from the group.

Practice
Practice as in the first round.

Play
Begin and manage play as in the first round.

How do you feel? (*to the demolition experts*)
  What were you feeling during this round?
  What's changed since the last round?

How do you feel? (*to the guides*)
  What were you feeling during this round?
  What's changed since the last round?

What happened? (*to the efficiency experts*)
  What did you notice going on?
  What happened next?
  What happened after that?

What values were evident? (*to the group*)
  If we start with the assumption that our values drive our behaviors, what values may have been driving the behavior of the demolition experts?
  What values drove the other behaviors you observed?

What did you learn? (*to the group*)
  As you reflect on what you observed and what the demolition experts have told us about their feelings and their choices, what general principles might you come up with to explain what you observed? (Elicit several responses.)
  What else?

How does this relate to the real world? (*to the group*)

Assume for a moment that this game is a metaphor for something you experience every day in each of your jobs. What do you experience in your jobs that is governed by the same principles we discussed?

Round 3: Negative Ideas

Setup

1. Set up as before.

2. Explain that in the third round all rules stay exactly the same as before except the role of the guide.

3. Ask for new guides from each team. Thank the old guides.

4. Explain the role of the guides:

   a. The new guides and the demolition experts will continue to act as teams.

   b. Pass out the Negative Idea Direction Cards (Form C) to everyone.

   c. Explain that in the third round guides may not give any feedback or make any positive recommendations to the demolition experts. Guides may only offer negative ideas about what the demolition experts should do, beginning each statement with, "You should not...."

   d. Define negative ideas as recommendations about future actions not to try.

   e. Review the examples on the Negative Idea Direction Cards (Form C).

   f. Elicit three or four other examples of negative ideas from the group.

Practice

Practice as before.

Play

Begin and manage play as before.

Debriefing Questions

How do you feel? (*to the demolition experts*)

What were you feeling during this round?

What's changed since the last round?

How do you feel? (*to the guides*)
What were you feeling during this round?
What's changed since the last round?

What happened? (*to the efficiency experts*)
What did you notice going on?
What happened next?
What happened after that?

What values were evident? (*to the group*)
If we start with the assumption that our values drive our behaviors, what values may have been driving the behavior of the demolition experts?
What values drove the other behaviors you observed?

What did you learn? (*to the group*)
As you reflect on what you observed and what the demolition experts have told us about their feelings and their choices, what general principles might you come up with to explain what you observed? (Elicit several responses.)
What else?

How does this relate to the real world? (*to the group*)
Assume for a moment that this game is a metaphor for something you experience every day in each of your jobs. What do you experience in your jobs that is governed by the same principles we discussed?

Round 4: Positive Ideas

Setup

1. Set up as before.

2. Explain that in the fourth round all rules stay exactly the same as before except the role of the guides.

3. Ask for new guides from each team. Thank the old guides.

4. Explain the role of the guides:

    a. The new guides and the demolition experts will continue to act as teams.

    b. Pass out the Positive Idea Direction Cards (Form D) to everyone.

    c. Explain that in the fourth round guides may not give any feedback or make any negative recommendations to the demolition experts. Guides may only offer positive ideas about what the demolition experts should do.

d. Define positive ideas as recommendations about future actions.

e. Review the examples on the Positive Idea Direction Cards (Form D).

f. Elicit three or four other examples of positive ideas from the group.

Practice
Practice as before.

Play
Begin and manage play as before.

How do you feel? (*to the demolition experts*)
    What were you feeling during this round?
    What's changed since the last round?

How do you feel? (*to the guides*)
    What were you feeling during this round?
    What's changed since the last round?

What happened? (*to the efficiency experts*)
    What did you notice going on?
    What happened next?
    What happened after that?

What values were evident? (*to the group*)
    If we start with the assumption that our values drive our behaviors, what values may have been driving the behavior of the demolition experts?
    What values drove the other behaviors you observed?

What did you learn? (*to the group*)
    As you reflect on what you observed and what the demolition experts have told us about their feelings and their choices, what general principles might you come up with to explain what you observed? (Elicit several responses.)
    What else?

How does this relate to the real world? (*to the group*)
    Assume for a moment that this game is a metaphor for something you experience every day in each of your jobs. What do you experience in your jobs that is governed by the same principles we discussed?

Round 5: Choose 2

Setup

1. Set up as before.

2. Explain that in the fifth round all rules stay exactly the same as before except the role of the guides.

3. Ask for a new guide from each team. Thank the old guides.

4. Explain the role of the guides:

   a. In the fifth round the guides may use any two of the four coaching tools: Negative Feedback, Positive Feedback, Negative Ideas, or Positive Ideas.

   b. Remind the guides that this is the last chance they have to reduce the team's score. The BMWs are still up for grabs.

Play

1. Don't allow practice for this round.

2. Begin and manage play as before.

Final Scoring

1. When the round is over, total the scores from each of the rounds. The team with the lowest score is the winning team.

2. Award prizes: cash or the keys to the new BMW.

Final Debriefing Questions

How do you feel? (*to the demolition experts*)
   What were you feeling during this round?
   What's changed since the last round?

How do you feel? (*to the guides*)
   What were you feeling during this round?
   What's changed since the last round?

What happened? (*to the efficiency experts*)
   What did you notice going on?
   What happened next?
   What happened after that?

What values were evident? (*to the group*)
   If we start with the assumption that our values drive our behaviors, what values may have been driving the initial behavior of the demolition experts?
   What values drove the other behaviors you observed?

What did you learn? (*to the group*)

As you reflect on what you observed and what the demolition experts have told us about their feelings and their choices, what general principles might you come up with to explain what you observed? (Elicit several responses.)

What might we suggest as the optimal situation in which to use negative feedback alone?

What can we say about how to combine the different feedback tools? What else?

How does this relate to the real world? (*to the group*)

Assume for a moment that this game is a metaphor for something you experience every day in each of your jobs. What do you experience in your jobs that is governed by the same principles as we discussed?

What if? (*to the demolition experts*)

What if we increased the number of bombs? How might that have changed your choices?

What if we decreased the time you had to defuse the bombs? How might that have changed your choices?

What if we increased the penalty for making mistakes? How might that have changed your choices?

What next? (*to the group*)

What might you do differently as a result of what you learned here?

How might you apply the principles you learned here to how you coach your people?

How might you apply the principles you learned here to how you receive coaching from your coaches?

Variations

1. Abbreviated: This exercise can be compressed by eliminating less critical rounds. When pressed for time, you may eliminate Round 3 or Round 5 and develop those insights in the "what if" phase of the final debriefing. The richness of each round depends heavily on the time allocated for debriefing.

2. Houston Control: This game can be played with any exercise in which one person depends on another for information, advice, or instructions. In a recent variation we used an electronic switch box to simulate a space adventure. One participant (the Astronaut) was required to throw 36 unmarked switches in a designated, patterned order. A second participant (Houston Control) called out instructions regarding which switches to throw in what order. A buzzer sounded if the switches were thrown in the wrong order.

In Houston Control we used the same series of Negative Feedback, Positive Feedback, Negative Ideas, Positive Ideas, and Choose 2 to communicate instructions, and we used the same debriefing questions to expand the learning.

NEGATIVE FEEDBACK DIRECTION CARD: FORM A

Guides and demolition experts will act as teams. The demolition expert's goal is to defuse all of the bombs in the bomb zone and return to the starting line as quickly as possible. In this round, guides may not make recommendations or offer encouraging feedback. Guides may only offer demolition experts **negative judgments about past events** such as:

What Guides May Say	What Guides May Not Say
You shouldn't have turned left.	Turn right. Don't turn left.
You shouldn't have turned right.	Turn left. Don't turn right.
You shouldn't have walked past that spot.	Keep going in that direction.
You should not have raised [lowered] your hand.	Raise [lower] your hand.
	That's right, keep raising [lowering] your hand.
	Move your hand 30 degrees to the right.
You should not have leaned over so far.	Lean over farther.
You should not have sped up [slowed down].	Speed up [slow down].

POSITIVE FEEDBACK DIRECTION CARD: FORM B

The demolition expert's goal again is to defuse all of the bombs placed around the room and return to the starting point as quickly as possible. Guides may not tell demolition experts to speed up, slow down, or turn. Guides may only offer demolition experts **positive data about past events** such as:

What Guides May Say	What Guides May Not Say
Turning left was a good idea.	Turn left. You shouldn't have turned right.
Turning right was a good idea.	Turn right. Don't turn left.
You were right to slow down.	Slow down. You shouldn't have been walking so fast.
You were right to have raised [lowered] your hand.	Raise [lower] your hand.
That's right, keep raising your hand.	Move your hand 30 degrees to the right.
You were right to have leaned over so far.	Lean over farther.
You were right to have sped up [slowed down].	Speed up [slow down].

NEGATIVE IDEA DIRECTION CARD: FORM C

Guides and demolition experts will act as teams. The demolition expert's goal is to defuse all of the bombs in the bomb zone and return to the starting line as quickly as possible. In this round, guides may not make recommendations or offer encouraging feedback. Guides may only offer demolition experts **negative judgments about past events** such as:

What Guides May Say	What Guides May Not Say
You shouldn't turn left.	Turn right. You shouldn't have turned left.
You shouldn't turn right.	Turn left. You shouldn't have turned right.
You shouldn't keep going in that direction.	Keep going in that direction. You shouldn't have stopped.
You should not raise [lower] your hand.	Raise [lower] your hand.
	That's right, keep raising [lowering] your hand.
	Move your hand 30 degrees to the right.
You should not lean over so far.	Lean over farther.
You should not speed up [slow down].	Speed up [slow down].

POSITIVE IDEA DIRECTION CARD: FORM D

The demolition expert's goal again is to defuse all the bombs placed around the room and return to the starting point as quickly as possible. This time guides may tell demolition experts to speed up, slow down, or turn. Guides may only offer demolition experts **positive, future-oriented ideas or suggestions about future actions** such as:

What Guides May Say	What Guides May Not Say
Turn left.	Don't turn right. You shouldn't have turned right.
Turn right.	Don't turn left. You shouldn't have turned left.
Keep going in that direction.	Don't keep going in that direction. You should have stopped.
Raise [lower] your hand.	Don't raise [lower] your hand.
	Don't move your hand 30 degrees to the right.
Lean over farther.	You were right to lean over farther.
Speed up [slow down].	Don't speed up [slow down]. You should not have slowed down [sped up].

4

DELEGATING WITH STYLE

Carol Harvey

Overview Many supervisors and managers find it difficult to successfully delegate tasks to subordinates. However, much of the success of delegation depends on how well people learn to carry out whatever tasks they are being asked to perform. This activity presents a new approach to delegation by utilizing learning theory to teach managers how to improve their delegation success rates. It has been used successfully in supervisory training programs and in time management seminars.

Suggested Time 30 minutes

Materials Needed
✔ Flip chart and markers
✔ Form A (What Is Your Style?)
✔ Form B (Role Play), cut into sections
✔ Form C (Learning Style Guidelines)

Procedure
1. Distribute Form A.
2. Explain that each participant should complete this sheet by choosing the most appropriate answers. There are no right or wrong answers, so participants should choose the answers that *best* describe how they would usually prefer to handle each situation.
3. Instruct the participants to add up their total number of A, B, and C answers.
4. Ask the participants to list their first names and A, B, and C scores on the flip chart.
5. Without explaining what these scores mean, select up to two sets of participants with *dissimilar* learning styles and place in dyads. For example, pair the participant with the highest A score with the participant with the lowest A score. This activity works best

Contact Information: Carol Harvey, Assumption College, 500 Salisbury St., Worcester, MA 01615, 508-767-7459, charvey@eve.assumption.edu.

when you have opposite letter scores between the members of the dyad. For example, pair a person who has an A score of 7 or higher *and* a low B score with someone who has a B score of seven or higher *and* a low A score. Listing the group's scores on the chart pad makes it easier for you to select the two pairs with the most striking differences in learning styles.

6. Hand out the *appropriate sections* of Form B to the 4 participants, who will participate in the role play. Give them a few minutes to read their roles as outlined in Form B. Their task is to prepare a 5-minute role play illustrating the situation presented to them. Partners should *not* discuss their roles with each other.

7. Distribute Form C to the rest of the class, who will act as observers.

8. Conduct the role plays.

9. Facilitate a discussion in which you explain that this activity illustrates that how we prefer to learn often influences how we expect others to learn. Write the following on the flip chart: Participants who had

—more *A* answers prefer to learn by *seeing*.

—more *B* answers prefer to learn by *hearing*.

—more *C* answers prefer to learn by *doing*.

Some participants will have more than one category that are scored particularly high, such as 5 A's, 2 B's, and 5 C's. This means that this person is comfortable learning new information in more than one way.

When a participant's answers are fairly evenly divided into A's, B's, and C's, this person does not have a strong preference for any one particular style of learning. These participants take in new information by all three processes.

10. Ask the observers for examples of behaviors from the role plays that illustrate each of these learning styles (e.g., people who prefer to learn by seeing often draw diagrams, take notes, use phrases like "see what I mean," etc.). Facilitate a discussion of the added difficulties one encounters when trying to get a person to do an unfamiliar task, if it is taught in a way that makes it more difficult for that person to learn. Ask the group to provide examples from their own experience.

11. Ask the participants what they have learned about (a) how they learn new information, and (b) how this relates to teaching others new tasks.

WHAT IS YOUR STYLE?: FORM A

For each situation, circle the **one** answer that best represents how you would usually prefer to act.

1. You have just purchased a complicated new piece of electronic equipment in your home. The easiest way for you to learn how to operate it would be to

   A. carefully watch the instructional video that came with the product.

   B. ask your next-door neighbor who has the same model to explain how it works.

   C. just start tinkering with it.

2. You are lost and late for an important meeting. You would be more apt to

   A. ask for directions, write them down, and then follow them.

   B. ask for directions, listen, and then try to follow the directions.

   C. just try to find the site by driving around.

3. Your company has purchased new equipment that is important to performing your job. You have your choice of how to learn it. You would tend to prefer to

   A. go to a class, take notes, and use the manual.

   B. go to a class, listen to what the instructor has to say, but take hardly any notes

   C. skip the class and try to learn by using it.

4. You are trying to improve your ability to remember names. In a meeting with several new clients you

   A. keep glancing at their business cards.

   B. listen to the names that they call each other.

   C. try to use their names more in the conversation.

5. You are having trouble with a piece of machinery at your work site that you need to master ASAP. The first action that you usually take is to

   A. consult the instruction manual.

   B. call the manufacturer's toll-free help line.

   C. fiddle with it and try to get it working by yourself.

6. If you had to master a new foreign language for an overseas assignment, the easiest way for you to do that would be to

   A. read the text and/or take lots of notes in class.

   B. listen to others speak it and/or listen to tapes.

   C. practice speaking the language.

WHAT IS YOUR STYLE?: FORM A (CONT.)

7. You are in a phone booth and call information for a phone number. You usually

   A. write it down immediately as the operator gives it to you.

   B. don't write it down but repeat it out loud to yourself as you dial.

   C. just dial it.

8. You have to memorize a speech. The easiest way for you to do that would be to

   A. keep reading it over and over.

   B. put it on tape and listen to it over and over.

   C. keep saying it out loud.

9. You want to learn the latest dance craze. The easiest way for you to learn it would be to

   A. watch someone do it.

   B. listen to directions on how to do it.

   C. just try to do it.

10. You feel more comfortable in a class when the instructor begins by saying:

    A. "Here are some handouts that outline what I am going to do."

    B. "There is no need to take notes, just listen to what I am going to tell you."

    C. "This is a hands-on class."

11. Which do you tend to remember best?

    A. What you have seen.

    B. What you have heard.

    C. What you have done.

12. How do you think that you usually learn best?

    A. By watching someone do something

    B. By listening to someone tell you how to do something

    C. By doing it yourself

Add up your total number of A's, B's, and C's.

Number of A's   _____

Number of B's   _____

Number of C's   _____

ROLE PLAY: FORM B

ROLE PLAY FOR HIGH A, B, OR C SCORERS

Assume that you are going on a four-week cruise vacation. Your boss has made it clear that in order to get so much time off, you must show your assistant how to do your job in your absence. In a five-minute role play, go over a task that he or she will be performing for the first time in your absence. You may choose to teach any relevant task, such as how to complete a report, run a machine, etc. Your goal is to teach this employee how to perform any task that will be delegated to him or her in your absence. You may do this in any way that is comfortable for you.

- CUT HERE -

ROLE PLAY FOR LOW A, B, OR C SCORERS

Assume that your boss is going on a four-week cruise vacation during which you will need to do the job in his or her absence. In a five-minute role play, you and your partner will go over some of the tasks that you will be performing for the first time in his or her absence. Remember, this is your only opportunity to learn how to do this work, so your goal is to understand the instructions. Be sure that you are clear about what you will need to do in his or her absence.

LEARNING STYLE GUIDELINES: FORM C

Most people tend to prefer one way of taking in information over others. Some people need to learn by seeing, or through hearing, or through doing, or a combination of these. All three ways are equally valid. However, we tend to teach other people new tasks using the methods that *we prefer* to use to acquire new information, which may be the hardest way for them to learn. This is particularly important to be aware of when we try to delegate unfamiliar tasks to others. If people are unsure of what to do or how to proceed, they will be less successful at learning the delegated task. Sometimes what we perceive as an unwillingness to accept delegation is just a colleague's inability to learn the task the way we are teaching it. This problem develops when there is a mismatch between learning styles.

Since you have been provided with the scores of those involved in the role plays, you are to watch for examples of how people in these role plays instruct another person in an unfamiliar task in the way that they prefer to learn.

Jot down observations that illustrate this behavior. For example,

—High A scorers use words and phrases that indicate learning through *seeing,* such as "watch how I do this," etc. They tend to provide written instructions, draw diagrams, and refer the learner to the manual, etc.

—High B scorers encourage *listening* to the instructions rather than doing, showing, or providing written instructions about how to accomplish a task. They often discourage others from taking notes or trying to do the task.

—High C scorers teach by actually *doing* a task with the learner.

OBSERVATION NOTES:

5
ASSIMILATING THE NEW TEAM LEADER

Ed Betof

Overview This process is designed to help a new team leader (newly hired, appointed, or promoted) to rapidly develop a strong positive relationship with the team. It promotes immediate, open, two-way communications between the leader and the team. The process is appropriate for either highly or less experienced leaders.

The process provides the leader with an opportunity to hear first-hand the initial questions, issues, and concerns that exist in the team's mind. It also gives the leader the opportunity to talk about his or her business philosophy and to share his or her expectations for the organization. Many leaders have used it again and again as they progress in an organization. Associates say that the program makes them feel more appreciated and valued.

Typically, the process should involve the entire team, including any administrative assistant. It may also include an extended staff if the larger team is critical to success. The process works best when it takes place within the first several days after the leader has taken responsibility for the team.

Read the facilitator guidelines on Form A before beginning the process.

Suggested Time Approximately 3 to 3½ hours for the staff and 4 to 5 hours for the leader, including the preparation and debriefing meeting

Materials Needed
- ✔ Form A (Facilitator Guidelines)
- ✔ Form B (Sample Leader Letter 1)
- ✔ Form C (Sample Participant Handout with Questions)
- ✔ Form D (Sample Feedback to Leader)
- ✔ Form E (Sample Leader Letter 2)
- ✔ Form F (Overview of the Process)
- ✔ Form G (Follow-Up Process)

Contact Information: Becton Dickinson, 1 Becton Drive, MC 057, Franklin Lakes, NJ 07417, 201-847-4502, edward_betof@bd.com

Procedure

1. Contact the new leader to recommend and explain the assimilation process. It is essential that the process be used voluntarily. If the leader is forced to use it, the leader's reluctance will show in his or her conduct and will defeat the purpose of the process.

2. Ask the new leader to invite the staff by letter to attend an "assimilation" meeting, and to clarify the reasons for having it. (See Sample Leader Letter 1—Form B.)

3. The new leader usually kicks off the assimilation, explaining the objectives for the meeting. He or she introduces you as the facilitator, and then leaves the room for 1 to $1^{1}/_{2}$ hours. Without the leader present, the group feels more comfortable to speak freely.

4. Once the leader leaves the room, reiterate the group's objective. Then lead the staff through an icebreaker exercise designed to get the participants comfortable with sharing personal information and getting to know each other better. A sample exercise might be to ask each person to share with the group the answers to some simple questions. The questions are:

   • What is your home town?

   • What is your favorite nickname (or your middle name)? Why is it your favorite nickname (or why were you given the middle name)?

   • Where would you travel on vacation if you could go anywhere? Why?

   • What leadership characteristics do you most admire in your ideal leader? Why? (List the leadership characteristics on a flip chart for the group to view. Later, review that list with the leader.)

5. Following the icebreaker, lead the group through the questions from the leader's letter of invitation. Raise the questions, but do not indicate your feelings on any of them. Try to get a sense of whether each comment is an individual one or whether the group overall agrees with the response. Guarantee confidentiality, in terms of not identifying who made specific comments. The participants' responses are noted on a flip chart. (See Sample Participant Handout with Questions—Form C.)

6. The group is given a 30- to 45-minute break, while the leader returns to the room (alone with the facilitator) to review the staff questions and comments. At this point, make sure that the leader understands the points raised. Coach the leader, if appropriate, on possible responses to some of the more difficult questions, or at least recommend the thought processes the leader should work

through in forming responses to the questions. The key point is that the leader must not feel the need to be an expert in all areas; the group doesn't require or expect this. It is, however, quite important that the leader come across as a good, thoughtful listener. It is also very important that the leader not dominate the follow-up session. The most effective sessions are really dialogues, where the leader will make some comments, pause, seek additional data from the group, and then respond, so that it becomes an active exchange between the new leader and the team, building the kind of relationship that will serve them well in the future.

7. At the second session, the leader and team meet to review the notes that were generated in the first session. As facilitator, you will also participate in both facilitating and monitoring modes. Try to get a sense of the questions that were not asked, but nevertheless are on the minds of the group. Ensure that the leader is addressing the questions raised by the group and that the questions and answers are clear to both the leader and the group.

8. The leader closes the meeting by thanking the team for their help in the assimilation process, and tells the group that the notes from the meeting will be distributed to the attendees. The information that has been gathered can be used as the basis for the agenda for a follow-up meeting, or to establish a schedule for resolution of action items. Depending on the time of day, having a group lunch or going out to dinner together after the New Leader and Team Assimilation process promotes continued team building (bonding).

9. Meet with the leader for a debriefing session on the process. This is an ideal time to provide feedback on what the leader did well in the session, comment on areas for improvement, and provide guidance for action planning and team development. (See Sample Feedback to Leader—Form D.)

10. The leader writes a letter commenting on highlights of the assimilation meeting and thanking the participants for their help, and includes a copy of the meeting notes. (See Sample Leader Letter 2—Form E.)

11. The New Leader and Team Assimilation Meeting is Stage I (See Overview of the Process Form F) of development and assimilation with the team. Stage II involves periodic follow-up meetings with the leader and staff on the action items. The leader solicits feedback on his or her performance and provides feedback to the staff on their action items. Stage III is the New Leader and Team Assimilation Follow-up Process usually conducted six to nine months after the new leader's appointment. For instructions on the New Leader Assimilation Follow-Up Process, see Form G.

FACILITATOR GUIDELINES: FORM A

Facilitator Do's

- Clarify and restate.
- Pump, prime—for instance, repeat the question.
- Ensure all individuals actively participate.
- Test for consensus of views on key topics.
- Use pauses and silence to gain additional comments.
- Keep the confidentiality of the data.
- Remember, the immediate leader is your *key* client.
- Give the leader feedback on what was said and how it was received.

Facilitator Don'ts

- Let one person dominate.
- Put words in a person's mouth.
- Rephrase comments unless you have the agreement of the speaker.
- Tell the leader who said what.
- Tell higher-level leaders what occurred in the sessions.

SAMPLE LEADER LETTER 1: FORM B

Memo: To: Staff

From: Newly Appointed Leader

Copy To: HR Facilitator

Subject: New Leader and Team Assimilation Meeting

On (day/date) (facilitator name) will facilitate our team through the initial stages of the process of New Leader and Team Assimilation (NLTA). This program has been used by thousands of leaders to help in the rapid development of a strong, positive working relationship between a new leader and the team. The process is based on the premise that an effective relationship needs a considerable amount of shared understanding, developed primarily through open, two-way communication.

The NLTA meeting will consist of two sessions. On (day/date), in our first session, we will have the opportunity to focus on the following questions:

1. What do we already know about _____?

2. What don't we know, but would like to know about _____?

3. What are our concerns about _____ becoming our manager or leader?

4. What do we want most from _____?

5. What does _____ need to know about us as a group?

6. What are the major problems _____ will be facing during the first year?

7. What are the major challenges the _____ team and _____ will be facing over the next year? (Prioritize list.)

8. What commitments are we willing to make to support _____ and ensure that major challenges are successfully met?

You will find it helpful to give some thought to each question before our session. I am interested solely in an open, free flow of information; in the responses and ideas generated during this initial meeting, not in who says what. Accordingly, I will not attend this part of our meeting (session one). (Facilitator name) will facilitate this session.

At the conclusion of session one, (name of facilitator) will review your anonymous responses to the questions and discuss them with me.

SAMPLE LEADER LETTER 1: FORM B (*CONT.*)

At our second session, on the same day (day/date), I will have the opportunity to respond to your answers and we will have a chance to discuss other questions and issues.

I look forward to a productive, thought-provoking meeting. This is an excellent opportunity for each of us to set our courses and to help build a strong, cohesive team.

Regards,

xxxxxxx

SAMPLE PARTICIPANT HANDOUT WITH QUESTIONS: FORM C

New Leader and Team Assimilation
(Leader Name)
(Date)

1. What do we already know about _____?

2. What don't we know, but would like to know about _____?

3. What are our concerns about _____ becoming our leader?

4. What do we want most from _____?

5. What does _____ need to know about us as a team?

6. What are the major problems _____ will be facing during the first year?

7. What are the major challenges the _____ team and _____ will be facing over the next year? (Prioritize list.)

8. What commitments are we willing to make to support _____ and ensure that major challenges are successfully met?

SAMPLE FEEDBACK TO LEADER: FORM D

STRENGTHS DEMONSTRATED IN NLTA PROCESS

- Appropriate use of humor to put the group at ease.

- Handled constructive feedback without becoming defensive.

- Positive reinforcement of the team for candid comments.

- Adaptability demonstrated; good on your feet.

- Handled a large volume of data well and effectively synthesized it.

- Positively demonstrated decisiveness.

- Exhibited self-confidence; spoke with authority.

- Effectively probed for more insights and understanding of data.

DEVELOPMENT OPPORTUNITIES

- Put relationships on equal level with tasks—the personal touch is important. Use whatever method is comfortable for you; e.g., birthday meetings.

- Recognize incremental improvement, particularly with your team. Stopping to smell the roses is important for you and your team or organization, in order to maintain morale.

- More coaching of your team; e.g., preparation for last site presentation.

- More emphasis on "full delegation" and less emphasis on detail.

- Focus on building and reinforcing staff self-confidence and self-esteem—keys to their ability to take on more challenges.

- Develop greater openness; watch out for the mailbox feedback. This is very important so you can monitor your efforts at style refinement. Invite feedback in any form.

GOOD START ON THE JOURNEY TO LEADERSHIP EXCELLENCE!

SAMPLE LEADER LETTER 2: FORM E

TO: Team Members

FROM: Newly Appointed Leader

CC: HR Facilitator

SUBJECT: NEW LEADER AND TEAM ASSIMILATION NOTES

Attached please find the notes from the New Leader and Team Assimilation meeting we held on (_____).

First, I would like to thank everyone for their active participation in the process and the effort put into the meeting. I believe we were able to gain an in-depth perspective of ourselves as the (_____) team and the challenges we face together for the future. I hope it was of value to the group and opens the door for our future working relationship together as a winning team. I certainly found it of great value and appreciate your honesty as we worked through the topics. It will be important for our team development to have follow-up meetings during the coming year.

Many thanks also to (HR facilitator) for being a great facilitator throughout the program.

Regards,

OVERVIEW OF THE NEW LEADER AND TEAM ASSIMILATION PROCESS: FORM F

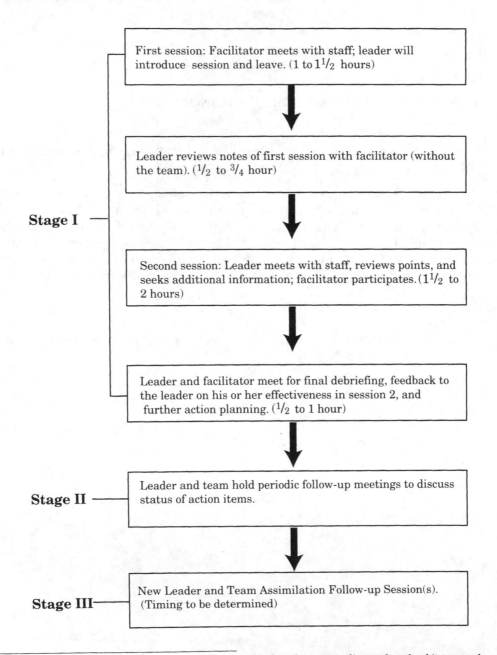

Stage I

First session: Facilitator meets with staff; leader will introduce session and leave. (1 to $1\frac{1}{2}$ hours)

Leader reviews notes of first session with facilitator (without the team). ($\frac{1}{2}$ to $\frac{3}{4}$ hour)

Second session: Leader meets with staff, reviews points, and seeks additional information; facilitator participates. ($1\frac{1}{2}$ to 2 hours)

Leader and facilitator meet for final debriefing, feedback to the leader on his or her effectiveness in session 2, and further action planning. ($\frac{1}{2}$ to 1 hour)

Stage II

Leader and team hold periodic follow-up meetings to discuss status of action items.

Stage III

New Leader and Team Assimilation Follow-up Session(s). (Timing to be determined)

NEW LEADER AND TEAM ASSIMILATION FOLLOW-UP PROCESS: FORM G

There are three goals for the Leader and Team Follow-Up Process:

- To provide feedback to the leader in terms of adjusting his or her leadership style to the needs of the group.

- To help in further aligning the leader and team.

- To promote team development and increase their collective effectiveness.

Ideally, this assimilation follow-up process takes place six to nine months after the leader started the assignment. It can also be used at any time by established leaders who want feedback on their leadership style. Some leaders use it annually with their teams to be sure they are receiving candid feedback. It also may be used following a 360-degree feedback process to pinpoint specific behaviors to modify.

The steps are similar to those for the New Leader and Team Assimilation meeting. The first section is done without the leader attending; then the leader is briefed, and the second phase of the program is a dialogue between the leader and the team. Each section takes about $1^1/_2$ hours, and the leader briefing requires about 30 minutes. If the leader has completed the New Leader and Team Assimilation meeting notes from the initial meeting, the facilitator may want to distribute copies to the staff at the beginning of the follow-up meeting. The HR partner acts as facilitator for the session.

The following questions are used:

1. What is (____) doing that we value and want him or her to continue doing?

2. What actions is (____) not taking that we would like him or her to start taking?

3. What is (____) doing that we want him or her to modify or stop doing?

4. What are we (the team) willing to do to help (____) grow and succeed in the position?

5. What do we need to start, stop, or modify in our actions to become a higher-performing team?

The debriefing with the leader following the session is designed to capture the key learning and action items. After it, the leader sends a letter to the staff noting session highlights, including the session notes, and suggesting plans for follow-up actions.

6

TRAINING LEADERS FOR SUCCESS

Ed Rose and Linda Becker

Overview   Employees are often promoted into leadership roles with very little prior experience. This exercise is a warm-up activity intended to set the stage for a leadership training intervention. It has universal application, depending on the structure of the debriefing questions posed.

Suggested Time   30 minutes

Materials Needed   ✔ Form A (Coaching for Success), one for each team
✔ Form B (Team Debriefing), one for each team
✔ Room large enough to allow breakout areas

Procedure   1.   This activity can be used with both large and small groups. If you have a large group, separate the participants into teams of 5 to 10. If you have a small group, you may decide to combine the team and overall debriefing sessions.

2.   Hand out Forms A and B, one of each per group. Instruct the teams to take the next 5 minutes for someone in the group to read the story out loud to the rest of the team; and then to take about 15 minutes to fill out the debriefing form and be prepared to share answers with the entire group.

3.   Give the teams a 5-minute warning before the time is up.

4.   Begin debriefing the exercise by asking question 1, then question 2, and so on, from Form B. Make sure that every team has an opportunity to share its responses. There is no single right answer; each person will contribute answers based on his or her own experiences. The more answers are shared, the more learning opportunities for the entire group.

Contact Information: Ed Rose, AET, Inc., 1900 S. Harbor City Blvd., Melbourne, FL 32934, 321-223-9640, edrose@cfl.rr.com.
Linda Becker, Intersil MS 53-217, 2501 Palm Bay Road, Palm Bay, FL 32905, 407-724-7560, lbecker@intersil.com.

5. End the session by asking the overall debriefing questions. At this point, you can tailor the material to lead into the topic of the class or workshop.

Debriefing Questions

1. If you were a farmer in your organization, how would you grow your people?

2. If plants need sun and rain and food to grow, what do employees need?

3. How well would a plant thrive if it received these things only once or twice a year?

4. If we equate coaching with providing sun, rain, and food to your employees, how important is it that they get a regular schedule of these nutrients?

COACHING FOR SUCCESS: FORM A

Once upon a time, a man named Ed inherited some land. Never having been a landowner before, Ed decided to visit his property. Along the way he came across a vegetable stand. The asparagus was firm; the watermelon was full; the herbs were full of fragrance.

"Good madam," Ed called to the vegetable peddler, "where did you acquire such marvels?" Pleased with the compliment, the vendor replied, "Why, I grew them in my fields down the road." Ed thought a minute. "Good madam," he said again, "to what do you attribute your success?" Laughing, the vegetable peddler—whose name was Linda—replied, "Why, to the blessing of this fine earth, the rain, and the sun!"

An idea took hold in the mind of the new landowner. He was going to grow magnificent vegetables! When Ed came upon a seed vendor, he asked for one of everything and went to locate his property. Being an organized man, Ed decided to plant his seeds in furrows 6 inches deep and spaced 12 inches apart, in rows 3 feet apart, so that he had room for all the seedlings. After the planting was done, Ed went back to town. Now he knew that his seeds needed the sun, the rain, and the good earth, so every morning he went out to assess the day. To his great pleasure, the sun came up every day and by afternoon a gentle rain came upon the land.

When it was harvest time, Ed approached his property with great anticipation. His mouth simply watered with thoughts of his first crop. To his dismay, he found that his herbs looked like weeds, his asparagus was a skimpy harvest at best, and his watermelon had overrun a major portion of the garden.

Distraught, the landowner ran back to the vegetable stand with samples of his crops. Once again he was struck by the magnificence of what the vendor had to offer. He blurted out, "Linda, I do not understand. We both used the sun, the rain, and the good earth. Why do you have abundance when I have so little?"

The wise vegetable farmer sized up the situation. Taking the asparagus in hand she said, "This asparagus should not be cut for another two years. You must give the plant time to thicken. During the third season, you will be able to cut it and enjoy the harvest for a full month." Taking up what was left of the herbs, she said, "If herbs are harvested incorrectly or at the wrong time, their value is lost, like the herbs you have here." Taking up the watermelon, she said, "This is a very vigorous plant, requiring at least eight feet between hills. That is why it took over your garden."

Ed then asked, "Why didn't you tell me this before? You said it was the rain, the soil, and the sun that would make my plants grow!"

Linda replied, "What I told you was correct. I didn't know what your plans were, so I didn't see any need for more detail. You know, Ed, vegetables are just like people. They all have different strengths and weaknesses and require different nourishing to be the best that they can be."

TEAM DEBRIEFING: FORM B

1. Describe some of the analogies you see between this story and your organization:

   a. The earth, the rain, and the sun—The type of environment the person thrives in; what the person's embedded life interests are (long-held, emotionally driven passions that you can attempt to feed in different job assignments, etc.).

   b. Watermelon, herbs—Different types of people exhibit different brain strengths, cultural diversity, gender.

   c. List others:

   _____

   _____

   _____

2. Why didn't Ed get the same results as Linda? Did he err in selecting the environment? Strategy? Planning? Mentoring?

3. In Linda's metaphoric connection of vegetables to people, how are vegetables like people?

4. If you are to coach people to their fullest potential like Linda did with the vegetables, why does it help to understand the people you are coaching?

7

GIVING FEEDBACK TO LEADERS

Michael Bochenek

Overview   Often, it is difficult for team members to give feedback to their leader without a sense of permission. Sometimes, a structured exercise provides the context for such an exchange. This activity allows individuals to observe various leader styles and provide feedback about their effectiveness.

Suggested Time   60 minutes

Materials Needed
- ✔ Several sheets of $8^1/_2 \times 11$-inch paper
- ✔ Form A (Leadership Checklist)

Procedure
1. Inform participants they will work on a toy-designing task that examines leadership and problem-solving behaviors.
2. Randomly form teams of 3 to 6 participants.
3. Ask each team to select as leader the person who has the highest or lowest Social Security number or phone number, without area codes.
4. Ask the teams, under the guidance of a leader, to design, sketch, and name a toy that meets several criteria:
   - Sells for $12 or less.
   - Fits into a normal size backpack.
   - Is appropriate for children between the ages of 8 and 12.
   - Engages players and has educational value.

   Provide 15 minutes for this task.
5. After toys have been designed, distribute the Leadership Checklist (Form A) to the leaders and to team members. Direct the leaders to meet in a separate room or hallway to complete the

Contact Information: Michael Bochenek, Elmhurst College, Center for Business and Economics, 190 Prospect Avenue, Elmhurst, IL 60126, 630-617-3119, michaelb@ elmhurst.edu.

checklist and discuss what they did to help or hinder the design process.

6. During this time, ask the teams to review what their leaders did to help or hinder the design process. Have them complete the Leadership Checklist and plan how they will give feedback to the leader.

7. Ask the leaders to rejoin their teams and share their perceptions. The team then gives the leader feedback on his or her behavior.

8. Solicit a summary of leadership behavior observed in each team, seeking patterns of agreement and disagreement.

9. Ask the teams to present their designs and talk about the processes that produced the ideas. (Allow 5 minutes.)

10. Summarize the discussion and give a brief lecture on leadership models (e.g., traits, behavior style, contingency, transformational), referring to the Leadership Checklist. (Allow 10 minutes.)

Variations

1. Select leaders to meet a specific learning goal of the workshop (e.g., trust, listening, decision making) or to address incidents (e.g., unresolved conflict, domination) from earlier activities.

2. Have teams develop an ad, slogan, or bumper sticker to promote their toy designs.

3. Have the entire team develop criteria for the most visually appealing, innovative, or marketable designs, and then select winners in each category.

LEADERSHIP CHECKLIST: FORM A

Use the checklist below to appraise leader behavior during the toy design activity. The information is based on *Fundamentals of Management*, 9th ed. (1996) by Donnelly, Gibson, and Ivancevich, McGraw-Hill.

1. **Traits**—features that predict success. Circle the degree to which the leader displayed the following traits.

Drive	Low	Moderate	High
Motivation to lead	Low	Moderate	High
Integrity	Low	Moderate	High
Self-confidence	Low	Moderate	High
Intelligence	Low	Moderate	High
Knowledge of organization	Low	Moderate	High

2. **Behavior (style)** —specific actions of leaders. Circle the behaviors that best describe the leader.

   Autocratic decision making   vs.   Democratic decision making

   Task-centered   vs.   Person-centered

3. **Situational (contingency)**—Appropriate behavior is based on the situation or context. Was the leader:

Aware of the task demands and skill level of members?	Yes	No
Flexible in handling the design task?	Yes	No
Able to manage the changing needs of task and team members?	Yes	No

4. **Transformational**—change-oriented behavior that addresses more than task completion. How much did the leader:

Respond effectively to crisis?	Little	Moderately	To a Large Degree
Transform followers?	Little	Moderately	To a Large Degree
Provide intellectual stimulation?	Little	Moderately	To a Large Degree
Articulate a vision?	Little	Moderately	To a Large Degree
Communicate clearly?	Little	Moderately	To a Large Degree
Build trust through fairness?	Little	Moderately	To a Large Degree
Exhibit a positive self-regard?	Little	Moderately	To a Large Degree

---

8
DEVELOPING NEW TEAM MANAGERS

Deborah Hopen

Overview   When organizations begin to use teams in their workplaces, managers need to learn new roles. Managing a problem-solving or self-directed work team requires different skills than managing employees in a more traditional, hierarchical work setting. These three scenarios describe situations that teams and their sponsoring managers might face. As the participants consider the scenario questions and discuss their responses, they will discover ways to work effectively with teams. (You may also use this exercise in individual coaching sessions.)

Suggested Time   30 minutes

Materials Needed   ✔ Form A (Three Scenes from an Organization)
✔ Form B (Discussion Guide)

Procedure
1. Divide the participants into teams of 2 or 3.
2. Give each team a copy of Form A.
3. Have them read the scenarios and formulate their responses.
4. Ask the teams to appoint a presenter to share and discuss their responses with another team. Thus, if there are two teams, the member appointed would visit the other team and share how his or her group viewed each scenario. If there are three or more teams, rotate presenters one time so that each team is visited once.
5. Reconvene the entire group. Share the key points on Form B and compare them with the views of participants.

Contact Information: Deborah Hopen Associates, 1911 S.W. Campus Drive, Federal Way, WA 98023, 253-927-6668, debhopen@aol.com.

1. Create three subgroups. Assign one scenario to each group.

2. Ask each subgroup to select a member to serve on a "panel" of group reporters.

3. Convene the panel and ask each reporter to discuss the scenario assigned to them and how they would respond.

THREE SCENES FROM AN ORGANIZATION: FORM A

SCENARIO 1

The newly formed green team was having trouble making progress. The desired results were stated clearly, and management had given the team adequate resources and a reasonable amount of latitude in its approach to the task.

Nevertheless, they've been floundering from the beginning. They suffered through several false starts and directionless activities. They finally settled on an approach, but are now having trouble moving from one step to the next. They tend to postpone intermediate decisions or conclusions because they feel they need more information or more time or more resources.

How can you help the team get on track?

SCENARIO 2

In an effort to stimulate team activities, you establish a "Team of the Month" recognition program. Although there was a lot of excitement and many new teams formed during the first month of the program, the pace of business improvements associated with team activities has declined sharply in the past quarter.

Two months ago, you increased the reward from a $25 gift certificate for each team member to an overnight stay at a local resort hotel; however, this produced no noticeable improvement in results.

How can you best stimulate team performance?

SCENARIO 3

An ongoing team has been established in the food services department you manage. The first problem the team decided to tackle involved petty theft of utensils. You shared with the team at its formation that $650 of stainless steel flatware has disappeared since the beginning of the year. This constitutes a negative effect of 0.69% on the cafeteria profit margin. Everyone on the team is quite concerned about this situation. And as the department manager, you are experiencing significant pressure from the owners to solve this problem. On a recent business trip, your large key ring set off the metal detector at the airport. It immediately occurred to you that installing a metal detector in the exit door frame could quickly identify anyone leaving with stolen spoons. You suggested this approach at the next team meeting, but the team leader asked you to save your recommendation until the team had collected more data. You pointed out that the company's money was "walking out the door" while the team was wasting time when a perfectly good solution was staring it in the face. The team leader thanked you for your comment and the team returned to data collection planning.

What should you do now?

DISCUSSION GUIDE: FORM B

SCENARIO 1 KEY POINTS

✔ *Ask the team members if they need any further clarification of or changes to the task agreement.*

Are the expected outcomes clear? Are the performance indicators easy to measure? Could they be better defined? Are the targets reasonable? Are the team members able to devote sufficient time to the task? Are more members or members with different skills needed? Is the team hampered by financial restrictions or management approval cycles?

✔ *Ask the team to identify and quantify exactly what is holding the group up.*

What needs to be increased? What needs to be decreased? What actions have been completely successful? What actions have been only partially successful?

✔ *Ask the team to examine its group process.*

Has the team established explicit norms? Is the team checking its behaviors against the norms? Does the team have any consistent behavioral issues?

✔ *Ask the team to review its progress.*

Has the team established a formal action plan? Is the team checking its progress against the action plan? If interim results fall short of targets, is the team recycling through the agreed-upon steps?

✔ *Ask the team how you can help.*

SCENARIO 2 KEY POINTS

Have you considered the pitfalls of your current program?

✔ Creating competition instead of cooperation—rewarding teams or members who withhold information others could use in an effort to gain an advantage.

✔ Limiting the number of groups or employees that can be recognized at one time—when one team wins, the other teams all lose.

✔ Letting every team have its "turn"—it's difficult to recognize the same successful team over and over.

✔ Focusing on nuances—it's also often difficult to differentiate among performances.

DISCUSSION GUIDE: FORM B (*CONT.*)

What other reinforcement techniques are you using?

✔ Providing regular feedback—compliments for even small accomplishments.

✔ Recognizing milestones—public acknowledgment of intermediate results.

✔ Chatting informally with team members—listening with respect, not taking action, and recommending that any problems discussed be solved through the team structure.

SCENARIO 3 KEY POINTS

Have you forgotten that you should leave your manager's hat outside the room when you are a member of the team?

✔ Do nothing.

✔ Honor the process.

✔ Participate as a cooperative member of the team and let the solution arise from the data and root-cause analysis.

✔ Don't narrow your viewpoint prematurely.

✔ Build off other team members' suggestions.

Have you forgotten why the team was formed?

✔ Management wanted to tap into the creativity of a cross section of the organization.

✔ Management perceived the problem was more complex than one person could permanently solve.

✔ Management felt that commitment could be built more effectively if the entire department participated in the process.

Are you worried that the team won't solve the problem fast enough? Cheaply enough?

✔ Trust—Do you have more faith in your own abilities than those of the team members?

✔ Respect—When the team is successful, do you think your superiors will lose respect for you as an individual?

9

TAPPING THE COLLECTIVE POWER OF A GROUP

Leigh Mundhenk

Overview Today's great leaders have learned that a facilitative style of leadership is more effective than the traditional directive style. With the traditional style of leadership, the leader creates the vision, determines the goals, and makes the decisions for the group, focusing on generating support for these decisions and managing the group in the accomplishment of the goals. In contrast, the facilitative leader helps the group develop a common vision, set goals, and make its own decisions. The facilitative leader uses process interventions to facilitate rather than direct the group, serving as a resource, coach, mediator, and challenger as the group works together to accomplish its goals. This style of leadership promotes creativity and risk-taking, and optimizes human interaction and organizational learning. Thus it can greatly enhance organizational performance and help organizations succeed in today's competitive business climate.

This interactive, hands-on activity will help middle and senior managers learn when and how to use the facilitative model of leadership to enhance the quality of outcomes while generating strong stakeholder involvement and commitment. Participants will have the opportunity to learn:

- how a facilitative leadership style can enhance productivity;
- how and when to choose between a facilitative or traditional leadership style;
- skills needed to become a facilitative leader;
- how to assess their skills as facilitative leaders; and
- how to use, through practice, selected skills based on an assessment of their needs.

Suggested Time 60 to 90 minutes

Contact Information: Leigh Mundheuk, University of Southern Maine, Lewiston-Auburn College, 51 Westminster St., Lewiston, ME 04240, 207-753-6581, mundhenk@usm.maine.edu.

Materials Needed   ✔ Form A (Assessing Your Skills As a Facilitative Leader)

✔ Flip chart and tape

Procedure

1. Open discussion by asking participants what is meant by participative leadership.

2. Go over the background information presented in the Overview to give participants a brief understanding of participative leadership, including how it differs from traditional leadership and the value it has in generating quality outcomes by enhancing stakeholder involvement and commitment.

3. Make the following points about the traditional leader, using a flip chart and then taping the flip chart page on the wall.

   The traditional leader:

   • Creates the vision, determines goals, and makes decisions for the group.

   • Focuses on building support and commitment for implementing these decisions.

   • Manages the group in implementing and accomplishing the goals.

4. Make the following points about the facilitative leader, using a flip chart and then taping the flip chart page on the wall next to the one describing the traditional leader.

   The facilitative leader:

   • Encourages the group to use its creativity and knowledge in creating a common vision and goals.

   • Uses process skills to help the group do its own work.

   • Acts as a resource, coach, mediator, and sometimes challenger to assist the group in its work.

5. Conclude this discussion by stating that facilitative leadership:

   • Encourages and rewards risk-taking.

   • Facilitates a high level of human interaction.

   • Promotes self-management by encouraging the group to take responsibility for its own work.

   • Promotes organizational learning, which leads to enhanced organizational performance.

6. State that having both leadership styles as tools to work with gives leaders options to use in different situations.

7. Lead a discussion on choosing a leadership style by asking participants when one style of leadership is preferred over the other.

65

Make the following points if they are not mentioned in the discussion.

a. Managers should use a traditional leadership style when they need control; when they want to:

1. Create the vision.

2. Determine the action plan.

3. Have control over the outcome.

4. Use their expertise and authority because it is needed for the best possible outcome.

b. Managers should use a facilitative leadership style when they have no specific agenda or desired outcome; when they want to:

1. Generate a high level of creative input.

2. Create a high level of ownership.

3. Maintain neutrality, and are willing to support any decision the group makes.

4. Abdicate their expertise and authority for the opportunity to help their group members grow professionally.

8. Form groups of 3 and ask participants to discuss situations when they would choose one style over the other and give reasons why. Ask for volunteers to provide examples.

9. Conclude by stating that it is very important to choose the right leadership style for each situation; considerable harm can come to a manager's credibility if he or she empowers people and then retracts that empowerment by overriding decisions made by the group.

10. Shift to a discussion of the skills used by facilitative leaders.

11. Form groups of 4. Give each group two sheets of flip chart paper and tape. Have them select a scribe and a reporter, and ask them to brainstorm a list of skills facilitative managers need to have, writing the skills on the flip chart paper and taping it to a wall when finished.

12. Distribute copies of Form A to all participants. While remaining in their groups, participants should review Form A and identify skills listed on their flip chart paper that are not on the assessment. Each group should report only those skills not on the assessment. Ask participants to add these skills to Form A.

13. Conduct a general discussion about the skills needed to be an effective facilitative leader. Be aware that terminology may be used that is unfamiliar to some members of the group.

Participants should be encouraged to ask questions to get clarification.

14. Tell participants that they are now going to have an opportunity to assess their own skills as facilitative leaders.

15. Instruct participants to follow the instructions on Form A, placing a check in the appropriate place beside each skill indicating their level of competence at using the skill. Finally, ask participants to circle the three skills they feel are the most important for them to develop.

16. State that while most of these skills are basic and require practice to improve, some are more sophisticated and may require some instruction. Ask if any participants need instruction and offer help, using the other participants as resources: Demonstrate with another participant how the skill can be used.

17. Conduct a role-play practice session. Form groups of 6, and ask group members to each lead a portion of a meeting. Ask participants to tell the group what skills they plan to practice. Each group member will lead the meeting for 15 minutes, rotating turns. When done, ask them to discuss their practice skills with their group members and get feedback.

    Meeting Scenario: You are a customer service group, comprised of one manager and five customer service representatives. You are planning to have a daylong retreat where you will discuss problems facing the department and possible solutions. The purpose of this meeting is to decide on a date, time, location, and overall goals and outcomes for the retreat.

18. Reconvene the group and process the role play by asking some or all of the following questions:

    a. What was the experience like?

    b. What went well?

    c. What was difficult or awkward?

    d. How well did the role play help you to feel more confident using the skills?

    e. What do you need to do to further increase your confidence with these skills?

19. Conclude by stating that developing masterful facilitative leadership skills allows managers to tap the knowledge and energy of their entire group and inspire increased productivity.

ASSESSING YOUR SKILLS AS A FACILITATIVE LEADER: FORM A

Rate your competence in each of the following skills by placing a check mark in the high, medium, or low column. Circle the three skills you most want to improve.

SKILL	Competence HIGH	MEDIUM	LOW
• creating a welcoming environment			
• clarifying the purpose			
• helping the group establish norms or ground rules			
• helping the group determine roles			
• actively listening			
• giving effective instructions			
• identifying problems			
• encouraging full participation			
• providing a safe environment			
• keeping the group on task			

- acknowledging and handling conflict and difficult situations
- giving process feedback or suggestions
- drawing out opinions
- using affirmation
- suspending judgment and maintaining neutrality
- summarizing progress
- guiding the group in coming to conclusions

_____

_____

_____

_____

_____

_____

_____

10

PRACTICING HOW TO COACH

Doris Sims

Overview   We all know one of the best ways to develop management coaching skills is to practice, practice, practice. This activity provides a wide variety and a large quantity of scenarios that occur between employees and managers, so even with a large group you will not run out of different situations to role play!

In addition to the 50 coaching scenarios, a feedback form is included with this activity for the observers in the group to provide written positive and constructive feedback for participants following their role-play positions as coaches.

Suggested Time   15 minutes per role play

Materials Needed   ✔ Form A (Coaching Skills Practice—Scenarios)

✔ Form B (Coaching Skills Practice—Feedback)

Procedure   1. Divide the class into trios and distribute Forms A and B. Designate several scenarios or allow trios to select one to use from Form A.

2. For each scenario, one person should take the role of *manager/coach* (all scenarios are written from the perspective of the coach), another person takes the role of the *employee*, and the remaining member of the group will become a *feedback giver* to the manager/coach using the Coaching Skills Practice—Feedback Sheet (Form B).

3. During and after each role play, the feedback giver will complete Form B and give it to the participant acting in the manager/coach role.

4. Rotate these roles for each scenario so that each person plays each role at least once.

Contact Information: Doris Sims, Alcatel, 100 Coit Rd., M/S HRD7, Plana, TX 75075, 972-477-2916, dmsims@attbi.com.

Variations

1. The scenarios can be chosen by the facilitator and read to the groups to create a more impromptu situation, or the group members can read and select the scenarios they would like to role play.

2. The groups can contain more than one feedback giver.

COACHING SKILLS PRACTICE— SCENARIOS: FORM A

1. Annette is responsible for obtaining monthly productivity statistics and creating the quarterly update report. The report is always accurate and Annette turns the report in on time, but those who use the report have complained to you that the format of the report makes it hard to read and understand. You decide to talk with Annette about the problem.

2. Brian is interested in becoming a supervisor. He has many leadership characteristics, and you agree he will make an excellent supervisor. The only issue you see is that others perceive him as somewhat arrogant because he frequently interrupts others to present his own ideas. He has no previous supervisory experience, and he has requested your help in achieving his goal.

3. Beverly and Mark are very effective, highly productive employees—unless they have to work together. They avoid communication with each other and often don't share information that is critical to the other, and their conflict is hurting the overall effectiveness of the team. They have recently been assigned to work together on a project to solicit vendors for an upcoming conference, and Mark has just entered your office to protest the joint project.

4. Bettina has been an employee with the company for 12 years, and she is a very productive, dependable employee who works well with everyone on your work team. However, now that the department has switched to personal computers rather than terminals to process work, she has been unhappy and her productivity is now much lower than the productivity of others in the department. Like others in the department, she has attended a computer training class and has been using the computer for a month, and she has now come to you asking to go back to using the terminal to process her work.

5. Crystal's wedding is one month away. Normally she is your most successful sales representative, but lately she has been busy with wedding preparations—during work hours. You have documented that she is spending an average of 80 minutes every day on the phone with her mother and various wedding preparation businesses. You have decided to talk with her about this issue.

6. Ben has been one of your employees for six months. He has a positive attitude, wants to learn new skills, and has a perfect attendance record. However, you have noted his error rate is 10 percent higher than that of other employees in your department over the last six months. You decide to discuss this with him at his standard weekly meeting today.

7. Casey has been with the company for two months. When she applied for the job, she indicated she had used spreadsheet software in her previous job to produce reports. As you have reviewed her work, you have found several calculation errors in her spreadsheets, and you are wondering if she knows how to use the spreadsheet formulas correctly. She seems quite happy in her job and she is an excellent team player in your group. You decide to meet with her to discuss the spreadsheet errors.

8. Chris is a data entry processor. The quality of his work has dropped significantly in the last two months. He has been a dependable employee with the company for three years, and this is the first time his performance has dropped below a satisfactory level. You've been documenting errors each week to see if improvement will take place without meeting with Chris, but the error rate is not improving, and you decide to meet with him.

9. Jack is an excellent employee with a positive attitude. However, he sometimes dresses inappropriately according to the company's dress code policy. He sometimes wears jeans when it is not casual Friday, and today he has on sandals, which violates a safety rule in the company. You ask him to meet with you to discuss this issue.

10. Dana's fingernails are so long they interfere with her typing on the computer. Her documents contain an average of five errors, and when you go into her cubicle to talk with her informally, you notice as she is typing that her fingernails hit different keys than her fingers are aiming for. She has an excellent knowledge of the company's industry, which is so critical to this position, and she knows the department procedures thoroughly, but the errors need to be addressed. You decide to discuss what you've observed at your next weekly meeting with her.

11. Hector has excellent technical knowledge; he is extremely helpful to the other employees in your department, fixing computer problems and answering software questions, and everyone, including you, appreciates his knowledge. The problem is that often he is so busy helping others with technical problems, he doesn't complete his work goals. In the last month, you've documented that he has reached his daily call numbers only 70 percent of the time. You decide to discuss this with Hector.

12. Normally Robin has excellent attendance, and she has been with the company for six years. However, in the last three months, she has been absent ten days altogether. Because of this, your department did not meet a project completion deadline, which you have had to explain to your manager. Robin has just entered your office asking for three more vacation days next week.

13. Carol has been promoted to team leader in your group. She has natural leadership skills, but she does not know how to organize and lead a project through to completion, or how to create a project plan. You need her to lead a new procedure change for the group, and you call her into your office to explain the procedure change and to discuss the project management skills she needs as a team leader.

14. David is a new on-the-job trainer in your department. He has created excellent training materials, and he has been meeting with new employees to go over department procedures. However, two of the most recent trainees have complained that he goes over the procedures too quickly and they don't have time to ask questions or to practice their new skills. You decide to meet with David to give him this feedback and to determine a plan of action together to address this issue.

15. Mark has been in your department for eight months. He seems eager to learn and to perform well, but he is in your office every 30 minutes asking for help prioritizing his work. Mark has just entered your office again asking for help.

16. Heather is a knowledgeable, competent employee, and she has been with the company for five years. However, when your group holds a department meeting, she never offers her ideas and opinions, which you know would be very valuable to the group because of her experience and insight. Today is your standard weekly meeting with Heather, and you decide to address this issue.

17. Jesse's job is to check the final documents for errors. Jesse has been with the company for three months. He is on time every day and appears to be working hard at his desk. The problem is that he is missing too many errors in his quality checks. In the random checks you conducted this week, you discovered six obvious errors that should have been caught during the quality check. Because Jesse is a new employee, you ask him to meet with you to determine if he is aware of his quality check goals, and to see if he has attended the training classes he was scheduled to attend.

18. You have just started as a new supervisor in the company, and you really enjoy your new job and your new work group. Hannah does the most accurate work in the department, and you really appreciate that. However, because of her perfectionist tendency, her speed is very slow. She is processing 13 customer research issues daily, while your other employees average 20 customer research issues daily. You decide to meet with her to discuss this issue.

19. Judith has expressed an interest in moving in her career path to a position as a trainer for the department. Judith is a natural people person, so you agree she would enjoy and succeed in this type of position. Her speaking skills are superior. The area she needs the most improvement in is her written communication skills, which will be important for the trainer position because new training materials need to be created and kept up to date. Judith has just entered your office to ask for your ideas about what training and skills she needs to reach her trainer career goal.

20. Wesley always puts in more than 50 hours a week, and his work is of high quality. However, you never know when he is going to arrive in the morning. While your department has a flex-time policy, Wesley didn't arrive this morning until 9:45 and you had no message he would be late. In fact, he has arrived after 9:30 four times in the last two weeks. He has been with the company for two years, and he is a very valuable employee, but this problem has been worsening recently. You decide to talk with him about it to see what has changed to cause this to happen.

21. Melanie has been with the company for four years, and she is one of your most knowledgeable employees. However, her desk organizational skills need work; for example, last week she found an investor's check in her drawer that everyone had been looking for all week. When she was absent earlier in the month, no one could find anything on her desk to complete two of her most urgent tasks. You ask her to meet with you this afternoon to talk about this problem.

22. Joseph is one of your supervisors. His employees seem to like working for him, and you feel the group looks up to him as a leader. You would like to see his time management skills improve. He forgot to attend two important meetings this week, and he doesn't prioritize his work well. Just last week he forgot an urgent project task item, and this has delayed a company project by two weeks. You decide to talk with him at his normal weekly meeting this afternoon about improving his time management skills.

23. Sarah is a whiz on the computer, she always has a smile on her face, and everyone enjoys working with her. Because of her strong system skills, she is often selected to work on project task teams. Her attendance at the meetings is consistent, but you've received three complaints in the last two months about her inability to follow through and complete specific project tasks assigned to her. This is causing some delays in major system conversion projects. You schedule a special meeting with her to discuss this.

24. Mike is one of your most effective supervisors. He has been with the company for five years, and he has just become a father for the first time. He has just entered your office to request a more flexible work schedule to allow him to come home earlier in the afternoon to spend time with his wife and new daughter.

25. Veronica is one of your supervisors. She has strong coaching skills and does an excellent job of ensuring departmental safety procedures are accurate and followed by employees. Her department safety record so far this year is 100 percent. However, one of her employees recently came to talk with you about problems that are occurring during meetings that Veronica leads. Veronica never seems to have a real agenda for her meetings, and when the meeting is over, no one seems to know what was decided or whether any tasks were assigned to the attendees to follow up on. You decide to talk with Veronica about this issue at her next weekly meeting.

26. Susan is going out on medical leave for six weeks. She has requested a meeting with you to go over the dates of her leave and the company medical leave procedures and policies. She does not know who to notify that her leave will start next week. She is also concerned about how her job responsibilities will be handled while she is out of the office. She has just entered your office to discuss these items.

27. Steven is an excellent customer service representative. His call productivity rate is high, and you've even received two complimentary letters from customers in the three months he has been here. The only problem is that the three employees sitting next to him have complained to you about the strong cologne he wears, and they've asked you to ask him to reduce the amount of cologne he puts on. Steven has just entered your office for his weekly meeting.

28. Andrew is a technical help desk employee who has been with the company for one year. His technical knowledge is excellent and he is able to help customers resolve problems easily, as long as the customer doesn't get upset or angry. He needs help learning to ease the anger of irate customers and then lead them into the information he needs to resolve the problem. Otherwise you are afraid he is going to leave the company, because his stress level is very high and he is becoming increasingly frustrated in his job. He has asked to speak with you this afternoon about his frustration.

29. Maria would like to cut back on her hours and move into a part-time position. She is a steady, loyal employee who has been with the company for nine years. She has just entered your office to talk to you about her request.

30. Lonny always gets his work done and normally exceeds all his performance objectives. Customers and coworkers alike love Lonny's friendly attitude. The only problem is the monthly statistical report you need every month to present to the senior management committee; every month you have to ask him for the report because he has never given the report to you by the due date. The report is due today, so you decide to meet with him to ask for the report but also to discuss why this is happening.

31. Darlene has noticed a new position in the marketing department she is interested in. She has only been in her current position for four months, and the company policy states all employees must have at least one year of tenure in a position before transferring to another. She has just entered your office to ask you to complete the transfer paperwork.

32. Jenny is a new loan collector; she has only been with the company for one month. She is a very quick learner and she follows procedures precisely. However, she gets very emotionally upset every day working with the customers and worries about their problems every night. You think she is an excellent employee for the company, but the loan collector position may not be the best fit for her. You ask her to meet with you to talk about this.

33. Kirk has taken on a new job responsibility within the department, and he is very excited about it. It requires him to meet with a variety of people in various other departments. He does not know any of the people he will be working with, and the other project team members don't know each other, but the success of the project depends upon the key people working together closely and effectively. He has come to you asking for advice on getting started with the new project.

34. Jade has been an employee of the company for four years, and she has just transferred into your department. She is learning your department procedures quickly, and she gets along well with everyone in your group except for John. You know that John is a little impatient and likes to get right to the bottom line quickly, and you have observed that Jade is very expressive and enjoys talking through details and many different ideas. You believe that might be the source of the communication problem. Jade has just stepped into your office, asking for your advice as to how to work more effectively with John.

35. George has ten years of experience working with system conversions; he has been in your department for eight months. He is so knowledgeable you know the department can really benefit from his experience and ideas. If only he would voice his ideas! Whenever you have a department or project meeting, he never says a word. But after meetings he has come to you with new ideas that you wish he had presented in the meetings for discussion. This just happened again today, and he has just entered you office to talk about another idea that was discussed at the meeting.

36. Riley has been filling out his timesheet incorrectly. He has been with the company for only two months, so you believe he is not filling it out incorrectly on purpose, but that he just doesn't understand how to fill it out correctly. You ask him to come into your office to discuss the errors you've been finding on his timesheet.

---

37. Max sometimes has a problem using inappropriate language on the job. Yesterday when you were walking by his cubicle with an excellent candidate for the open position in your department, you overhead him swearing on the phone, and so did the job candidate. Today you asked him to meet with you to talk about this issue.

38. You have received complaints from customers about Marti, who has not been returning phone calls. This month, three customers specifically called to complain that Marti had not called them back in over a week. You decide to talk about this problem with Marti today during her weekly meeting.

39. In your department, it is important that employees arrive on time so the customer phone call queues are covered adequately. Aaron has been with the company for four years, and his customer service skills are excellent. But in just the last two months, you notice he has arrived late to work several times. Last week you noted that he was more than 20 minutes late three times. You decide to talk with him to see what is causing the late arrivals.

40. Linda is a supervisor who reports to you. Her peers in the company respect her abilities and ideas, and she is a team member on several project task teams working to resolve issues. But you've had two employees who report to Linda complain that their performance reviews and salary increases are several weeks overdue. They both say they've talked to Linda about it with no result. You call Linda and ask her to meet with you about this issue.

41. Nick is an account manager who reports to you. He handles several of the company's important accounts, and his clients respect him very much. In fact, you've had two other clients request him as their account manager. However, he seems to have a difficult time on many days prioritizing his work, and asks for your advice and help prioritizing his work and making judgment calls an average of three times daily. He always seems to have good ideas to solve his client's problems, but he just seems to lack the confidence to make the decisions on his own. Or, maybe he is not aware that you trust him and would like for him to make these decisions on his own. He has just walked into your office to ask how you would like him to handle the latest customer issue.

42. Sharon is upset about a company policy that has just changed, causing her to lose vacation time she thought she would gain when she reached her five-year anniversary with the company next month. She is very angry and has just come into your office to tell you she is going to go talk to the Human Resources director.

---

43. Walter is a special projects leader in your group. He will be presenting a new idea to the senior management team next week, and he is a little nervous. You know he has researched his idea thoroughly, and the idea is excellent. However, when he practiced the presentation for your work group earlier in the week, everyone had a difficult time hearing him, and he read the presentation directly from his notes word for word, even though you know he knows the presentation material inside and out. He has just entered your office to ask for your feedback on the practice presentation.

44. Melanie is working an average of three hours of overtime each day, but her productivity is the same as others in the department who are not working overtime. The quality of her work is excellent. But because Melanie earns time and a half pay for her overtime hours, and because you've been documenting in the last two weeks that she is taking excessive breaks, you've asked her to meet with you this afternoon.

45. Sean is new in your department; he transferred from the customer service area, where he worked for two years. He has now been in your department for two months, and he seems to be working well with the other employees in your group. However, you were notified this morning that he did not attend the required safety course last Thursday, and he wasn't working at his desk that day either. You ask him to come into your office to determine what happened last Thursday.

46. Veronica is one of your most dependable and knowledgeable supervisors. Last Monday during your weekly meeting with your supervisors, you told them about a new company product line that would be announced next week. You asked all of the supervisors to keep the information confidential until the announcement. However, after the meeting, the news spread through your division about the new product line, and Veronica's employees tell you they heard the news from Veronica. You decide to ask Veronica about the situation.

47. Craig is known for his sense of humor, and usually this fills a positive role in your work group, because he helps others lower their stress level and keeps everything in perspective. Unfortunately, today he went too far when he played a joke on another employee by giving her a dribble cup. The other employee was very upset about the stain on her clothing, and asked you to "do something" about Craig. You decide to ask Craig to meet with you about this specific incident.

48. To William, everything is a crisis. The good thing about this is that William is quick to handle all problem situations, but you find it difficult to tell when a situation really is a crisis and when it is not. Sometimes William jumps to conclusions before researching the problem. William has just entered your office to apply for the open supervisor position in the group. You feel he is an excellent candidate, but he really needs to learn how to evaluate situations more carefully before reacting if he is going to be a supervisor.

49. Zoe is one of your most knowledgeable and dependable customer service representatives. She just transferred from another department in the company a few months ago, and she has been with the company for seven years. When you monitor her phone calls, you find that she always provides accurate information to the customer. However, her customer service skills need improvement; some customers have complained that she has been rude to them. On the phone conversation evaluation sheet you completed after monitoring her calls, you have noted she needs to remember to greet the customer and ask how she can help them, and thank customers for their business. You've asked her to meet with you this morning to talk about this.

50. Zane is your most creative manager. He always has good ideas for new products and he is a creative problem solver as well. Last year the new product line he developed was the company's best seller. However, he is required to fill out specific paperwork for his employees and to track his budget each month, and he consistently "forgets" or is late turning the paperwork in. You decide to talk with him this afternoon to come up with a solution to this issue.

COACHING SKILLS PRACTICE—
FEEDBACK: FORM B

Directions: Please complete this feedback sheet for each person in the group who acts in the role of coach by circling the answer that corresponds with your observations. Provide comments as applicable to support the answer you choose.

The name of the coach I am observing is: _____

1. Did the coach provide both positive and constructive feedback during the coaching session?

    A. Yes, both positive and constructive feedback was provided.

    B. Only positive feedback was provided.

    C. Only constructive feedback was provided.

    Comments: _____

2. Did the coach provide factual information (what has been observed or heard, and the factual result(s) of the employee's actions) or subjective information (judgment statements based on feelings or personal perspective) about the problem?

    A. The coach stated the problem and the desired behavior using factual information.

    B. The coach stated the problem and the desired behavior in a subjective manner.

    C. The coach stated the problem both factually and subjectively.

    D. The coach stated the problem but not the desired behavior.

    E. The coach stated the desired behavior but not the problem.

    Comments: _____

3. Did the coach ask for and listen to the employee's perspective (or "side of the story") on the problem?

    A. The coach asked for the employee's perspective and listened attentively.

    B. The coach did not ask for the employee's perspective at all.

    C. The coach asked for the employee's perspective, but could have listened more attentively by _____.

    _____

    Comments: _____

4. Did the coach ask for and listen to the employee's ideas for solving the problem?

   A. The coach asked for the employee's ideas and listened attentively.

   B. The coach did not ask for the employee's ideas at all.

   C. The coach asked for the employee's ideas, but could have listened more attentively by

   _____

   Comments: _____

5. Did the coach provide ideas for improvement or possible solutions?

   A. Yes, the coach provided at least one idea or possible solution.

   B. No, the coach did not provide any ideas or possible solutions.

   Comments: _____

6. At the end of the coaching session, did the coach schedule a follow-up meeting with the employee in the future to review the employee's improvement and the impact of the solutions or ideas implemented?

   A. Yes, the coach scheduled a follow-up meeting.

   B. No, the coach did not schedule a follow-up meeting.

   Comments: _____

   Overall Comments: _____

   _____

   _____

PART

EMPLOYEE DEVELOPMENT

11

GETTING A QUICK READ ON YOUR TRAINING GROUP

Carolyn Balling

Overview As a trainer it's always helpful to know about your participants' experience, background, or opinions related to the topics of a course. Even without time to gather data ahead, you can learn about your group quickly using this simple, interactive assessment exercise.

Suggested Time 10 minutes

Materials Needed ✔ One flip chart page for each of several questions

✔ Tape

✔ ½-inch adhesive dots or other stickers for each participant, one dot per flip chart page per participant

✔ Form A (Sample Assessment Questions)

Procedure 1. Before the session, prepare 3 to 7 flip chart pages with questions related to participants' experience with or opinions about course topics. Include a rating scale with each item.

Refer to Form A for examples of questions and rating scales that could be used in a train the trainer workshop on techniques for assessing and evaluating learners' progress.

2. Post prepared flip chart pages. (Allow space between posted pages because participants will be moving between pages to affix their dots.)

3. Introduce the activity by acknowledging that participants bring experience with and opinions about course topic(s) to class, and stating that to make the course best meet their needs you want to find out something about their experience. Review the questions

Contact Information: Carolyn Balling, Training That Fits, 6743 Banning Drive, Oakland, CA 94611, 510-339-9039, Balling@pacbell.net.

and rating scales on the posted flip chart sheets to illustrate the type of information you want to find out now. Clarify posted questions and rating scales as needed.

4. Distribute adhesive dots or stickers to participants. Explain that you want group members to place one sticker on each of the rating scales on each of the flip chart pages to indicate the answers that best describe their experience or opinion.

5. Set a time limit of 3 minutes for participants to place stickers on posted pages.

6. Monitor the group as individuals place stickers on flip chart pages. Answer questions or assist with decision making as needed. Note the time remaining, and extend it as needed.

7. Call time after 3 minutes, or after most participants have finished.

8. In front of the group, review and interpret responses. Ask for confirmation or clarification of your interpretations as needed. Ask group members to explain dot placement, such as any dots placed beyond the range of the rating scale.

9. To conclude the exercise, summarize group responses and experience in relation to the course topics and agenda. Note adjustments you will make in the course to best fit the group's background and needs.

Variations

1. When reviewing the results, ask for specific questions or needs group members would like addressed related to each question.

2. Assign small groups to review the responses to each different question. Ask groups to interpret the results as well as list expectations or needs they have related to their assigned question.

3. Use a similar technique at the end of the session or course as an evaluation.

SAMPLE ASSESSMENT QUESTIONS: FORM A

1. I like the idea of taking progress checks of learners' work and of my training and instructing:

No, sounds like extra work.	No, evaluations at the end tell me enough.	Maybe, if it's easy and painless.	Yes, without a doubt.

2. I'd characterize my knowledge of assessment techniques as:

Never heard of them.	Know about them but don't use any.	Know about and use only occasionally.	Know about and use regularly.

3. My comfort level with using assessment techniques is:

Low —or— Never used them	Lower than higher	Higher than lower	High

4. When I use an assessment technique and gather data, I report the results to the group:

Never; it never occurred to me or I never gathered data.	Sometimes, if it's good news.	Most times, most data.	Every single time, and everything I find out.

5. I use a wide variety of methods to determine whether learners are learning:

No; little or no variety or no method used	Small variety	Medium variety	Yes, wide variety

12
GIVING AND RECEIVING FEEDBACK

Francesco Sofo

Overview This activity is a strategy to learn about five principles of giving and receiving effective feedback. Instead of engaging in an activity and then moving on to something else, participants are asked to discuss in detail from several perspectives two principles of giving and receiving feedback and then share those outcomes in a group before reporting the findings to the whole group. By focusing in detail on feedback and then expressing this in concrete form to share with the whole group, the participants learn about a set of principles of giving and receiving feedback.

Suggested Time 90 minutes

Materials Needed
✔ Form A (General Functions and Principles of Feedback)
✔ Form B (Five Principles for Giving and Receiving Effective Feedback)
✔ Form C (Five Roles for Discussing Feedback)
✔ Flip chart and markers

Procedure
1. Inform participants that this exercise will give them the opportunity to learn about a set of principles for giving and receiving effective feedback.

2. Distribute Form A and ask participants to read it to themselves. Conduct a brief discussion on the general functions and principles of effective feedback.

3. Divide the whole group into five Home Teams of five members or conduct the exercise with one or more intact teams.

Contact Information: Francesco Sofo, Adult Education/Human Resource Development, University of Canberra, P.O. Box 1, Belconnen, ACT 2616, Australia, 616-2015123, franks@education.canberra.edu.au).

4. Distribute a copy of Form B to each Home Team member. Each team member is to select one of the five principles for giving and receiving effective feedback from Form B. Ensure that each of the five principles is selected only once.

5. Ask all participants who chose the same principle to form an Expert Team to discuss that principle. There will be five Expert Teams as there are five principles on Form B. (You may call them Expert Teams 1, 2, 3, 4, and 5.) If there are fewer participants than required, then select fewer than five principles.

6. Distribute a copy of Form C to each member of the Expert Teams. Allow members to adopt one of the roles listed on Form C. They should discuss the feedback principle with this role in mind.

7. Instruct the Expert Teams to discuss the principle they selected from Form B. Inform them that they have 10 minutes to ensure that the team members share all the knowledge they have and their understanding of the principle and relate their own experiences about it. As far as possible they should adhere to the role function prescribed for them during the discussion.

8. Ask everyone to go back to their Home Teams to contribute their findings from the Expert Teams. (Time allocated for this is 15 minutes.)

9. Invite each Home Team to make a summary on flip chart paper and report it to the entire group.

[If time permits, use the following additional steps.]

10. Using the principles just learned, ask all group members to form pairs and to give each other feedback on this exercise.

11. Elicit comments from members of the whole group on how they felt they were able to apply the feedback skills.

GENERAL FUNCTIONS AND PRINCIPLES OF FEEDBACK: FORM A

As well as verbal messages, feedback consists of nonverbal messages including silences. Feedback is information that is given to the speaker concerning the listener's reactions to the message. Once people's attention is obtained, all responses and reactions are regarded as feedback. Feedback begins from the moment feed forward (the introduction) is initiated. Feedback has a number of functions in social interaction. Feedback:

✔ provides information about different people's reactions;

✔ acts as a group memory by recalling events;

✔ maintains equilibrium within the relationship(s);

✔ encourages people to appreciate complexity and difference;

✔ stimulates people to gain insights;

✔ achieves self-knowledge and identity of individuals and groups;

✔ assists in knowledge, skills, and attitudes acquisition;

✔ creates possibility for improvement at individual, group, and system levels.

Some general principles for giving feedback are useful when engaging in a social interaction. A general first principle for giving feedback is to demonstrate genuine respect to all members of the group. Respect is demonstrated by:

✔ giving recognition to strengths;

✔ being open and impartial to possible outcomes;

✔ offering different explanations for problems;

✔ asking the person(s) being observed how they think they used their skills;

✔ execution of the specific role by each participant.

This type of feedback is designed to encourage inquiry and curiosity through observation and description. Feedback is most useful when it involves formulating and testing hypotheses. This requires adoption of an open-minded attitude and maintenance of a stance of neutrality.

FIVE PRINCIPLES FOR GIVING AND RECEIVING EFFECTIVE FEEDBACK: FORM B

Giving information or feedback can be used as a way of giving help. It can be a learning mechanism for people who want insights into how well their behavior matches their intentions as perceived by the participants or audience. Feedback can be a means of establishing one's identity for answering, *Who am I?* The famous sociologist Charles Cooley said that we come to know who we are by the reflection others give us of ourselves. The following are five principles of giving and receiving effective information (feedback).

PRINCIPLE 1

Giving Feedback

Feedback describes behavior rather than evaluates behavior.
Describing one's own reactions to another's behavior leaves the other free to use the feedback or not use it, as he or she sees fit. Avoiding evaluative language reduces the need for the individual to react defensively (learning is difficult when one is defensive).

Here is an example:

Your head nodded a lot and I noticed you yawning six or seven times during the discussion (behavior); not, *You looked bored and disinterested* (motive).

Receiving Feedback

Encourage feedback by asking questions that indicate you want feedback.
Obtaining information about yourself from others can help you know yourself better and enable you to interact more effectively in groups. Your reactions to feedback should encourage others to provide it freely. Ask:

✔ *Are there other benefits people think may result from this communication exchange?*

✔ *What did you notice about my performance / behavior?*

✔ *How did I come across just then?*

FIVE PRINCIPLES FOR GIVING AND RECEIVING EFFECTIVE FEEDBACK: FORM B (*CONT.*)

PRINCIPLE 2

Giving Feedback

Feedback describes specific behaviors.
In giving feedback, try to avoid making general and categorical statements about behavior. Telling people they were "domineering" gives a categorical interpretation of their behavior and may not be very useful to them. A more useful statement would be:

Just now when we were deciding the issue, I felt that you did not listen to what others said and that you were expecting me to either accept your point of view or face attack from you.

Receiving Feedback

Ask about the specifics of your own words and behavior.
If people say you were "okay" or "good" or use other evaluative terms such as "awful" or "enjoyable," you will need to ask them about specific behaviors or words you used to give them that reaction. Ask:

What sort of things did I do and say that made you feel it was okay?

PRINCIPLE 3

Giving Feedback

Effective feedback expresses consideration toward the receiver.
Feedback can be destructive when it serves only your own needs as giver and fails to consider the needs of the person on the receiving end. During the social interaction endeavor to notice the purposes and motivations of the speakers. Instead of assuming what they were endeavoring to achieve, ask them to express what their needs and motivation were during the interaction. Then you can more accurately frame your feedback with their orientations and perspectives in mind.

Receiving Feedback

Ask probing and clarifying questions.
Make sure you understand comments others make about your behavior. You can do this by asking them probing questions such as questions of clarification and qualification. Ask:

Can you give me an example of that?

What assumptions did you identify in what I said?

Were there times I did not engage in that behavior?

FIVE PRINCIPLES FOR GIVING AND RECEIVING EFFECTIVE FEEDBACK: FORM B (*CONT.*)

PRINCIPLE 4

Giving Feedback

Feedback should be tentative and focus on behavior that the receiver can modify.
Try to develop a sense of what is within the power of people to change within themselves. For example, personality characteristics are not points of focus that people generally would want to address or change about themselves. Frustration is only increased when people are reminded of some shortcoming over which they have no control.

Receiving Feedback

Avoid reacting and becoming defensive to feedback you receive.
You should withhold your own judgments, reasons, or explanations when feedback is provided by accepting others' responses to you without justifying your actions or words. If you try to justify your actions, others may think that you are defensive and they may then be reluctant to give you further feedback or to clarify points they made.

PRINCIPLE 5

Giving Feedback

Once expressed, ownership of the speaker's utterances may be assumed by the listener as well.
The speaker should express thoughts and feelings about the other person's behavior. Everyone needs to assume responsibility for telling each other the impact of behaviors on them. Frame your feedback in terms of your own feelings and thoughts rather than the other person's assumed feelings. Example:

I felt frustrated when I heard the conversation return to the same issue three times.

Receiving Feedback

Use this sequence of action after you receive feedback:

a. Take ownership of the feedback and reflect on it.

b. Decide if and how you can grow from the feedback.

c. Say "Thank You" to the person giving the feedback.

FIVE ROLES FOR DISCUSSING FEEDBACK: FORM C

ROLE 1: CRITIC

Apart from contributing your own ideas about the principle of giving and receiving feedback, you should try to ask critical thinking questions both of your own assumptions and of the ideas expressed by others in the group. (Play the devil's advocate.) Use the following types of questions to help you be a critic in the discussion:

What are you assuming when you say that?

What is likely to happen if everybody adopted that view or procedure?

How is your idea similar to the ideas already expressed?

What are your reasons for saying that?

How can we judge the value of that idea?

ROLE 2: IMAGE MAKER AND SCRIBE

Apart from contributing your own ideas about the principle of giving and receiving feedback, you should endeavor to keep a record of the discussion in words and picture/diagram format. As well as scribe, your role is to suggest metaphors or images for the ideas that best symbolize the thinking of the group. For example, if people express an idea that a feedback principle is not very useful, you may want to suggest an image for this idea such as "no through road," that is, a "dead end," or a "rubbish bin for waste."

Listen to people's language as you may find people use figurative expressions and your role may be to simply highlight the images enunciated for all the group to note. You may suggest that some of the images are worth exploring in order to help everyone clarify the meaning.

ROLE 3: IDEAS THREADER

Apart from contributing your own ideas about the principle of giving and receiving feedback, your role is to encourage people to link their own contributions to the discussion already expressed. Encourage the group to build a coherent and unified set of explanations clearly showing the links among all the contributions. Help to clarify and consolidate the ideas. Ask people how their ideas are similar to or different from other ideas already shared. Your role is to make overt the thread that ties together all the ideas expressed. Ask the group to help you identify the nature of such a thread.

ROLE 4: CRITICAL REVIEWER

Apart from contributing your own ideas about the principle of giving and receiving feedback, your role is to encourage people to critically review their contributions. You may appeal to particular individuals in the group or to the group generally and ask them if new information presented in the discussion has made any difference to their initial ideas.

Just before the discussion ends, ask people how their ideas have changed as a result of the discussion. Then ask them if they are happy to accept any conclusions the group has arrived at; for example, would they use the ideas themselves?

ROLE 5: FACILITATOR AND TIME KEEPER

Apart from contributing your own ideas about the principle of giving and receiving feedback, your role is to encourage all people in your group to contribute equitably. You may do this by noticing which group members tend to be reticent and inviting them to express their view of what has already been said and any views of their own on the topic. About two minutes before time is to expire for the discussion, you should inform the group that it may be a good idea to summarize their discussion. The critical reviewer (role 4) may wish to ask the group a question to consider.

In short, your role is to ensure that the discussion remains focused, that all contribute equitably, and that people are aware of the need to achieve the group goal within the given time.

13

IMPROVING LISTENING SKILLS

Kat Koppett

Overview   Listening is a critical skill that can all too often be taken for granted. There are many techniques designed to enhance our ability to listen effectively. However, we are unlikely to employ them unless we recognize how complicated listening is and how flawed our assumptions can be, based on our inaccurate and incomplete interpretations of messages. This exercise is designed to spur discussion and insight into the listening process. It can highlight the pitfalls of assuming that what we think we heard is what we actually heard. It can underscore that people communicate not just data or facts, but emotion and intent, and that we must listen for these too. Finally, this exercise can make us more conscious about our inferences and more motivated to improve our listening skills.

The good news is that listening is a muscle. It can be exercised and developed. Through practice and awareness, communication can indeed be enhanced.

Suggested Time   45 to 60 minutes

Materials Needed   ✔ 3 × 5-inch cards
                      ✔ Pens

Procedure   1. Pass out the 3 × 5-inch cards and pens.

2. Assign each participant a number and have them write the number on the card, as large and as legibly as possible.

3. Have the participants find a partner and decide who will be A and who will be B.

4. Have the A's tell the B's a story from their lives. The stories should be:

Contact Information: Kat Hoppett, Story Net LLC, 1774 Great Highway, San Francisco, CA 94121, 415-752-0217, kat@thestorynet.com, www.thestorynet.com.

    a. true;

    b. about 60 to 90 seconds long; and

    c. from any period or aspect of their lives (e.g., something that happened this week, or something that happened in childhood).

5. The B's should *listen only*. They should not interrupt or ask questions.

6. When the A's finish, have the B's tell a story.

7. Have the partners exchange 3 × 5-inch cards. Each person now has the card with the number of the story they just heard.

8. Ask everyone to find a new partner.

9. Each person now tells the story that he or she just heard, but in the first person (i.e., "I took the goldfish...") as accurately as possible, as if it is his or her story. Stress that each participant is to attempt to tell the story exactly as it was heard. (*Note:* Refrain from telling the participants that they will have to repeat their partners' stories until this point.)

10. When both participants have told their stories, ask them to exchange 3 × 5-inch cards and find a new partner.

11. This time, ask people to make sure that they are not paired with someone who has a card with a number they have already seen. This process ensures that people will not get their own stories back or hear the same story more than once.

12. Again, have the participants exchange stories (as above) and swap cards.

13. Have the participants form a circle, and one by one tell the stories that they just heard.

14. Debrief the activity, using these tips:

    Have the participants share randomly, rather than around the circle. This will enhance their ability to stay present and be receptive.

    Ask people to listen to the stories without commenting or "claiming" their own stories, until all of them have been told. The impulse may be strong to correct the stories in the moment, but the flow will be smoother and the debriefing richer if the participants can wait until everyone has told their stories.

Debriefing Questions

- How many of you felt your story remained accurate?
- Did anyone not recognize his or her story?

- Did you listen differently after you knew you were going to have to repeat the story you heard?
- How did it feel to have your story repeated in its current form?
- How did it feel to tell someone else's story?
- What kinds of things can we listen for? (Facts, emotions, the intent or point of the story.) Which were the easiest to discern? Which were the most important? How do they relate to each other? Which are the most "real"?
- What kinds of things did we change in our telling? Why? (We forgot; we wanted to make connections to close logic gaps; in telling the story as our own, we inadvertently or deliberately made it more personal, for example, by changing the genders of key people.)
- What did we "make up" that we were sure we heard?
- How did the tellers interact with the listeners who were silent?
- Did you change the story based on the nonverbal signals of the listener? Why or why not?
- Why bother listening if no one truly gets it right?
- How is it we are able to function in the workplace when we misunderstand?
- What should we do with this information about the effectiveness of our listening?
- How can we listen more effectively?

Variations
1. If there are more than 16 to 20 people in the group, split the group into more than one subgroup. Make sure you do this at the beginning of the process, so that each subgroup will be sharing all the stories that they told. You need not have a facilitator for each subgroup. The only part of the process for which the entire group needs to be divided is the last round of sharing stories in a circle.
2. Pick four people to work in front of the rest of the group: A, B, C, and D. Send C and D out of the room. Have A tell a story to B. Then invite C back into the room and have B repeat the story as exactly as possible to C. Then invite D in, and have C tell the story. Finally, have D tell the story to the whole group. This version takes less time and allows the participants to watch the process of how the story changes.
3. Do variation 2 in two rounds, in subgroups of eight, four participants relating the story and four watching. Then switch. This will allow everyone to participate and watch without taking an inordinate amount of time.

14
COLLABORATION AT ON-LINE SESSIONS AND WEB CONFERENCES

Alain Rostain

Overview A key success factor in on-line collaboration and creative thinking is getting participants to listen to each other's input and build on each other's ideas. It is very easy for participants to become distracted by other things in their physical environment, or to be off in their own worlds. This activity works best when you can break participants into virtual groups of no more than 5 or 6 people. Placeware Conference Center, for example, allows each row in the virtual audience to create its own chat session.

Use this exercise:

- to increase listening and spontaneity, and
- to explore storytelling.

Suggested Time 10 minutes

Materials Needed ✔ Software that allows for subgroups to create chat sessions
✔ A concurrent teleconference session for the facilitator to run the exercise

Procedure
1. Set up your participants in virtual groups of no more than 6.
2. Have each group create its own chat session. (The procedure and capacity for this depends on the software you use, of course.)
3. Have each group assign a player order (which player goes first, second, and so on). A simple way to do this is to have each player enter "Here" in the chat window at the same time, and see how the order comes out.
4. Groups then tell stories, each player contributing one word at a time, using the preestablished order.

Contact Information: Alain Rostain, Creative Advantage, Inc., 26 Laurel Glen Terrace, San Rafael, CA 94903, 415-499-5100, alain@creativeadvantage.com.

5. Continue for a couple of minutes, or until the story comes to a natural conclusion, and try it again. Use the same order or create a new order.
6. The setup (context) and side coaching are critical to this exercise's success. Side-coaching prompts might include:
   - Say the first thing that comes into your mind.
   - It's alright if it doesn't make sense.
   - Avoid "and."
   - Finish sentences.
7. Debrief the exercise by asking:
   - What was that like?
   - What happened?
   - What obstacles did you encounter? What helped?
   - What did you learn?
   - What did it take for you to be successful?

Variations Instead of the group telling a story one word at a time, use any of the following:

- Lesson of the Day: Each player goes exactly once, summarizing the biggest lesson of the day or meeting.

- Proverb: Similar to the original game, but it needs to make even less sense.

- Expert Panel: Select one player as the interviewer, and have the others act as one expert. They answer questions from the interviewer one word at a time.

- Haiku.

- Two words at a time.

- A sentence at a time.

15

SEEING THROUGH ANOTHER'S EYES

Dave Arch

Overview   Often we disagree not because of anything that's right or wrong, but rather because of a difference in perspectives. Seeing the issue through the eyes of another can bring us to the understanding necessary to value the other person's opinion. Here is a simple exercise to demonstrate this point.

Suggested Time   10 minutes

Materials Needed   ✔ Form A (What Is It?) *Note:* Make two duplicates, enlarging them both so that everyone in your group can see them. However, during the enlargement process, please make sure that you keep them both as squares. If you plan to use this activity frequently, you might also wish to laminate them both.

Procedure   1. Invite two volunteers from your group to come to the front of the room and sit in two chairs. For maximum impact, have the two chairs quite a distance from each other.

2. Show the person on your left one of the pictures (so that only he or she can see it). Have the picture turned so that it looks like a picture of a duck. Ask the person to remember what the animal in the picture was, then place the picture face down in the person's lap.

3. Take the other picture to the other person and have the picture turned so that it looks like a rabbit. Ask the person to remember what animal was in the picture, and place the picture face down in the person's lap.

4. Now ask both people to reveal the animals in their pictures. Of course, one will say the picture was a duck and one will say that it was a rabbit. Boldly declare that you will now cause the pictures

Contact Information: Dave Arch, The Bob Pike Group, 7620 78th St., Edina, MN 55439, 800-383-9210, ext. 686, Darch@bobpikegroup.com, www.bobpikegroup.com.

to change places. Clap your hands, go to the person on the left, and lift the picture to show it to the person (again, so others can't see) in such a way that it now shows a rabbit. Ask what picture is now seen, and the person will indicate a rabbit. Go to the other person and show the picture turned so that it looks like a duck. The person will indicate that the picture is now of a duck.

5. Bow to the thunderous applause...and then turn both pictures around to show the audience the secret to this miracle.

6. Ask participants what can be learned from the "magic of perspectives." This is a wonderful opening activity any time you want people to share their opinions honestly in a meeting. Everyone needs to realize that we will not all agree on what we are seeing. However, others' perspectives are as valid and valuable as our own!

WHAT IS IT?: FORM A

16
INTRODUCING HUMAN PERFORMANCE TECHNOLOGY

Sivasailam "Thiagi" Thiagarajan

Overview This activity uses a children's game to introduce the critical steps in human performance technology. A volunteer from the audience demonstrates his or her less-than-perfect performance for a few minutes. All participants then use a checklist to analyze the performance gap, causes for the gap, and appropriate interventions.

Suggested Time 45 minutes

Materials Needed ✔ The engine to get this activity going is any simple children's game from the toy store that involves motor skills under timed conditions and can be played alone. We prefer Milton Bradley's Perfection. This game includes a plastic tray with a 5 by 5 array of slots of different shape (squares, rectangles, circles, triangles, stars, and other shapes) and plastic pegs of the same shapes to be placed in these slots. Before the game, the player removes the pegs from the slots, turns a built-in timer to zero, presses down the tray, and begins placing the pegs in the correct slots. The timer clicks ominously as the player races to fill all the slots with the correct pegs. If the player is unable to complete the task within 60 seconds, the tray springs back with a loud noise, throwing out all the pegs.

✔ Form A (Performance Technology Intervention Selection Checklist)

Procedure 1. Select a volunteer. Look for a friendly person with self-confidence and a sense of humor. As you bring the person to the front of the room, whisper your thanks and announce that the activity may involve some good-natured teasing of his or her performance. (To simplify our description, let us assume that your volunteer is Joan, a trainer from a retail store outlet.)

Contact Information: Sivasailam Thiagarajan, Workshops by Thiagi, Inc., 4423 East Trailridge Road, Bloomington, IN 47408, 800-996-7725, thiagi@thiagi.com, www.thiagi.com.

2. Introduce the play equipment. Show the Perfection game tray and the 25 pegs. Demonstrate how to put the pegs in the correct slots. Ask Joan to try out a couple of pegs and praise her performance extravagantly.

3. Begin the activity. Set the timer, press down the tray, and invite Joan to begin placing the pegs in the correct slots. Invite other participants to surround the table and cheer Joan on. Give a play-by-play commentary on Joan's progress. Do everything you can to distract Joan without being obviously obnoxious.

4. Conclude the activity. Invariably, time will run out before Joan completes her task (unless she has been secretly practicing this game with her children). The tray will spring up with a loud bang, startling Joan. Thank Joan for her valiant and enthusiastic effort. Lead a round of applause as you escort her back to her seat.

5. Announce the disappointing results. Count the number of pegs that Joan was not able to place in their slots. Tell the audience how many pegs Joan was able to fit in the slots within the 60-second time limit.

6. Distribute a copy of Form A to each participant. Explain that you will use Joan's performance as a case study to explore the initial steps in the human performance technology process.

7. Refer to the first two questions on the checklist. Explain that performance technology defines a need as a gap between desired and actual performance, and defines potential for improved performance as the difference between the actual performance of typical individuals and that of a master performer. Tell the participants, in a tongue-in-cheek fashion, that you have a 9-year-old daughter (or nephew) who can correctly place all 25 pegs in their slots within 27 seconds. Discuss these facts with the audience and elicit the conclusion that there is both a performance gap and potential for improved performance.

8. List causes for the performance gap. Ask the audience, "Why was Joan unable to perform as effectively as a 9-year-old child?" Wait for responses from the audience and write them down on a sheet of flip chart paper. Encourage a wide assortment of possible causes, including off-the-wall suggestions. If participants appear to have run out of ideas, ask more probing questions to suggest different types of potential causes.

Here are sample responses that we usually get from our audiences:

- Lack of interest.

- Too much pressure.
- Her hands are too big for the tiny pegs.
- Too many people looking over her shoulders.
- Not a part of her job specification.
- The work surface is too low.
- Objectives were not spelled out clearly.
- It's too soon after lunch.
- The ticking of the timer was too loud and disruptive.
- She has a headache.
- Not enough team support.
- She was not involved in the goal-setting process.
- Unfamiliar with the task.
- The pegs are too much like each other.
- Old age.
- Not enough practice.
- The facilitator did not give clear instructions.
- Too much feedback.
- Lack of self-confidence.
- The room is too cold.

9. When you have accumulated a list of 30 to 50 causes for the performance problem, ask participants to help you classify these items into different types. Listed below are eight types of causes that performance technologists often identify. Name each type and ask participants to select examples from the list that was developed for Joan. Encourage participants to identify additional causes that belong to each type. Point out that these eight types can be organized into four pairs, each with an internal and external counterpart of the same basic cause.

- Lack of skills and knowledge
- Lack of information and instruction
- Lack of interest and motivation
- Lack of rewards and incentives
- Lack of physical and mental capacity
- Lack of tools and facilities
- Lack of interpersonal skills
- Lack of interpersonal support

10. Explain that the selection of a suitable performance improvement strategy depends on identifying the primary cause among different possible causes. Work with participants to identify the primary type of cause. Depending on the group, you may end up with lack of knowledge (unfamiliarity with the game) or lack of motivation. Point out that different performance technologists may identify different primary causes.

11. Explain that most performance gaps are created by more than one cause. Even if there is a clear primary cause for a performance gap, it may be a good idea to identify some secondary causes that strongly contribute to the problem. Work with participants to identify some types of secondary causes.

12. Explain that strategies for improving human performance are called interventions in the performance technology jargon. Training is one intervention, but there are several other interventions. Ask participants to name different interventions that could be used to improve Joan's performance and to bring it closer to that of your daughter (or nephew). In the beginning, encourage wild speculations.

Here are some sample interventions from our audiences:

- Offer a $1,000 prize for breaking the previous record.
- Disable the timer.
- Arrange the pegs in the correct array before starting the timer.
- Work with both hands.
- Work with a team of five members.
- Practice in a quiet location for several days.
- Hypnotize the worker.
- Have a child coach the adult performer.
- Begin the task with a self-affirmation statement.
- Provide therapy to get insights into the performer's childhood trauma.
- Improve primary education to encourage hand–eye coordination activities.
- Arrange the work area to be more efficient.

As the brainstorming of interventions continues, ask the participants to select the best set of interventions that directly addresses the primary cause of the performance gap. Narrow down the ideas to the most effective intervention. Point out that not everyone may agree on a single best intervention. Explain that if enough time is available, a performance technologist can design alternative interventions and select the best one on the basis of pilot testing data.

13. Explain that in addition to the primary intervention, a performance technologist may select some secondary ones. There are two reasons for doing this: 1) The performance gap may have more than one type of cause. 2) The primary intervention may require other interventions to support it. (For example, if the primary intervention were to provide repeated practice, you may need a secondary intervention that provides incentives for sustaining practice.)

14. Point out that you have specified the performance gap, identified the primary cause, and selected a suitable intervention. You still have to design, develop, evaluate, and implement the intervention. But you are off to good start with an objective choice of intervention. Explain to the participants that real-world performance analysis and intervention selection activities may take several days or months. However, the same procedure used for analyzing Joan's play performance can be applied to large-scale, real-world performance gaps.

15. Suggest a follow-up activity. Ask participants to select a small-scale performance gap that is currently bugging them. Suggest that they spend some time analyzing that gap and selecting a suitable intervention by using the same checklist.

PERFORMANCE TECHNOLOGY INTERVENTION SELECTION CHECKLIST: FORM A

1. Is there a performance gap?
2. What are the desired and actual levels of performance?
3. Is there potential for improved performance?
4. Is there a difference between typical performers and master performers?
5. What types of causes hinder effective performance?
   - Lack of skills and knowledge
   - Lack of information and instruction
   - Lack of interest and motivation
   - Lack of rewards and incentives
   - Lack of physical and mental capacity
   - Lack of tools and facilities
   - Lack of interpersonal skills
   - Lack of interpersonal support
6. What is the primary cause of the performance gap?
7. What are some secondary causes?
8. What is the appropriate intervention?
   - Training
   - Education
   - Job aids
   - Motivation
   - Incentives
   - Feedback
   - Recognition
   - Employee selection
   - Better tools
   - Ergonomics
   - Team support
9. What supporting interventions are needed?

17
LINKING EFFORT AND PERFORMANCE TO VALUED OUTCOMES

John Sample

Overview In business and industry, much of the reward system is prefaced upon the relationship between hard work, high performance, and attaining valued outcomes. Identifying valued outcomes other than financial rewards is often a challenge for managers. This activity will enable participants to understand the relationship between performance goals and valued outcomes for employees and managers. This activity is based upon Vroom's motivation theory of expectancy. Having completed the activity, managers will better understand how to identify valued outcomes for employees and how to develop plans for linking such outcomes to effort and performance.

Suggested Time Approximately 60 minutes

Materials Needed
✔ Form A (Worksheet: Expectancies ➡ Effort ➡ Performance ➡ Valued Outcome)
✔ Form B (Implications for Management)
✔ Form C (Motivation Strategies)
✔ Pens and pencils
✔ Flip chart, overhead projector, or whiteboard

Procedure 1. Begin the session by stating that there are many theories of motivation useful to managers and employees, and that this exercise will focus on a motivational theory that links employee effort with performance goals in return for valued outcomes. Vroom's theory of expectancy motivation has enjoyed wide acceptance for over thirty years (Vroom, 1964).

Contact Information: John Sample, Adult Education/HRD Program, College of Education, Florida State University, Tallahassee, FL 32309, 850-644-8176, Sample@coe.fsu.edu.

2. Provide participants with Form A (Worksheet: Expectancies ➡ Effort ➡ Performance ➡ Valued Outcome) and explain the fundamental tenets of Vroom's cognitive theory of motivation.

According to Vroom, human beings in the workplace are constantly thinking about

✔ the effort to perform the job,

✔ the performance realized from the effort, and

✔ the valued outcome realized by the employee from the job performance.

Vroom's approach to motivation assumes that we behave in the present based on valued outcomes to be realized in the future if certain levels of job performance are attained. If there is no foreseeable valued outcome of interest to the employee, then effort and performance may decline to levels of marginal acceptance by managers. If a valued outcome is identified and attainable, then employees are more likely to increase **effort** to **perform** their jobs so that **valued outcomes** are realized.

3. Draw the diagram below on a flip chart. Use the examples below or generate an example by soliciting information from the group.

Effort ➡ Performance ➡ Valued Outcome = MPS (Motivational Potential Score)

	E ➡ P ×	P ➡ O	×	**VO** Money, Promotion, Raise
Example 1 MPS = 5.04	0.7 ×	0.8	×	9 Directs own project. More autonomy. Valued assignment. Training.

Effort ➡ Performance ➡ Valued Outcome = MPS (Motivational Potential Score)

	E ➡ P ×	P ➡ O	×	VO
Example 2 MPS = 0.63	0.7 ×	0.1	×	9 Directs own project.

Request from participants examples of valued outcomes other than money, raises, or promotions, and then list each contribution in the right-hand column under the heading *VO* for *Valued Outcome*. Other examples could be 1) an opportunity to direct a large-scale project, 2) more autonomy, 3) a valued assignment, 4) specialized training and development. Make sure that participants understand the nature of a valued outcome, which is something tangible for which one is willing to demonstrate *Effort* to *Perform* on the job.

111

4. Choose one of the valued outcomes from the list and request that the participant who offered the example rate the value of the outcome using a number between 1 and 10 (10 denoting the highest value for the outcomes). For purposes of explanation, assume for the moment that the participant said, "The opportunity to direct my own project from start to finish is something I have been wanting for a long time. I will give it a value of 9." Write "9" next to the valued outcome.

5. Having established the value of the outcome, then ask the participant to determine the likelihood that working hard (*effort*) will result in a job well done (*performance*). In essence, you are asking the participant to establish a practical probability coefficient between two variables—effort and performance. Be careful how this question is asked because participants may become confused by the language of statistical probability. One way to generate this information is to ask the participant to estimate the likelihood (i.e., probability) using a question such as, "What are the chances that if you put forth the effort, you will be able to perform well—one chance in ten, three chances in ten, eight chances in ten...?" Convert the participant's response to a probability coefficient by placing a decimal in front of the number. For example, if the participant says that the likelihood is seven chances in ten that effort will result in high performance, then write "0.7" under the E ➡ P in example 1.

6. Ask the participant to estimate the likelihood that performance will be instrumental in realizing his or her valued outcome. For example, if the participant says that the likelihood is eight chances in ten that performance will result in obtaining a valued outcome, then write "0.8" under P ➡ O in example 1.

7. To determine the Motivational Potential Score, ask someone in the group to multiply $0.7 \times 0.8 \times 9.0$. The MPS for the first example is 5.04. Discuss with participants the power of such a cognitive process to explain why some employees and managers appear to be highly motivated. They have been able to realize valued outcomes by exerting their effort to perform well, and the performance was instrumental in obtaining the valued outcome.

8. Now change one of the numbers in the equation by saying to the participant who values the opportunity to direct a project, "What would happen if you believed that performance would not be instrumental for a valued outcome? Assume for the moment that even though you know that effort would lead to performance on your part, you also believed that performance would not result in a valued outcome. Let's assume that you believe the likelihood of

performance resulting in a valued outcome was one chance in ten (0.1). For the second example, let's multiply $0.7 \times 0.1 \times 9.0$."

9. The MPS for example 2 is 0.63. Ask participants if the difference between 5.04 and 0.63 is significant. Explain that the two scores are the result of changing only one of the three variables—the likelihood of performance resulting in a valued outcome. Are they surprised that the scores could change so dramatically? Does this explain why some talented employees who began their employment with zest began a downslide in effort and performance?

10. Ask to what extent participants in the group know what the valued outcomes for their employees are, and the extent to which effort and performance are related to valued outcomes. Many, if not most, will indicate that they are not sure! Discuss the implications of expectancy theory for managers and employees by using Form B.

11. Provide participants with copies of Form C (Motivation Strategies). Listed in the left-hand column are possible outcomes that have value for many employees. Participants may add valued outcomes at the bottom of the list. Request that they select any three employees they supervise or manage and, based on their knowledge of each employee, select one to three outcomes they believe to be important to each employee. Ask them to place an X in the appropriate columns to designate their selections. Then, for each employee, ask them to develop a short plan of action that links Effort ➡ Performance ➡ Valued Outcome.

12. Arrange participants in teams of 4 to 6. Request that they exchange information about what they have identified as valued outcomes for their employees and the strategies they developed for each employee. At the end of the group discussion, discuss with all participants:

   ✔ There is great variety in terms of valued outcomes and the strategies necessary to obtain valued outcomes.

   ✔ Money, raises, and promotions are not always available, for any number of reasons.

   ✔ Strategizing linkages to increase effort and performance of individuals and teams results in reasonable expectations for managers and others in a position to influence performance.

   ✔ For this approach to be successful, managers must accurately assess the abilities of employees and clearly express their expectations about performance.

Variation   If managers and employees are participating together in this activity, separate them into a managers' group and an employees' group for step 12. Facilitate discussion between the two groups on valued outcomes. Do they identify similar valued outcomes?

References   Newsom, W. B. (1990) "Motivate, Now." *Personnel Journal*, 51–52.

Sample, J. (1986) "The Expectancy Theory of Motivation: Implications for Training and Development." In J. W. Pfeiffer and L. Goodstein (eds.), *The 1984 Annual: Developing Human Resources*. San Diego, CA: University Associates, 242–256.

Vroom, V. (1964) *Work and Motivation*. New York: John Wiley.

WORKSHEET: EXPECTANCIES ➡ EFFORT ➡ PERFORMANCE ➡ VALUED OUTCOME: FORM A

One of the most powerful theories of work motivation to be advanced over the past 30 years is based on the work of Victor Vroom (1964). He and many others have researched the effect of expectations on effort, job performance, and valued outcomes of employees. According to Vroom, human beings are constantly thinking about

✔ the effort to perform the job,

✔ the performance realized from the effort, and

✔ the valued outcome realized by the employee from the job performance.

Take a moment to think about several of the valued outcomes you might expect to obtain as a result of your job performance. Two of the most often cited examples are promotions and raises. List other valued outcomes that you might add to the list for yourself. Remember that a valued outcome is a reward you will receive for which you are willing to exert effort in order to perform on the job.

Valued Outcomes:

1. Promotion

2. Raise

3. _____

4. _____

5. _____

6. _____

7. _____

8. _____

Effort ➡ Performance ➡ Valued Outcome

$$E ➡ P \times \quad P ➡ O \quad \times \quad VO$$

Example 1
MPS* =

Promotion, Raise

_____

Example 2
MPS =

_____

Example 3
MPS =

_____

Consider your personal Effort to achieve the level of Performance necessary for you to obtain your Valued Outcome. What would occur if your Effort to achieve the level of Performance and a Valued Reward were realized? Would you conclude that the linkage between Effort and Performance and a Valued Outcome was evident where you work?

*Motivational Potential Score

IMPLICATIONS FOR MANAGEMENT: FORM B

Individual differences. Individuals attach different valences to different valued outcomes. It is not an unreasonable expectation of management to match rewards with individual valued outcomes whenever possible. If you are a manager, ask yourself if you truly know what the valued outcomes are for your individual contributors and team members. Don't assume that everyone is motivated by money.

Tie rewards to performance seen as valuable by the organization. For example, if the business values quality, reward for producing high-quality work.

Provide clear expectations, training, and encouragement. Remember that we have subjective hunches about our ability to increase performance through effort. Training and encouragement reinforce an individual's commitment to exert more effort to perform at higher levels. Clear goals help clarify expectations.

Present creditable evidence that the performance is directly linked to rewards. Managers must take notice of worthy performance when it occurs; reinforce that performance will be rewarded by the organization. Managers must listen carefully to understand the link individuals have perceived between hard work (effort) and the reward system (valued outcomes).

Explain the meaning and implications of outcomes. For example, if an employee who is interested in working on a special task force knows that assignment to the task force is linked to successful completion of a project, the individual will give special attention to the project. Managers must remember their responsibility to clear the path toward the goal and not to be an obstacle to performance.

IMPLICATIONS FOR EMPLOYEES

Pursue timely discussions with your manager. Request feedback about your manager's perceptions of your level of effort and performance. Provide examples of both to help your manager understand this important aspect of your work.

Communicate your valued outcomes. Money and promotions are important, but not the only valued outcomes for individuals. Some outcomes—such as managing big projects from start to finish—may lead to other valued outcomes. Don't assume that your manager knows what is important to you. Make this part of your discussion during goal-setting and performance appraisal meetings.

Analyze what is necessary for you to improve your performance. We often assume that additional training is the silver bullet for improving performance. This not usually the case; sometimes all that is required is additional information or upgraded equipment or software!

MOTIVATION STRATEGIES: FORM C

Outcome	Employee 1	Employee 2	Employee 3
Good Pay			
Job Security			
Promotion and Growth			
Working Conditions			
Interesting and Challenging Work			
Help with Personal Problems			
Loyalty to Employee			
Full Appreciation of Work Done			
Tactful Discipline			
Feelings of Being in on Things			

Individualized Strategy to Link Employee
EFFORT ➡ PERFORMANCE ➡ VALUED OUTCOME

Employee 1

Employee 2

Employee 3

18
LEARNING HOW TO LEARN

Angela Deitch

Overview This activity is a short, fun, and active experience that can be used to introduce participants to the notion of learning how we learn. The exercise can be expanded or contracted to fit a variety of time frames. In addition, it can be used as a stand-alone exercise, icebreaker, opener for a one- or two-day workshop on learning, or module in another skills workshop.

Suggested Time 1 to 2 hours depending upon the purpose for the exercise and type of processing desired

Materials Needed ✔ 3 lightweight pieces of fabric such as nylon net, purchased from a fabric store and cut into 18-inch squares, per participant

✔ Form A (Reaction Sheet)

✔ Flip chart and markers

Procedure 1. Introduce the exercise as an introduction to skills training, an icebreaker, or a change of pace activity. Don't tell participants they will be exploring their own learning strategies since *you will be observing participants' reactions at each step of the exercise.*

2. Have participants stand with enough space to move their arms freely. Move furniture if necessary.

3. Give each participant three squares of fabric. Explain that they will be learning to juggle, and that you will have them practice each movement after you demonstrate it.

4. First, demonstrate the motion of the arm alone. Raise each arm, one at a time, and pretend you are tossing the fabric into the air. Focus on the imaginary fabric in the air. Have participants practice the motion to get the feel of it.

Contact Information: Angela Deitch Consulting, 82 Lochatong Road, West Trenton, NJ 08628, 609-883-6327, adconsultg@aol.com, www.angeladeitchconsulting.com.

118

5. Next, starting with the *right* hand, toss one fabric square into the air above your head. Keep your eye on it, and watch it float down. Reach out and take it in the same hand. Have participants practice. Encourage them to get the feel of the motion, and to note how the fabric behaves when it is tossed in the air and floats down. After several tosses with the right hand, demonstrate the same movement with the *left* hand. Toss the fabric square, this time with left hand. Keep your eye on it as it floats down, then reach out and take it in the left hand. Have participants practice several tosses and catches with the left hand.

6. Next, have participants practice with two squares. Toss one square into the air with the *right* hand. As soon as the first square is in the air, toss the second into the air with the *left* hand. Keep your eye on the square in the air. Meanwhile, the first fabric square is floating down. Pick it out of the air with the left hand, the hand that has just tossed the second square. Repeat the movements, catching and tossing the fabric square with the *hand opposite* the one that has just tossed it. (One complete series would be: Toss with right hand. Toss with left hand. Catch/re-toss with left hand. Catch/re-toss with right hand.) Have participants practice for several minutes until most of them seem to be able to reproduce the movements.

7. Finally, add the third fabric square. (I usually hold the second and third with my left hand: One is held by my thumb, and the other is held by the small finger.) Begin by tossing the first fabric square into the air with the right hand. Then toss the second into the air with the left hand, releasing the square that is held by the thumb of the left hand. *Immediately*, toss and release the third square, which is held with the little finger of the left hand. (This will require some practice, to toss the second and then the third into the air with the left hand—two quick motions—*before the first floats down and must be picked out of the air with the same left hand*.) Once the three fabric squares have been tossed into the air, use one hand and then the other to take a square out of the air and toss it again.

8. Offer encouragement each step of the way. Have participants strive to complete several series of tosses and catches. When a fabric square falls to the floor, start the series over again. Demonstrate how you compete against yourself to successfully complete an increasing number of series. You may decide to end the exercise when most of the participants can successfully manipulate, i.e., juggle, the fabric squares five to ten times.

9. Ask participants not to discuss their comments with other participants. Distribute Form A and ask participants to indicate their responses.

10. Depending on the amount of available time, you may have participants discuss their responses in small groups *after* they complete Form A. A reporter would then speak for each group.

11. In the processing, ask for possible interpretations of the agree/disagree responses.

12. Have the reporter read the group's statements. Expect a number of responses such as:

"I felt nervous/anxious/frustrated/silly/angry/clumsy, etc."

"My hands began to get sweaty."

"I was afraid of making a fool of myself."

"Everyone else seemed to catch on, but not me."

"I'm not very athletic."

"I thought about when we used to choose sides to play baseball, and no one would choose me."

"My mother/father used to tell me I was a slow learner."

"My second-grade teacher said I was dumb."

13. Ask several participants to tell about their experiences, particularly as young children, when someone made fun of their physical or mental ability.

14. Note that some participants may report being eager or excited to learn to juggle: "I enjoy learning new things." A number of the others may nod in agreement, or repeat the thought. Some of these participants may have dismissed their anxiety, and wish to give the politically correct response. If you have carefully observed the participants as they practiced, you may have noticed a number of indications of anxiety: people watching each other, getting frustrated, making negative comments about their ability, questioning the appropriateness of the exercise for their particular group, people who give up or sit down, etc. Share your observations with the group; it's not necessary to attribute a particular behavior to a specific person.

15. Ask participants whether their private conversations (stories) help or hinder their learning. In what way?

16. Ask participants to describe how they learned to ride a bicycle or swim. What helped them learn? Have them describe the *learning process*. Note on a flip chart terms they associate with learning,

such as: time, observation, practice, repetition, improvement, longer, better, etc. Also: recognition, reward, emotion (happy, proud, etc.). Note, also, that teachers, parents, and relatives, the very people we look up to as children, may be associated with negative feedback. Point out that past experiences affect the way we view the world, change, challenges, and new behaviors. These affect our openness to learning, and serve as barriers or diminish our capacity to learn. As we become more aware of the stories that negatively affect our openness to learning, we can become more competent in the way we learn.

17. In the discussion that ensues, relate comments to the following concepts:

Learning how we learn: a process of developing our competence. Frequently our openness to learning is increased or diminished by our own interpretations of the situation and our personal and historical stories about our ability to learn.

Learning: the ability to repeatedly produce a new action at will. Learning is demonstrated by a change in the body, and takes time and practice. A person who says *she knows* how to swim *can provide evidence by demonstrating* a particular stroke in the swimming pool.

Competence: how well we perform a skill, based on the assessment of an expert. Someone who is a recognized authority in the performance of the skill can distinguish a number of different levels of proficiency. Use examples to describe different levels of competence. Example: "A young teenager takes out his parents' car and is involved in an accident." "The race car driver manipulated the vehicle around the track at lightning speeds." Ask participants to describe the young teenager's, the race car driver's, and other intermediary levels of driving skill. The purpose of this discussion about levels of competence as it relates to learning is to increase participants' awareness that learning—of all skills—is a process that takes time and practice and that is improved with coaching. (Refer to coaches of professional athletes.) The more adept we are at learning how we learn, the more we can facilitate our learning of functional skills, work-related skills, and the yet undetermined skills of the future workplace.

REACTION SHEET: FORM A

Please do not discuss the exercise until after you have completed the Reaction Sheet.

Part I. Write a statement that describes your feelings as you participated in the exercise.

_____

_____

Part II. Indicate your agreement/disagreement with the following statements that describe your feelings as you participated in the exercise.

Select:

(1) Strongly Agree ... (2)Agree ... (3) Neither Agree Nor Disagree ...
(4) Disagree ... (5) Strongly Disagree

1. Based on this exercise, I feel pretty good about my ability to juggle.	(1)	(2)	(3)	(4)	(5)
2. I was apprehensive about succeeding at the exercise.	(1)	(2)	(3)	(4)	(5)
3. I found myself checking to see how well other participants were doing the exercise.	(1)	(2)	(3)	(4)	(5)
4. There wasn't sufficient time to do the exercise well.	(1)	(2)	(3)	(4)	(5)
5. I thought of other incidents when I was judged on my physical ability to perform.	(1)	(2)	(3)	(4)	(5)
6. I would like to learn more skills, similar to this one or others that I haven't tried yet, just to experience new learning.	(1)	(2)	(3)	(4)	(5)
7. I prefer to stand in the back of the room so I can watch others' performance without being so visible myself.	(1)	(2)	(3)	(4)	(5)
8. I'm uncomfortable being called on to perform skills requiring eye–hand coordination.	(1)	(2)	(3)	(4)	(5)
9. It would have been helpful to read the directions before doing the exercise.	(1)	(2)	(3)	(4)	(5)
10. By the end of the exercise, I could juggle as well as, or better than, the other participants.	(1)	(2)	(3)	(4)	(5)

19
ASSESSING AND REINFORCING LEARNING

Susan Boyd

Overview   Review is an important part of training to reinforce concepts before new ones are presented. When skills and concepts are practiced and reviewed, they become an integrated part of the learner's developing skill set and increase the comfort level and confidence in using the new software for job tasks. Review activities also provide a way to assess the learner's grasp of the material and to spot mistakes that can be corrected before moving on to the next topic. This activity offers a varied approach to reinforcing and practicing the skills learned.

Suggested Time   Approximately 5 to 15 minutes for each activity

Materials Needed   ✔ Index cards

Procedure   **1. Independent Practice Exercises**

These are hands-on practice exercises that are job-focused and designed to allow the learner to use the skills and concepts presented in the preceding lesson. These exercises should be designed on two levels, with Part 1 covering the essential commands and features, and an optional Part 2 for additional concepts and practice. Allow a 15-minute time frame for the exercise; all learners should be able to complete Part 1 within this time limit. Faster learners will be able to complete the optional Part 2 also, within the same amount of time. Exercises can be combined with rest and lunch breaks to allow learners additional time if needed. Learners should be encouraged to use all available resources, such as the training manual, quick reference cards, on-line help, and user's manual. During the exercise, the trainer should make notes of problem areas, observe how learners solved the problems, and pro-

Contact Information: Susan Boyd Associates, 270 Mather Rd., Jenkintown, PA 19046-3129, 215-886-2669, susan@susan-boyd.com, www.susan-boyd.com.

vide guidance if needed. The trainer can extend the time frame if the majority of the class requires it for Part 1; also, provide clarification to the class if the exercise seems to be misleading or ambiguous. After the exercise is completed, the trainer can involve the learners in a brief discussion regarding the major learning points.

2. **Walk-Through Procedures**

Another review technique is to ask volunteers to do a step-by-step walk-through of how to complete a specific procedure or job task, using the software. The volunteer can review this for the whole class, or you can assign partners and ask one partner to guide another through all the steps. Typically this takes less than 5 minutes per procedure or job task.

3. **Stump the Class**

Assign teams of 3 to 4 people per team and give each team 3 index cards. They are to write a review question and answer on each card that would test the class's knowledge of the topics covered so far. They have 10 minutes to review all their training materials and come up with the questions. The trainer collects the cards and reads off a question, then tosses a ball randomly to a participant. The person who catches the ball may answer the question, confer with the team, or toss the ball to someone else. When the question has been answered correctly, the person who has the ball tosses it to someone else and the process continues until all the questions have been answered.

4. **Baseball Review**

This is a variation of the Stump the Class activity. Divide the group into two teams. Have them choose team names and give each team 20 index cards. The team members work together to write a question and answer on each card to test the other team's knowledge of the material covered so far. Set up bases in different corners of the room. There is a "pitching team" and an "answering and running" team. The pitching team asks questions. If the running team member answers correctly within the specified time limit, that runner advances one base, and continues to advance if the next person answers the next question correctly. If a team member misses a question, that's an out. When there are three outs, the teams switch. At the end of the game, the team with the most "runs" wins. If you feel this activity puts an individual on the spot, allow conferring with partners or the rest of team to help answer the questions.

5. Help Scavenger Hunt

This review activity is designed to have the learners work in teams to answer a list of written questions that involve using the Help resources available, including the on-line help facility, user's manual, and reference cards. This activity helps the learners become more independent by becoming familiar with the Help resources. Allow 10 to 15 minutes for this activity.

6. What Have You Learned So Far?

This activity is designed for teams to list all the skills, concepts, and topics they have learned so far in the course. The team with the most items will win a small prize. The learners are encouraged to go back to their notes, training manuals, user's guides, reference cards, and on-line help and also to look at the software screens and menus to come up with their lists. Allow 5 to 10 minutes so learners have to work quickly. Reward the team with the most items and then have everyone stand. Toss a ball and ask the person who catches it to state one thing he or she now knows how to do. As each person answers, have the person throw the ball, then sit down. The only rule is that you cannot repeat what someone else has already stated.

7. How Can You Apply This to Your Job?

Periodically during a course, have each team list on an index card three ways they can apply a particular software feature or command on the job. Allow 5 minutes for this activity. Collect the cards and send an e-mail list after the course, summarizing the important topics covered and how they can be used on the job.

8. Pictionary

Make a list of key software concepts or functions covered so far and print the items on separate index cards. Ask for volunteers to illustrate the items on a flip chart, using pictures only, and have the rest of the team guess what is pictured. Allow 15 minutes for this activity. This functions as a good review activity after a lunch break or as the morning review for a multiple-day class.

9. Homemade Reference Cards

If reference cards are not available for a particular topic or procedure, have the learners make their own. Provide a worksheet that lists the topics or commands, and leave space for them to fill in the rest of the information. Periodically, after teaching a topic, ask the learners to go back and fill in the steps on their reference cards. If reference cards are already made up, use the time to have learners highlight the commands or procedures they will use most often in their jobs.

10. But, What I Really Want to Know...

Before teaching a new topic or concept, ask teams to write three questions they have about the topic on index cards (one question per card). Then, after the trainer has presented the topic, ask the teams to review their cards to determine what questions are still unanswered. The trainer can decide whether the questions can be addressed now or at a later time.

11. Game Show Review

Using a format like Jeopardy or Concentration, create a game made up of questions that review a section of the course and have individuals or teams compete to answer the questions. Several game show software programs can be used to create the games electronically, or they can be created using poster board.

12. Relay Race

List a word or phrase vertically on flip chart paper. The word might be a key concept from the class or the software program name. (For example, you might use Formulas for a spreadsheet class or Merge Letters for a word processing class.) Post copies in the four corners of the room and divide the class into four teams. Each team lines up in a single file and the first person is given a marker to fill in a command, benefit, or concept learned for any letter in the word. As soon as the first person is finished, he or she must run back and hand the marker to the next person in line, then go to the end of the line. Anyone who is stumped can just pass on the marker and go to the back of the line. Repeat until all letters are completed. The team that finishes first wins a small prize. This is a fun way to energize an afternoon session, as it gets everyone moving and thinking.

PART

TEAM DEVELOPMENT

20

FORMING, STORMING, NORMING, AND PERFORMING

Tim Osgood

Overview   This tool is a strategy to learn about the four stages of team development that Tuckman* has labeled: *forming, storming, norming,* and *performing*. Instead of listening to someone lecture about the topic, participants are asked to classify events that occur in teams according to stage. By sorting cards that list these events, they learn about the different stages. The exercise also promotes discussion about how existing teams are progressing.

Suggested Time   30 minutes

Materials Needed
✔ Form A (Stages of Team Development)
✔ Form B (Events That Occur in Teams)
✔ Form C (Answers to Card Sort Exercise)
✔ Form D (Events Occurring at Different Stages)
✔ Decks of cards corresponding to the number of teams that you have

Procedure
1. Tell the participants that this exercise will give them the opportunity to learn about the stages of team development in an active way.

2. Distribute copies of Form A and ask participants to read it to themselves. Hold a brief discussion on the essential character of each stage.

3. Divide the total group into teams of 4 to 8 members or conduct the exercise with one or more intact teams.

4. Distribute to each team a set of 24 index cards that each contains one of the 24 statements listed on Form B. Place the number cor-

Contact Information: Tim Osgood, 7 Harmil Rd., Broomall, PA 19008, 610-325-8111, osgoodtr@voicenet.com.

*B. Tuckman (1965). Developmental Sequence in Small Groups, *Psychological Bulletin*, 63, 384–399.

responding to each statement in the upper right corner of each card. For example, the first card in each set will look like this:

```
                                                            1




   Members are concerned with
   acceptance.
```

5. Explain that there are 24 cards in each set. Exactly 6 cards contain statements referring to each of the four stages: *forming, storming, norming,* and *performing.* Inform teams that they have 15 minutes to sort the cards into four piles corresponding to the stages.

6. Call time and distribute copies of Form C to each team. Ask each team to obtain a score corresponding to the number of cards correctly classified. (If there is more than one team doing the exercise, declare the team with the highest score the winner.)

7. Distribute copies of Form D. Ask each team to study the correct answers.

8. Reconvene the total group and discuss the significance of the answers. If the teams participating in the exercise are actual work teams, invite them to assess the apparent stage of team development for their teams. Ask each team to explain the reasoning for its assessment.

STAGES OF TEAM DEVELOPMENT: FORM A

Forming: Transition stage, characterized by movement from individual to team member status. This is a period of confusion, testing behavior, and dependence on a team leader for direction.

Storming: Conflict stage, characterized by infighting, defensiveness, and competition. Team members respond emotionally to and resist task demands.

Norming: Cohesion stage, characterized by an acceptance of team norms and roles. Team members work to achieve harmony.

Performing: Work stage, characterized by maximum work accomplishment, high-level problem solving and decision making, as well as personal insight and constructive self-change.

EVENTS THAT OCCUR IN TEAMS: FORM B

1. Members are concerned with acceptance.

2. Delegation is the prevailing leadership style.

3. The team communicates openly.

4. Conflict continues to occur.

5. Goals are not clear, but clarity is not sought.

6. The team encourages innovation.

7. Cohesion and trust increase.

8. Members communicate in a tentative manner.

9. Clarification of goals begins.

10. Participation increases.

11. Member satisfaction increases.

12. Conflicts about values surface.

13. The team leader is seen as benevolent and competent.

14. Subgroups and coalitions form.

15. The team leader's role becomes more consultative.

16. Subgroups work on important tasks.

17. The team assumes that consensus about goals exists.

18. Subgroups and coalitions are rare.

19. Goal clarity and consensus increase.

20. Pressures to conform increase.

21. Dissent is tolerated.

22. Role clarification begins.

23. The team has defined its work.

24. Decreased conformity begins.

ANSWERS TO CARD SORT EXERCISE: FORM C

Forming   *Total Obtained*

1   5   8   13   17   18

Storming   *Total Obtained*

9   10   12   14   22   24

Norming   *Total Obtained*

4   7   11   15   19   20

Performing   *Total Obtained*

2   3   6   16   21   23

Team Score   _____

EVENTS OCCURRING AT DIFFERENT STAGES*: FORM D

FORMING

Members are concerned with acceptance.

Goals are not clear but clarity is not sought.

Members communicate in a tentative manner.

The team leader is seen as benevolent and competent.

The team assumes that consensus about goals exists.

Subgroups and coalitions are rare.

STORMING

Clarification of goals begins.

Participation increases.

Conflicts about values surface.

Subgroups and coalitions form.

Role clarification begins.

Decreased conformity begins.

NORMING

Conflict continues to occur.

Cohesion and trust increase.

Member satisfaction increases.

The team leader's role becomes more consultative.

Goal clarity and consensus increase.

Pressures to conform increase.

PERFORMING

Delegation is the prevailing leadership style.

The team communicates openly.

The team encourages innovation.

Subgroups work on important tasks.

Dissent is tolerated.

The team has defined its work.

*Based on Susan A. Wheelan, *Group Processes: A Developmental Perspective,* Needham Heights, MA: Allyn & Bacon, 1994.

21
BUILDING BRIDGES BETWEEN TWO TEAMS

Jean Haskell

Overview   Turning a diverse group of people into an effective, productive team is a challenge. Integrating two well-functioning teams to become one team poses a different set of problems. What are the perceptions that each team has of the other? What are the misperceptions? What are the stereotypes that team members hold of the other team? What are the fears and concerns that each team has about working with the other? What are likely to be conflict areas? What are the secrets that each team holds? How do team members feel about the change? In this team integration activity, members of each team have an opportunity—within a structure—to express their concerns, perceptions, and misperceptions, and to lay the groundwork for effective integration.

Designed to be the opening session of an ongoing team integration process, this activity allows all these issues to be raised by putting one team at a time into a "fishbowl" and asking each team member to complete a sentence that speaks to one of the issues, while the other team listens from outside the "fishbowl." It requires enough chairs for members of both teams, space large enough for one team to sit in a circle around the other, a quiet room so all can hear, and a flip chart for instructions and to record issues. All members of both teams, as well as the new team leader, must be present for this activity. The room should be set up with two large circles of chairs, one circle inside the other, not facing each other.

Suggested Time   Two hours (or longer as desired)

Materials Needed   ✔ Two flip charts on easels, and markers for each one
   ✔ Sentence handles (incomplete sentences) written on flip charts in advance

Contact Information: Jean Haskell, Haskell Associates, 2205 Panama Street, Philadelphia, PA 19103, 215-735-3348, Jeanrhaskell@worldnet.att.net.

Procedure

1. Begin by reminding the teams that in a fairly short span of time, they will be working together as one team and under one team leader. Acknowledge the particular difficulties and challenges that this poses, as well as the emotional impact (as appropriate) of "breaking up the old gang." Tell them that today's activity will give them an opportunity to express their concerns and plan ways to deal with them as needed.

2. Select a random method (e.g., drawing straws) to determine which team sits in the center circle first. Ask members of that team to take seats in the center circle. Ask members of the other team to take seats in the outer circle. Tell them that each team will have a specific amount of time to sit in the center circle, and each member will be asked to express his or her viewpoint by making statements directed to specific issues. The other team will sit in the outside circle and listen. At the end of the structured time the teams will switch, with the outside team going to the center circle.

3. Turn to the first flip chart page on which you have written a sentence handle to be completed and show the handle to the group.

   Always begin with a positive handle, for example:

   Two things I like most about being on this team are _____.

4. Ask each person in the center circle to complete the statement in 30 seconds. Select one person to begin and go around in the order in which they are seated. If they seem to be speaking softly, remind them that they are in a "fishbowl" and that the outside group must be able to hear them.

   Depending on the size of your group (10 to 15 people), allow the inner circle 5 minutes to complete the task. At the end of 5 minutes, call time and ask the groups to switch places. The new inner circle group must now complete the same sentence. Call time at the end of 5 minutes and have the groups change places again. It is important to keep strict time limits for this activity. It is helpful to use a gong or make some other noise to signify that time is up and the teams must switch places.

   Note: There is no discussion of any of the statements at this point.

5. Present the second handle written on the flip chart, and ask the inner circle group to complete it, each person speaking one at a time. For example:

   One thing I do not like about working on this team is _____.

   or

One thing I would like to change about working on this team is
_____.

Again, give the first group exactly 5 minutes for everyone to complete the statement, then move the outer group to the inner circle and repeat.

6. Ask each person to complete the sentence with just one statement at a time in each round; however, continue for as many rounds as time allows, to permit participants to express as many thoughts as they wish. Go around in the seating order, giving all participants an opportunity to speak. If some participants seem hesitant, you can allow them to pass for one round and move on. Participants who are hesitant will soon learn that they must speak up quickly and will do so when it becomes important to them. If some continue to pass, tell them that is important to hear from all team members. If participants seem to want to make more input than time allows, you can consider lengthening the inner circle time; however, the second group must be given the same amount of additional time.

7. Repeat the inner and outer circle process until team members have completed the following, or similar, sentence handles:

One thing I'm looking forward to about working with the other team is _____.

One thing I am not looking forward to about working with the other team is _____.

One thing I admire about the other team is _____.

I think that the other team sees us as _____.

I think that they think we see them as _____.

One disadvantage of our working together will be _____.

One real advantage of our working together will be _____.

One concern I have about our working together is _____.

One thing I think we need to do to help us get started is _____.

One hope I have for the new team is _____.

You can vary the sentence handles to meet the needs of a particular set of teams, as appropriate.

Option: Consider asking the group for additional handles.

8. During the process, stand at the flip chart and record critical issues, concerns, or problems that are mentioned repeatedly.

9. After approximately one hour, or when the group energy seems to quiet down, stop the process and read off the listing of issues that you have recorded on the flip chart. State that these are the issues that seemed to emerge over and over again, and ask the group for additional issues that should be included. Record their suggestions.

10. Divide the large group of two teams into groups of four, with two members from each team in each group. Ask each group of four to review the list of critical issues and prioritize them from most to least important in integrating the two teams. Allow 15 minutes to complete this task.

11. When all groups have completed their prioritization, have each group write its list on a flip chart paper and tape it to the wall. Review the lists to determine which items are given highest priority. Select the three or four items that have received highest priority, write each item on one flip chart paper, and tape each paper to one wall in the room so that the charts are a good distance from each other.

12. Ask for volunteers who are willing to work on each issue and have the volunteers stand in front of the flip chart page they have selected. Be sure that each group has equal representation from each team.

13. Have each group spend some time together to determine the time and place of their first meeting, and assure that all meetings are noted by the leader.

    Option: If all team members have volunteered and you have allowed time, give the groups 30 minutes to hold their initial meeting at this time, perhaps to discuss how they might get started.

14. End the session by asking both teams to make a large circle and have each participant finish the statement:

    One thing I appreciated about the session today was _____.

    Thank the team members for their participation, and wish them well.

22
CLARIFYING NEW TEAM PROJECTS AND INITIATIVES

Stephen Hobbs

Overview Whether a team is considering a new initiative or involved in one, it is helpful to clarify what the team members know about their involvement in the initiative. Expanding on the 5W's and H format of questioning (Who, What, When, Where, Why, and How), this activity provides three additional questions framed in a vision-system-people orientation. After the team reviews its answers to the nine questions, a team story evolves that captures the essence of the team's perspective on its involvement in the initiative.

Suggested Time 30 minutes to 2 hours, depending on the depth of dialogue

Materials Needed
- ✔ Overhead projector
- ✔ Flip chart and felt-tipped markers
- ✔ Form A (Perspective Map Descriptions)
- ✔ Form B (Blank Perspective Map)
- ✔ Form C (Vision-System-People Map)
- ✔ Form D (The *IF* Question: Scenario Mapping)
- ✔ Form E (Facilitator's Guide to Perspectives)

Procedure
1. Distribute one copy each of Forms A and B to each person.
2. Define the task: You are asked to answer the eight questions presented on Form A. Write your answers on Form B.
3. If the group members have difficulty in brainstorming ideas, use Form E questions and statements to help guide a facilitated dialogue. Usually, no prompts are necessary.

Contact Information: Stephen Hobbs, WELLTH Learning Network Inc., 2804 6th Avenue NW, Calgary, AB T2N 0Y3, 403-252-8188, stephen.hobbs@wellthlearning.com.

4. On separate sheets of flip chart paper (8 sheets minimum, set out as in Form A on the wall or desk), record what each person has to say. It is important to ensure that you capture exactly what the person says. Use your facilitation skills to determine the order to collect data in.

5. After all comments are collected, ask the team members to summarize the story found in the answers to the questions.

6. With the eight stories recorded, bring the stories together as shown in Form C:

To determine the team's perspective on its vision—What is the vision story?

To review the system the team works in and through—What is the system story?

To acknowledge the people involved with the team both internally and externally—What is the people story?

7. For the three stories, ask the *IF* question outlined in Form D and record the dialogue. In asking the *IF* question, the team provides insights useful for scenario planning. Depending on the need of the team, a more in-depth facilitation of scenario planning is encouraged.

8. Type all stories, and distribute them to the team. If possible, maintain the integrity of Form B when typing.

9. From these stories, each member should be able to pass the elevator test: While traveling on the elevator with the CEO of your company, you are asked, "Why does your team exist? How does it function? Who is involved?" Could you answer the questions?

Variations

1. Use Post-It notes to record answers to each question and post them on the flip chart paper. This saves time in recording; however, the print size is smaller.

2. At Step 5, split the team into smaller groups and assign several questions for storytelling.

3. At Step 6, split the team into three groups to develop the vision or system or people story for presentation.

4. Use this activity as a briefing activity before starting an initiative. The view will provide insight into the preperspective the team has of the initiative (the baseline).

5. Use this activity for debriefing after completing the initiative. This review will provide insight into the postperspective the team has of the initiative (the comparison).

6. Photo-enlarge the forms to create a wall map.

7. Copy the forms and give them to each team member to complete before attending the team meeting.

PERSPECTIVE MAP DESCRIPTIONS: FORM A

Ideological Perspective ... this perspective obtains answers to the question *Why does the team exist?*
> It summarizes the team members' beliefs, assumptions, perceptions and attitudes about the team ... provides an understanding of the team mindset.

Ecological Perspective ... this perspective obtains answers to the question *What is the fit of the team in the organization?*
> It summarizes what the team members identify as the role/function of the team in the bigger picture ... provides an understanding of the team mission.

Practical Perspective ... this perspective obtains answers to the question *How does the team go about its work?*
> It summarizes the ways the team members carry out their tasks ... provides an understanding of the structure of the team through its meetings, organization charts, etc.

Temporal Perspective ... this perspective obtains answers to the question *What is the influence of time on the team tasks?*
> It summarizes the team members' views of the effect of time on their work ... provides an understanding of when things get done.

Resource Perspective ... this perspective obtains answers to the question *What resources (except people) are available to the team members to carry out their tasks?*
> It summarizes the assets available and used by the team ... provides an understanding of the tangible supports for the team (finances, equipment, etc.)

Spatial Perspective ... this perspective obtains answers to the question *What is the influence of location on the team tasks?*
> It summarizes the members' view of the effect of space on work ... provides an understanding of where things happen by identifying the sphere of internal/external influence of the team

Team Member Perspective ... this perspective obtains answers to the question *What do the team members know about the capabilities-competencies mix of the team members?*
> It summarizes the knowledge and skills each team member offers to the team as it operates ... provides an outline of what is to learned by team members

Client/Customer Perspective ... this perspective obtains answers to the question *What do you know about the people who influence the team as the team completes its tasks?*
> It summarizes the characteristics of the stakeholders involved with the team ... provides an understanding of who is responsible and accountable for what

BLANK PERSPECTIVE MAP: FORM B

Ideological Perspective

Ecological Perspective

Practical Perspective

Temporal Perspective

Resource Perspective

Spatial Perspective

Team Member Perspective

Client/Customer Perspective

VISION-SYSTEM-PEOPLE MAP: FORM C

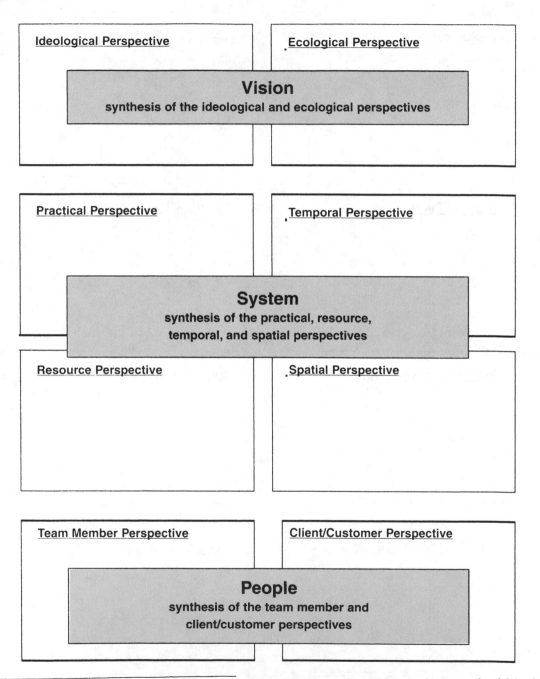

Ideological Perspective

Ecological Perspective

Vision
synthesis of the ideological and ecological perspectives

Practical Perspective

Temporal Perspective

System
synthesis of the practical, resource,
temporal, and spatial perspectives

Resource Perspective

Spatial Perspective

Team Member Perspective

Client/Customer Perspective

People
synthesis of the team member and
client/customer perspectives

THE *IF* QUESTION: SCENARIO MAPPING: FORM D

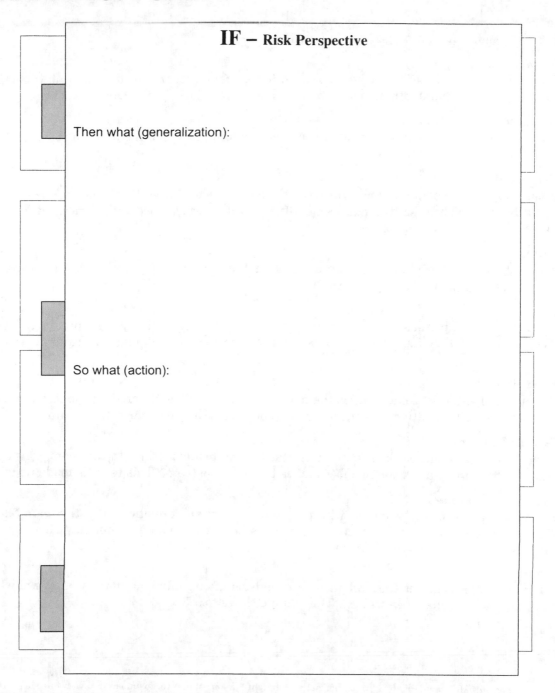

IF – **Risk Perspective**

Then what (generalization):

So what (action):

FACILITATOR'S GUIDE TO PERSPECTIVES: FORM E

Here are additional prompts. Add your own, too.

Ideological
About the philosophy of the team, its reason for existence, its intent, its proposal; considers the truth the team and others hold about the team as a whole. "This team exists because...."

Ecological
About the big-picture "fit" of the team; considers the uniqueness of the team in the organization. "This team exists to...."

Practical
About the arrangements through which the team undertakes its work—the steps, phases, tactics, schemes involved with standards, quantity, quality, performance; considers words ending in "-ing." "This team functions by...."

Resource
About the support available and access to it for the team to carry out its tasks, including finances, equipment, ideas. "This team uses...."

Temporal
About the cycles, periods, deadlines that affect the team in the delivery of its products or services; considers the time frames associated with the team. "This team operates according to...."

Spatial
About the place, area, zone in which the team operates to deliver its products or services; considers the specific location in which the team operates. "This team operates within...."

Team Member
About the knowledge, skills, and attitudes each team member brings to the team; considers what contribution each team member makes to the whole team. "This team is made up of...."

Client or Customer
About relationships the team has with people who affect and are affected by the team tasks. These people make up the contacts the team has in its external environment. "This team is affected by..." and "This team affects...."

Risk
About possible scenarios the team members envision after gaining an understanding of what they can do and what they will do. "This team chooses to...."

23

ENCOURAGING FEEDBACK

Mel Silberman and Freda Hansburg

Overview This activity demonstrates the importance of asking for feedback. Too often, people are reluctant to give us feedback and we have only ourselves to blame. When we let others know how much we value their feedback and specifically what we want information about, we have a better chance to improve upon our own effectiveness.

Suggested Time 20 minutes

Materials Needed
- ✔ Flip chart and marker
- ✔ Form A (Animal Feedback Form)
- ✔ Form B (Some Reasons Why People Withhold Feedback from Us)

Procedure

1. Ask participants if they are familiar with the Anderson fairy tale, "The Emperor's New Clothes." Typically, a few will not be. Briefly summarize the story: Once upon a time, there was a powerful emperor who was very vain and arrogant. All of his subjects feared him. One day, two would-be tailors came to town and proposed to make the emperor the most beautiful cloak that had ever been created, using a magnificent, sheer golden fabric. The emperor eagerly agreed and the two charlatans pretended to make the cloak. When they presented the nonexistent cloak to the emperor, he said at first that he couldn't see it. The charlatans explained that the cloth was so sheer and delicate that it was deceptively hard to see, but that the golden threads would reflect the light in a magnificent way. Persuaded, the emperor wore this imaginary cloak in a grand procession through the village. He was, in reality, parading naked through the town. All of his subjects were so intimidated by him that they remained silent, until one small boy

Contact Information: Mel Silberman and Freda Hansburg, PeopleSmart Products & Services of Active Training™, 303 Sayre Drive, Princeton, NJ 08540, 609-987-8157, mel@activetraining.com, freda@activetraining.com, www.activetraining.com.

cried out, "Momma, the emperor has no clothes!" at which point, the whole village laughed.

2. Say: "The story makes two points. It's helpful to get honest feedback (you may be naked!) and often other people withhold that feedback from you. Let's look at another example of this."

3. Distribute copies of Form A, Animal Feedback Form, to participants and review it with them.

4. Pair up participants and instruct them to select the animal that can best be compared to their partners. Tell them to consider both physical characteristics and the individual's personality. Tell them not to divulge their selections to their partners.

5. Ask: "Would it be all right with you if you never get to find out what animal your partner selected?" Some participants will protest. Hear them out.

6. Poll the group, asking, "How many are curious about what animal their partners selected? How many want to tell their partners what they selected?" Expect that more people will want to hear than tell.

7. Say: "The point of this activity is that your partner has feedback about you, but it is being withheld at my request. In the real world, other people often withhold feedback from us . . . even though they always have some feedback that can be shared. When that feedback is withheld, we wind up guessing about how others think of us. Some of us think the feedback is more positive than it really is. Some of us think the opposite. The best thing we can do to get an accurate picture is to ask for feedback more often. If we are proactive and ask for feedback, we will be in a better position to know how others view us, rather than making guesses."

8. Ask: "Why do we shy away from asking people for feedback? Why do some people withhold their real feelings, even when we ask for them?"

9. Record participants' responses on a flip chart.

10. Distribute copies of Form B, Some Reasons Why People Withhold Feedback from Us, and compare this list to the responses on the flip chart.

11. Ask: "How can we motivate people to give us feedback?"

12. Instruct participants to brainstorm with their partners at least two strategies they could use to overcome these obstacles and encourage others to give them feedback. Tell them that, after doing so, they may share their animal choices with their partners, if they wish to.

13. Record participants' ideas about how to encourage feedback on a flip chart.

14. Optional: If participants are willing, invite them to share their animal choices with the group.

ANIMAL FEEDBACK FORM: FORM A

Directions:

From the list, select the animal that most resembles your partner, considering both physical characteristics and personal qualities. Do **not** show your selection to your partner.

- ❏ Lion
- ❏ Squirrel
- ❏ Monkey
- ❏ Tiger
- ❏ Giraffe
- ❏ Kangaroo
- ❏ Bear (type?)
- ❏ Cat (type?)
- ❏ Dog (type?)
- ❏ Bird (type?)

SOME REASONS WHY PEOPLE WITHHOLD FEEDBACK FROM US: FORM B

- We are afraid of what they might tell us.
- We haven't let them know that we really want their feedback.
- We haven't been specific about the feedback we are seeking.
- They are concerned that we will become angry at them or seek reprisal.
- They don't want a close relationship with us.
- They feel they haven't earned the right to give us feedback.

Directions:

With your partner, look over the list in the box. Come up with at least two strategies you could use to overcome these obstacles and **encourage people to give you feedback:**

1. _____
2. _____

Other Strategies:

3. _____
4. _____
5. _____
6. _____

24
FORMING LEARNING TEAMS

Bonnie Jameson

Overview   A successful organization consists of individuals and teams who have achieved the skill of self-directed learning. The ability to learn independently from many different resources is essential to the autonomous learner. When independent learners come together as a team, they combine their ideas and produce synergy, which is defined as the whole being more than the sum of the parts.

     This exercise is a process that learning teams can use to describe the reason for being a team and the philosophical intent for creating the kind of organizational climate the team wants.

Suggested Time   60 minutes

Materials Needed   ✔ Form A (Individual Worksheet)

       ✔ Form B (Small Group Work Process)

Procedure
1. Hand out copies of Form A (Individual Worksheet). Instruct each person to complete the sentences on the worksheet. (6 minutes)

2. Give each team member a copy of Form B (Small Group Work Process).

3. Choose a group facilitator, a recorder, and a spokesperson.

4. Use the round robin discussion process (each person takes a turn to speak) to share the sentences written in the individual work. Each person should share before discussion begins.

5. Individuals on the team may want to take notes to capture ideas that are meaningful and important to them.

6. After everyone on the team has shared sentences, discuss how to put the best parts of each person's work together to form one mission statement.

Contact Information: Bonnie Jameson, 1024 Underhills Road, Oakland, CA 94610, 510-832-2597.

7. Process the exercise using the following questions:

✔ What have we learned about the value of mission statements?

✔ How does working together on a common task create motivation and productivity?

✔ How can we use this process and content to enhance our team's success?

✔ How can we take more responsibility for our own team learning?

Variation This same basic process can be used with large groups or multiple teams.

✔ Separate groups or teams and have each follow steps 1 to 7.

✔ After each group has completed the steps, bring the groups back together and have a spokesperson from each team report on its mission statement and what they have learned.

INDIVIDUAL WORKSHEET: FORM A

Please complete the following sentences.

This *learning team* exists to...

_____

_____

_____

We *value* ...

_____

_____

_____

Our *desired outcomes* (goals) are...

_____

_____

_____

We can *measure our effectiveness* when we are able to ...

_____

_____

_____

SMALL GROUP WORK PROCESS: FORM B

Your teamwork goal is to create a Mission Statement for your team that combines the best of all your individual ideas.

1. Choose a group facilitator, a recorder, and a spokesperson.

2. Using the round robin process, each person shares his or her completed sentences. Do not interrupt or discuss ideas until each team member has had the opportunity to share sentences.

3. Listen carefully to each person's ideas and take notes on ideas you feel are important.

4. After all sentences have been shared, the facilitator leads a discussion on the ideas and helps the team formulate a mission statement that describes the team and organizational standards, using everyone's best ideas.

5. Process the experience by answering the following questions:

   ✔ What have we learned about the value of mission statements?

   ✔ How does working together on a common task create motivation and productivity?

   ✔ How can we use this process and content to enhance our team's success?

   ✔ How can we take more responsibility for our own team learning?

25
SINKING OR SWIMMING TOGETHER

Sharon Bowman

Overview Participants experience their own team-building skills, communication strengths and weaknesses, and problem-solving choices in a simulated challenge that can only be solved by using those skills.

✔ This activity is especially useful with groups of people who already work together and who wish to assess their skills in these areas.

✔ The activity itself is dynamic, hands-on, and high-energy, with both physical and mental components. Participants observe, experience, and discuss the insights they reach as a result of this activity.

✔ It is more successful after the group has worked together and some knowledge and trust have been built. It may be too high-risk as an opening activity and is more effective as a middle or closing activity.

Suggested Time 45 to 90 minutes depending upon the size of the group and the amount of discussion time after the activity

Materials Needed ✔ Large blank white paper plates (total number about half the size of the group; i.e., for a group of 30 you'll need about 12 to 15 paper plates; for a group of 12 use 6 paper plates)

✔ Large felt-tip pens (1 to 3 per group)

✔ General reminders posted on a flip chart or overhead transparency so that the group can refer to them if necessary during the activity (See Procedure, Step Two for suggestions.)

✔ Form A (Group Discussion Questions)

Procedure 1. Although this game can work with groups of as many as 30 people, it's often more time and space efficient to divide larger groups into two smaller groups of 10 to 15 people each. With a training

Contact Information: Sharon Bowman, The Lake Tahoe Trainers Group, P.O. Box 564, Glenbrook, NV 89413, 702-749-5247, sbowperson@aol.com, www.bowperson.com.

group of 15 or fewer, do the activity as one group rather than splitting into two very small groups.

2. A large, empty space free from furniture or other physical obstacles is absolutely necessary for the success of this activity and the safety of the participants. A break-out area in the training room will work, as will another empty room, a very long, wide hallway, or an unobstructed space outside. Lay a long strip of masking tape at either end of the space to designate the shorelines. The space between the tape strips is the river. The larger the group, the longer this space needs to be. A good rule of thumb is: The space should be at least twice as long as the line of participants would be if standing side by side (e.g., about 30 feet for a group of 15 participants).

3. The activity is divided into three steps:

    Step One: Brainstorming

    Step Two: The River Crossing

    Step Three: The Post-Activity Discussion

    Regardless of the number of groups you have, each group does each step at the same time. Give the game instructions to the whole group one step at a time and set a time limit for each step. For the sake of the instructions, we'll assume that you have one group of about 18 participants. If your real group is larger than 18, lengthen the suggested time for each step by another 5 to 10 minutes.

Step One: Brainstorming (10 minutes)

✔ Tell the group they have about 4 minutes to brainstorm and write down all the important characteristics, elements, or pieces of information associated with the topic they've been studying.

✔ After about 4 minutes, stop the brainstorming and direct the group to discuss and agree on the nine most important elements from their brainstorming session. The group writes each of these elements on a paper plate (one element per plate) with a felt pen so that the element can be read from a distance.

✔ Since your hypothetical group is 18 people, nine plates are enough. If your group were larger or smaller, your number of plates would be larger or smaller also. After the group has written the nine most important elements or pieces of information, have them read them aloud. Then proceed to Step Two.

Step Two: The River Crossing (30 to 40 minutes)

✔ Direct the group to stand at the shoreline (behind the masking tape) at one end of the river (the empty space between shorelines), with their paper plates in their hands.

✔ Explain that the space between the masking tape lines is actually a raging river symbolizing all the things that can go wrong with *[insert the training topic here]*. Their challenge is to safely cross the raging river to the opposite shore. There are a few things they need to know before they get started on this adventure. *(As you go over the following rules of the game, if possible post a shortened version as "reminders" so that the group can refer to them during the game if necessary):*

- The entire group must make it safely to the opposite shore in the time allotted without losing any group member in the raging waters.

- No part of a person's body can touch or step into the river (the current is so strong that they'll be swept away, i.e., have to return to the starting shore).

- In order to cross the river, the group can use the floating river rocks *(the paper plates)* as stepping-stones. The rocks symbolize the elements that make *[insert topic here]* successful. The rocks will help them cross the raging river of things that can go wrong with *[insert topic here]*.

- The paper plates must be in contact with a human body part at all times. If not, they are swept down the river and into the hands of the "River Guardian."

✔ You, the trainer, are the "River Guardian." During the game it's your job to offer the participants encouragement and cheer them on. It's also your job to grab any river rock that's not in contact with a human body and hold that rock for safekeeping until the game is over. The "River Guardian" also lets participants know if they accidentally step into the water and need to return to the starting shore. *(You'll find that the participants quickly get the idea that, instead of a benevolent and helpful person, you're actually eager to snatch as many of the rocks away from them as you can, thereby making it harder for them to cross the river. You'll be called "River Troll" before the activity is over! The game soon becomes "them" against "you," which adds to the fun.)*

✔ Tell them they'll have 20 minutes to cross the river. *(You can shorten or lengthen the time depending upon the group size. You don't need to adhere to the exact time—the objective of the activity is to*

158

*practice team-building, communication, and problem-solving skills,
not to stick to a time limit.)* Remind them to cheer each other on
because it's a team effort. Then wish them luck, get out of their way,
and be very noncommittal when they ask you if this or that is the
way to do it. *(There are at least a half-dozen ways to cross the river.
They may come up with a really creative way. As long as the basic
rules are kept, there are many "right" ways to do it. You may see the
group forming a human chain as they cross the river in a straight
line using the paper plates as stepping-stones. Or they may put a
paper plate under each foot and slide across a few at a time. Or they
may figure out ways to cross three or four at a time, sliding the plates
as they go. They may carry each other across or form human chairs
with two people sliding across and carrying a third between them.
Or they may hop across, each using one plate. Let them come up with
the solutions.)*

✔ Be ruthlessly vigilant in snatching up rocks and sending people
back who step into the water. You can really ham it up and drama-
tize your "River Guardian" role if you wish. *(Note: If you have more
than one River Crossing group, you'll need to enlist the help of one or
more participants to be "River Guardians" with you so that each
group has a Guardian. Be sure to quietly clue the other Guardians
in as to what their covert goal is in snatching rocks and sending people back to the shore. If the group loses too many rocks and can't
make it across the river, you may let them "earn" some of their rocks
back by stating something they've learned from the workshop.)*

✔ When the whole group has made it across the river, lead a final
group cheer and applause time. The group energy will be very high.
Let the participants have a few minutes to do some spontaneous
clapping, laughing, and sharing of reactions and comments. If you
wish, pass out little toys or trinkets that symbolize their success
(whistles, compasses, edible treats, real rocks, toy boats, etc.). If you
need to call time and some group members haven't crossed the river
yet, give them a round of applause for effort or let them know you
have magically transported them to the other side.

Step Three: The Post-Activity Discussion (15 to 20 minutes)

✔ Direct the large group to form smaller seated groups of about four
or five people each.

✔ Pass out copies of Form A (Group Discussion Questions) to each person.

✔ First give them 3 to 5 minutes to individually write their answers
to the questions on the handout without discussing the questions
with others.

✔ Then allow the small groups about 10 minutes to discuss their responses together.

✔ Finally, lead a large group discussion, asking volunteers to share with the whole group some of the insights from the small group discussions. At the end of the discussion, wrap it up by summarizing their ideas, comments, and reactions, and tie it all to the training topic. You may want to conclude with one more round of applause.

Variations

1. Besides team building, communication, and problem solving, this activity can be used in any learning situation involving group interaction and group skills.

2. You can make up new rules or change the old ones as the activity progresses. Just remember that the learning takes place through the struggle and effort of the participants. Don't make it too easy for them to succeed.

3. The debriefing at the end of the activity is the most important part, because the insights shared become crucial to the learning experience. Be sure to ask questions that evoke deeper answers than "yes" or "no."

GROUP DISCUSSION QUESTIONS: FORM A

Please take a few minutes by yourself to read and answer the following questions. Then, with your group, discuss the questions together.

1. What role did you play during the activity?

2. What were your strengths? Your weaknesses?

3. What did you notice about the different ways people communicated within your group?

4. Were there any conflicts? How did you handle them?

5. How did the group solve the problems that came up during the activity?

6. What was the general feeling within the group?

7. As a team, how did you think the group functioned and why?

8. What did you learn about yourself and the others?

9. What connections can you make between this activity and the training topic?

10. Any other observations? Insights?

26

USING DIVERSITY IN TEAM DECISION MAKING

Dianne Saphiere

Overview Frequently, consultants or facilitators work with teams that are divided by differing viewpoints and approaches. We are often called in during a crisis, when one side is about to steamroll another or the team itself is about to explode. This method can be useful at such junctures. It defuses the situation enough to allow team members to listen to one another, and to reframe their disagreement as a positive opportunity for creating the best solution for the organization. Understanding and learning from differing viewpoints is a wonderful way to continuously improve processes for trust building, information sharing, and decision making within an organization.

Suggested Time 1 to 2 hours, depending on the complexity and emotional charge of the topic

Materials Needed ✔ Form A (Pros and Cons Analysis)

✔ Prepared flip charts or transparencies of Form B (Using Diversity to Remedy Organizational Liabilities)

✔ Form C (Using Diversity to Remedy Organizational Liabilities)

Procedure 1. Conduct a needs assessment prior to conducting this activity, and get to know the team and its players well.
2. Recreate Form A on a series of flip chart pages, an overhead transparency, or a whiteboard. Copies may be handed out to each team member as well.
3. Work with the group to define a work-related topic of disagreement in a neutral way. (See Form A.)
4. Guide team members to describe the two (or more) differing positions in a manner acceptable to representatives of those positions.

Contact Information: Dianne Saphiere, Nipporica Associates, 2516 West 90th Street, Leawood, KS 66206, 913-901-0243, dianne @nipporica.com, www.nipporica.com.

5. Ask those who actually represent Position One to remain silent, while actual representatives of Position Two complete the box, Pros to Position One. It often dissipates immediate tension to hear positive opinions from those opposed to one's position.

6. Ask representatives of Position Two to remain silent, while representatives of Position One complete the box, Cons to Position One. It often relieves opponents to know that advocates of a position can see the downsides of their position.

7. Steps 5 and 6 are repeated for Position Two with representatives of Position One listing the pros of Position Two, and advocates for Position Two explaining the cons of their position.

8. Provide team members some quiet time for reflection, or conduct a short "creativity" activity to assist team members to think "outside the box."

9. Discourage team members from "my way/your way" thinking, and encourage them to create new solutions or approaches that maximize the pros of each position while minimizing the cons. (See Form B.)

10. Have team members discuss their new options, generating additional ideas or integrating approaches. If possible, ask them to agree on next steps to take in their decision-making process.

Variation The facilitator asks the group to agree on one organizational weakness or liability: something that the organization is not very good at, an area around which there is tension or frustration. This topic is entered into Form B, Using Diversity to Remedy Organizational Liabilities. (See Form C for an example of a completed worksheet.)

The facilitator leads the group to agree on one specific example of the liability, an example that is an indicator of the larger issue. This example is entered into the appropriate space on Form B.

The perspectives, neutral descriptions of behavior, expectations and values of each side, and benefits and disadvantages of the behaviors are entered into the spaces on Form B.

As in step 9 above, the facilitator leads the team to create solutions that will incorporate the insights and experience of each perspective to strengthen the organization.

PROS AND CONS ANALYSIS: FORM A

Topic Description:

Position One Description	Position Two Description
Pros to Position One	Pros to Position Two
Cons to Position One	Cons to Position Two
Solution That Maximizes the Pros and Minimizes the Cons	

USING DIVERSITY TO REMEDY ORGANIZATIONAL LIABILITIES: FORM B

Liability:

Describe a specific situation demonstrating the liability:

Perspective A:	Perspective B:
Description of Behavior:	Description of Behavior:
Expectations and Values:	Expectation and Values:
Benefits:	Benefits:
Disadvantages:	Disadvantages:
Suggestions for Interculturally Effective Approaches:	

USING DIVERSITY TO REMEDY ORGANIZATIONAL LIABILITIES: FORM C

Liability:

Expertise of middle managers is underutilized; they feel their ideas and opinions are not listened to.

Describe a specific situation demonstrating the liability:

The Executive Committee of the San Francisco site was asked by Japanese management to recommend a name for the new restaurant. The name they recommended was not accepted.

Perspective A: Executive Committee	**Perspective B:** President & Katsudon KK
Description of Behavior:	**Description of Behavior:**
We were asked to recommend a name for the new restaurant and did. After making our recommendation we had no information on the decision-making process until the decision was final.	We asked the Executive Committee of the hotel to recommend a name for the new restaurant; we reported the new name back to the site management once the final decision was made.
Expectations and Values: Good managers make a clear recommendation and have reasons for it ready if requested; we expected to be informed of the process and how our recommendation would be used; we expected recognition of our recommendation. Rational, verbal, initiative.	**Expectation and Values:** The recommendation was clear but perhaps rather disappointing, as the recommended name didn't seem to fit the corporate vision. It will be considered along with other ideas/options. Corporate image is most important. We at the top see the macro view.
Benefits: Ownership of the name; managers feel valued; U.S. expertise is utilized; a name Westerners would welcome.	**Benefits:** New name is consistent with corporate vision; is attractive to Japanese.
Disadvantages: Narrower perspective doesn't reflect Tokyo concerns; doesn't fit vision of Japanese organization; seems "insubordinate" for Americans to expect to influence when their opinion is requested.	**Disadvantages:** Creates distrust; ruins management credibility; stifles creativity; reinforces a "you just work here/are not valued" attitude.

Suggestions for Interculturally Effective Approaches:

1. Executive Committee should ask "20 questions" before proceeding: clarify use, limits, procedures, timelines, etc.
2. Management must take time to be explicit: clarify what they want before asking or say "not sure/I need your help."
3. Mutually define parameters, i.e., is it a worldwide decision, just for San Francisco, etc.
4. Management ideas should be shared downward to be critiqued.
5. Ensure two-way dialogue throughout the process.

27
PROBLEM SOLVING BY DISTANT TEAMS

Catherine Sees and Lewis Welzel Jr.

Overview In today's world of ever-increasing technological communications and increasing cost concerns, organizations are turning to problem solving and team building through the use of telephone conference calls. Standard team-building and group exercises take on a different and unique twist when team members are unable to rely on face-to-face interaction. Many individuals fail to realize the importance they place on working with team members in the same physical location. This exercise allows team members to examine their personal reliance on nonverbal signals to accomplish team coordination on problem-solving tasks. It also allows them to work on developing better problem-solving skills while coordinating activities from distant locations. The exercise does not contain a specific "right answer"; it requires that the team set team values and goals before moving toward an operational consensus.

Time Suggested 90 minutes

Materials Needed ✔ Form A (Facilitator Guidelines)
✔ Form B (Compuboard Employee Fact Sheet)
✔ Form C (Exercise Questionnaire)

Procedure 1. Introduce the exercise using the facilitator guidelines contained in Form A.

Contact Information: Catherine Sees, McDATA Corporation, 310 Interlocken Parkway, Broomfield, CO 80021, 720-566-3521, csees@lamar.colostate.edu.
Lewis Weizel Jr., 1700 W. Plum #53F, Ft. Collins, CO 80521, 970-669-0114, lew @lamar.colostate.edu.

2. Separate the group into teams consisting of at least 6 members and a maximum of 9. (The groups do not need to be evenly divided.) Randomly assign a team leader within each team.

3. Have each team set up as far away as possible from the other teams and place their chairs in as tight a circle as they can manage; however, they must place the chairs **facing out** from the center of the circle so that their backs are to each other.

4. Instruct the participants that during the exercise, they are to minimize all interaction with their team members except by voice. They are not to turn and talk directly to the person on either side or engage in "sidebar" conversations.

5. Distribute a copy of Form B to each of the team members and ask them to review the information and fill in the chart at the bottom with the order in which they would promote the employees (1 for the first to receive advancement, 2 for the next promotion, etc.). Instruct them to let their team leader know when they have completed the ranking. Allow them a maximum of 10 minutes.

6. Once everyone is done individually, have the group leader simulate initiating a conference call for the group. Generally this provides a little initial levity. The leader will now conduct a "conference call" in which the group must arrive at consensus on a ranking of the employees for the upcoming promotions.

7. Allow a maximum of 45 minutes for this section of the exercise, and provide them time warnings after 30 minutes. Let them know when they have 10 minutes left, 5 minutes left, and finally when the time is up.

8. Once consensus is reached, have everyone on the team fill in the second half of the ranking chart on Form B with the team rankings, and then complete Form C, the exercise questionnaire. If consensus is not reached, explain to the group that this will be reviewed in the debriefing session.

9. Have everyone return the chairs to their normal positions. Then conduct a debriefing, referring to Form A (the facilitator guidelines).

Debriefing
1. When the participants have relocated to their normal group setting, begin the discussion by going through the questionnaire they completed.

2. Address each question and allow individuals to come forward with their thoughts and feelings.

3. Stress the fact that there was not a "right" answer as a conclusion, but each team answer relied upon the values that were agreed upon by the team.

4. Complete the debriefing with an examination of problem-solving steps. Stress the need for team structure and communication when groups are distantly located.

FACILITATOR GUIDELINES: FORM A

INTRODUCTION

- Introduce the nature of the exercise and the unique aspect of team problem solving from distant locations. Explain to the group that there are only a few promotions available and, while each of the individuals listed in Form B is eligible for promotion, these advancements cannot take place all at one time.

- Ask the group to rank the employees from 1 through 7. The employee ranked first will get a promotion first. The employee ranked second will get a promotion next, and so on until the last employee is promoted.

- Explain to the group that there may be hurt feelings and concern from the individuals who were not the first ones to be promoted. It is important that sound reasoning and teamwork be utilized when determining the ranking order of the employees.

- Do not reveal to the groups that the exercise does not have a singular correct answer. The answer that each team reaches through consensus will be a result of the value setting that takes place initially.

RULES

1. The information in Form B is all that is available.

2. Active listening is extremely important in this process, as it is easy to "overtalk" or interrupt other members of the distant team.

3. Explain to the teams that the information provided is accurate.

4. Inform them that there are no management requirements for how the selection is to be made by this group.

5. Promotion selections agreed to by this group will be implemented without further review.

6. The exact number of promotions is unknown at this time, so the ranking is critical.

NOTES

- Each team will normally launch into a selection of rankings by reviewing individual decisions without any structure or process. Ranking the first and last individuals is fairly easy. The second through sixth rankings can be more difficult. This may require the distant team to set up a value system to judge the employees' information.

FACILITATOR GUIDELINES: FORM A (CONT.)

- In a review of this experiential mode of telephone problem solving, stress the need for a structured process of steps (problem identification, brainstorming, solution prioritization, and solution implementation). Finally, stress the need for achieving consensus on team values for the problem before moving into the actual ranking process.

DEBRIEFING

- Be careful that teams or individuals do not become submerged in the actual rankings of the employees.

- Focus on the process used by teams.

- Focus on the difficulties experienced in losing face-to-face interaction.

COMPUBOARD EMPLOYEE FACT SHEET: FORM B

SCENARIO

The Compuboard Corporation is a medium-sized manufacturing company located in the suburbs of Denver, Colorado. This non-union company has worked hard at incorporating an objective performance review system that provides feedback to the employees. Its goal was to be objective and timely with frequent supervisor review.

Due to outside market conditions, Compuboard has won the bid for a major new contract. This new contract will require the hiring of more workers and thus the need to promote some of the best performers on the manufacturing assembly line to supervisory or management positions. This unit produces circuit boards that are sold to electronic firms. Management wants to be sure that they have been as fair as possible in presenting an objectively based decision to the employees.

OBJECTIVE

The following employees have been designated as the best performers on the assembly line and pertinent data is provided about their performance. Since the actual number of promotions is currently unknown, you are to rate the employees on the chart at the bottom in the order they are to be promoted (1 = first to be promoted, 7 = last to be promoted). At the conclusion of the team discussion, please fill in the chart with the ratings the team agreed upon.

EMPLOYEE INFORMATION

1. George White: white; age 42; two years of high school; 14 years seniority

2. Jan Jarney: black; age 37; widower; high school graduate; 8 years seniority

3. Jackie Cramer: black; age 24; high school graduate; 2 years seniority

4. Dave Darby: white; age 50; finished junior college while working; 15 years seniority

5. Cathy Levi: Native American; age 36; high school graduate; 3 years seniority

6. Ron Savgado: Hispanic; age 40; high school graduate; 4 years seniority

7. Donald Watsel: white; age 39; divorced; 2 years of college; 7 years seniority

COMPUBOARD EMPLOYEE FACT SHEET: FORM B (*CONT.*)

COMPUBOARD PERFORMANCE REVIEW DATA; FACTORS EVALUATED BY SUPERVISOR:

Employee	Average Weekly Output	% Rejects	Absences	Cooperative Attitude	Loyalty
George White	39	4	6	Very good	Very good
Jan Jarney	43	5	7	Fair	Good
Jackie Cramer	35	0	0.4	Excellent	Very good
Dave Darby	40	4	13	Excellent	Excellent
Cathy Levi	40	9	9	Fair	Good
Ron Savgado	39	3	6	Very good	Good
Donald Watsel	36	4	5	Very good	Very good

Average Weekly Output: higher score = more output

% Rejects: lower score = fewer rejects

Absences: lower score = fewer absences

Full range of subjective ratings: fair, good, very good, excellent

COMPUBOARD RATING FORM

Employee	Individual Rating	Team Rating
George White		
Jan Jarney		
Jackie Cramer		
Dave Darby		
Cathy Levi		
Ron Savgado		
Donald Watsel		

EXERCISE QUESTIONNAIRE: FORM C

Was the project clear? Why or why not?

Were you able to communicate effectively with the other group members? Why or why not?

Did the group spend any time defining the problem before launching into rankings? Would this have helped? Why or why not?

How did members differ in the criteria used to promote people?

Was there any resistance among team members to changing their positions?

How were the differences resolved?

To what extent was the group decision really based on consensus? If you did not reach consensus, why?

If your rankings for the employees were different from what finally emerged from the team meeting, what changed? Were you comfortable with the change?

What principal thing would you change in the process of solving this problem to improve similar conference call sessions in the future?

28
BUILDING STRENGTHS IN VIRTUAL TEAMS

Heather Robinson

Overview Some of the characteristics associated with successful virtual teams include shared vision, clear information, and thorough feedback. Organizations that swap virtual team members to the counterpart location often find that those people not only carry with them the understanding of their home location, but quickly come to understand the views held by their host location team members, thus increasing understanding, compassion, and camaraderie in the organization. This exercise allows virtual teams to leverage their face-to-face time by using "virtual" swaps, thus gaining some of the benefit of real swaps.

This activity evolved during a two-day team-building session for a virtual team of software developers and testers, some of whom were located in Frankfurt, Germany, and some of whom were located in Bangalore, India. The team had been experiencing a great deal of frustration regarding lack of shared definition of deliverables, lack of understanding of the differences in work processes in the two locations, and differences in styles of communicating information. During the session, the team had done work with their location-specific groups but really weren't developing much understanding for the viewpoints of their counterparts from the other location. Something needed to be done! We strategically assigned both German and Indian participants to both a Frankfurt team and a Bangalore team, making sure we had a good mix of locations and functions on both of the "virtual" teams. Since the issue of deliverables was the most concrete, we chose that as our focus, realizing that many of the other issues would arise out of the groups' work together. We invited the participants to work during the exercise in the virtual teams, formulating answers to four questions and reporting to the other team between questions. We asked an Indian team member to report for the Frankfurt group and a German team member to report for the Bangalore group. The questions were:

Contact Information: Heather Robinson, Success Across Borders, 23723 51st Avenue S, Kent, WA 98032, 253-852-0903, har5055 @aol.com.

1. What do you want in the way of deliverables from Frankfurt? Bangalore?

2. How will you recognize them when you get them (what will they look like, how will they be evaluated, how will they be specified, etc.)?

3. What stops you from getting these deliverables (what are the challenges, what has happened in the past, etc.)?

4. What are you willing to do to get what you want (what are action items, commitments you are willing to make, support or information you are willing to offer, etc.)? What are you willing to stop doing to get what you want? [Make sure that action items account for exactly who will carry out the action and by when.]

The polite and, up until this point, somewhat disinterested group came alive! They went to work and barreled through the questions and reports for four hours straight, turning down all offers for an official break time. The richness of the information they developed was astounding and the new-found identification with the "other" was touching. Asking an Indian to report for the German location and vice-versa also had an interesting effect: To represent their counterparts' viewpoint meant that during the group work they had to listen carefully to what their counterparts were saying, ask lots of clarifying questions to make sure they understood correctly, and then be witnessed as representing their counterparts by both the counterparts and their same-location colleagues. This exercise was the heart of building the trust and understanding that fostered a very productive work team.

You can use this exercise to address goals and project outcomes as well as less concrete notions such as vision, mission, and communication norms. Be sure to adapt the questions so that they make sense for your group's focus. Finally, make the most of debriefing the activity—the lessons learned can have lasting effects!

Suggested Time   90 minutes to 4 hours

Materials Needed   ✔ 2 flip chart stands and pads

Procedure   1. Form two teams made up of members from both counterpart locations. Deliberately call them Location A Team and Location B Team, using the names of the actual sites; for instance, the Chicago Team and the Seattle Team. Choose teams carefully to ensure power equalization; this may require attention to the proportion of team members from the two locations, position in the organizational hierarchy, and strength of personality. All things being equal and using our example, this generally means that half of the members on the newly formed Chicago Team will actually work in Chicago and half of them will actually work in Seattle. Tell them they can pick anyone to report, as long as the reporter in actuality works at the counterpart location. Also, they must choose a new reporter for each round.

2. Write the first question for the group on a flip chart. If, for example, the group needs clarity on deliverables to be exchanged between the locations, the first question might be, "What does Chicago need to deliver to Seattle and what does Seattle need to deliver to Chicago?"

3. Give the teams a realistic yet challenging amount of time to frame their responses to the question and prepare a presentation.

4. The teams present their answers to each other.

5. Write the second question for the group on a flip chart. The teams then develop their answers and present to one another. Continue with the third and fourth questions. Customize the four rounds of questioning based on these questions:

   a. "What do you want?"

   b. "How will you recognize it when you get it (what will it look like, sound like, feel like)?"

   c. "What stops you from getting it (what are the challenges, what has happened in the past, what do you need to do your job, etc.)?"

   d. "What are you willing to do to get what you want (what are the action items, commitments you are willing to make, support or information you are willing to offer, etc.)?" "What are you willing to stop doing to get what you want?" [Make sure that action items account for exactly who will carry out the action and by when.]

6. Debrief the teams' processes. Ask questions such as, "How was this exercise for you?" What happened?" "What was it like to work in the other location?" and "What did you realize about their situation?" For those who were in their "home location," ask "What was it like to work with people from the other location as though they were part of your location?" Finally, ask all, "What did you learn that will be helpful as you continue your work together?"

29
SHARING INFORMATION IN TEAMS

Don Simpson

Overview   This activity, for teams of 5 to 7, illustrates the need to share information and generate a plan toward solving problems. There are five similar worksheets with different information, which must be shared to make the correct decision.

Suggested Time   Approximately 40 minutes

Materials Needed   ✔ Forms A, B, C, D, and E (Decision Worksheets); one set per team

✔ Form F (Specification Sheet); one sheet per participant

✔ Form G (Reactions Worksheet)

✔ Form H (Solution Grid)

✔ Form I (Your Role As Coach and Coach's Guidelines Worksheet)

✔ Form J (Coach's Observation Worksheet)

Procedure   1. Introduce the activity: *To address the issues facing your team, you must share information and process it effectively. This activity gives you practice in addressing a common problem. Each of you must decide what information to share, and when and how to share it. You must also work together to process the information toward your objective. Read the background. Agree on your expected output and how you will approach your task. Then begin. You'll have twenty minutes to complete your task.*

2. Distribute *Decision Worksheets* (Forms A to E). Each team member gets a *Decision Worksheet* that contains slightly different information from other worksheets. Also distribute Form F (*Specification Sheet*) to each member. If the subteam size is more than the number of worksheets, two team members may have the same information. It is very important, however, that all the work-

Contact Information: Don Simpson & Associates, 40 Mulberry Street, Rochester, New York 14620-2432, 716-442-6501, TrainOD@aol.com.

sheets be available to each team. Do not call attention to what information is different—that's for the participants to discern. Participants need not know anything technical about the problem that is not provided in the *Decision Worksheets*. There are ambiguous elements for discussion. The *Decision Worksheets* intentionally contain some elements the team must discuss—Is "ship in one week" the same as "immediately available"? Is "5 seconds acquisition time" the same as "instant-on"?

3. If there are no administrative questions, begin the activity.

4. At the end of the time, or when the team completes its task, stop the activity.

5. Ask participants to complete the *Reactions Worksheet* (Form G) as individuals.

6. Use the *Reactions Worksheet* to conduct a discussion to process the activity. Processing usually takes at least as long as the activity itself.

7. Distribute Form H (*Solution Grid*) and explain the solution. Often participants do not need the solution; they are confident they already have the right choice. The solution is arrived at by a process of elimination. Only one contender meets all the decision criteria.

Variations

1. During the activity, you or a colleague may observe the team or individual members (especially those in practice leader or facilitator roles) in order to provide feedback during the processing phase.

2. Often, the trainer or facilitator cannot spend adequate time with all the subteams or teams to provide valid feedback. Experienced members from the organization (perhaps those who have already completed the training) may serve as coaches. Coaching becomes a developmental experience in itself, reinforcing skills learned earlier. Coaches for participant teams are especially helpful if the teams are developing expertise in team roles, problem-solving skills, or consensus-seeking skills. Brief the coaches on their role (see Form I, *Your Role As Coach* and Form J, *Coach's Observation Worksheet*).

3. You may ask for a commitment check before you provide the correct solution. Ask: *On a scale from one, low, to five, high, how confident are you that this is the correct answer?* Post participant responses. Later, during processing, ask, *What could you as a team have done to increase some of the low feelings of commitment?*

LASER SPEED DETECTOR PURCHASE DECISION WORKSHEET: FORM A

You are a police department team chartered to determine the best laser handheld speed detection device for use by the road patrols. Your team has narrowed the decision to five promising models. They are listed on the Specification Sheet.

The laser gun is especially useful for speed detection in clear weather. Its laser beam is more difficult to detect than traditional radar. Also, the laser device can employ an instant-on. By the time a speeding motorist detects the beam, it's too late. The instant-on feature is an especially desirable advantage of this device.

An absolute requirement by the department is that the laser device have zero EMF emissions. This requirement is for the health and safety of the officers using the device.

The range of the device must be at least 750 yards. Minimum range is not a critical factor. There must be ±3 miles per hour accuracy at midrange.

LASER SPEED DETECTOR PURCHASE DECISION WORKSHEET: FORM B

You are a police department team chartered to determine the best laser handheld speed detection device for use by the road patrols. Your team has narrowed the decision to five promising models. They are listed on the Specification Sheet.

The laser gun is especially useful for speed detection in clear weather. Its laser beam is more difficult to detect than traditional radar. Also, the laser device can employ an instant-on. By the time a speeding motorist detects the beam, it's too late. The instant-on feature is an especially desirable advantage of this device.

An absolute requirement by the department is that the laser device have zero EMF emissions. This requirement is for the health and safety of the officers using the device.

The cost of the device must be not more than $1,500.

LASER SPEED DETECTOR PURCHASE DECISION WORKSHEET: FORM C

You are a police department team chartered to determine the best laser handheld speed detection device for use by the road patrols. Your team has narrowed the decision to five promising models. They are listed on the Specification Sheet.

The laser gun is especially useful for speed detection in clear weather. Its laser beam is more difficult to detect than traditional radar. Also, the laser device can employ an instant-on. By the time a speeding motorist detects the beam, it's too late. The instant-on feature is an especially desirable advantage of this device.

An absolute requirement by the department is that the laser device have zero EMF emissions. This requirement is for the health and safety of the officers using the device.

The device must be immediately available, in anticipation of the busy motoring season just ahead.

LASER SPEED DETECTOR PURCHASE DECISION WORKSHEET: FORM D

You are a police department team chartered to determine the best laser handheld speed detection device for use by the road patrols. Your team has narrowed the decision to five promising models. They are listed on the Specification Sheet.

The laser gun is especially useful for speed detection in clear weather. Its laser beam is more difficult to detect than traditional radar. Also, the laser device can employ an instant-on. By the time a speeding motorist detects the beam, it's too late. The instant-on feature is an especially desirable advantage of this device.

An absolute requirement by the department is that the laser device have zero EMF emissions. This requirement is for the health and safety of the officers using the device.

The cost of the device must be not more than $1,500. It must be immediately available, in anticipation of the busy motoring season just ahead.

LASER SPEED DETECTOR PURCHASE DECISION WORKSHEET: FORM E

You are a police department team chartered to determine the best laser handheld speed detection device for use by the road patrols. Your team has narrowed the decision to five promising models. They are listed on the Specification Sheet.

The laser gun is especially useful for speed detection in clear weather. Its laser beam is more difficult to detect than traditional radar. Also, the laser device can employ an instant-on. By the time a speeding motorist detects the beam, it's too late. The instant-on feature is an especially desirable advantage of this device.

An absolute requirement by the department is that the laser device have zero EMF emissions. This requirement is for the health and safety of the officers using the device.

The range of the device must be at least 750 yards. There must be ±3 miles per hour accuracy at midrange.

LASER HANDHELD SPEED MEASURING DEVICES SPECIFICATION SHEET: FORM F

HotShot 1200
Source: HotShot Electronics, Inc., Chicago
Weight: 4 lbs, 6 oz
Range: 10-900 yards
Accuracy at Midrange: ±3 mi/hr
EMF Emissions: Zero
Special Features/Information: Fog/clear settings. Instant activation. Safety lens.
Ship in one week.
Cost: $1,400

Zapper Trooper Model
Source: Minnesota Law Enforcement Equipment Co., St. Paul
Weight: 4 lbs
Range: 10-800 yards
Accuracy at Midrange: ±2 mi/hr
EMF Emissions: Zero
Special Features/Information: Instant activation. Safety lens.
Will be available in about six months.
Cost: $1,250

White Lightning
Source: White Electronics, NYC
Weight: 4 lbs, 8 oz
Range: 10-600 yards
Accuracy at Midrange: ±3 mi/hr
EMF Emissions: Zero
Special Features/Information: Instant activation.
Immediately available.
Cost: $1,050

ZOT Model 55-Alive
Source: Zebra Operating Technologies, Inc., Los Angeles
Weight: 4 lbs, 10 oz
Range: 10-850 yards
Accuracy at Midrange: ±3 mi/hr
EMF Emissions: Zero
Special Features/Information: Fog/clear settings. Instant activation. Safety lens.
Ship in one week.
Cost: $1,700

X Model 5640
Source: Prison Industries, Jolliet, IL
Weight: 4 lbs, 3 oz
Range: 10-800 yards
Accuracy at Midrange: ±3 mi/hr
EMF Emissions: Zero
Special Features/Information: Fog/clear and psychic settings.
Immediately available.
5 seconds acquisition time.
Cost: $1,400

REACTIONS WORKSHEET: FORM G

As an individual, please answer the following questions. You'll have the opportunity to share your feelings and suggestions with the rest of your team.

1. How confident are you that the team solution is correct?

1	2	3	4	5
Not Confident				Very Confident

2. What did you do that helped the team achieve its goal?

3. What did you do that didn't help, maybe even hindered, the team?

4. What did you learn about yourself and the way you interact with others on the team?

5. What emotions did you feel during this activity?

6. Some personal feedback you would like to provide (one to one):

    To: _____

    _____

    _____

    To: _____

    _____

    _____

LASER SPEED DETECTOR PURCHASE DECISION SOLUTION GRID: FORM H

Requirement \ Model	Hot Sot 1200	Zapper Trooper	White Lightning	ZOT 55-Alive	X-Files 5640
Range > 750 yds	900 yds	800 yds	600 yds	850 yds	800 yds
Cost < $1,500	$1,400	$1,250	$1,050	$1,700	$1,400
Instant-On	Yes	Yes	Yes	Yes	No
Zero EMF	Yes	Yes	Yes	Yes	Yes
Immediately Available	Yes	6 mo	Yes	Yes	Yes
Midrange Accuracy ±3mi/hr	±3mi/hr	±2mi/hr	±3mi/hr	±3mi/hr	±3mi/hr

☐ Eliminates this option.

YOUR ROLE AS COACH: FORM I

The most important part of this training session is the practice meetings. Participants get the opportunity to facilitate a task-oriented meeting, either as designated facilitator or as secondary facilitator. You can help the awareness and learning process in your role as coach for participants.

Do:

- Stay back. Don't get heavily involved.

- Be objective. Use behavioral observations.

- Use in-and-out interventions.

- Ask questions to get participants to think the situation through.

- Reinforce the principles and techniques from the classroom session.

- Conduct a feedback session for the team leader or facilitator. Give focused, behavioral feedback to participants, using your sensitivity.

Don't:

- Get involved with the content (task) of the team activity.

- Tell people what to do.

- Take over from the participant facilitator or team manager.

- Be a rescuer. Let participants learn from their actions.

Facilitating a Feedback Session:
Guidelines for Coaches

As you facilitate the feedback session, remember that you are not delivering a report card. Rather, you are eliciting participation from the team members. Here's a suggested agenda:

1. Review the processing agenda with the team. Select a scribe and a timekeeper.

2. Ask the team leader or facilitator:

   - *How do you feel about the meeting?*

   - *What went well? What would you do differently?*

   - *Before we solicit feedback from the team, on what behaviors would you like some specific feedback?*

   Have the scribe list the responses on a flip chart.

YOUR ROLE AS COACH: FORM I (*CONT.*)

3. Ask the team:

   - *What went well for you as team members?*
   - *What specific suggestions would you like to offer to the leader or facilitator?*

Have the scribe list the responses on a flip chart. During this part of the session, ask the leader or facilitator only to acknowledge the team's observations, not to respond.

4. Ask questions to make the comments from the team useful to the facilitator. Avoid overkill; try to sense when there has been enough feedback. If in doubt, ask the team facilitator. Throughout the session:

   - Keep it specific.
   - Keep it timely.
   - Keep it task-related.

5. You may add observations of your own after the team provides its feedback. Don't repeat a previous observation.

6. Ask the team leader or facilitator:

   - *Would you like to comment on any of the feedback?*

   The leader or facilitator may identify feedback on which he or she will take action, or may just say "Thank you" to the team. Avoid putting the individual on the spot or creating a situation in which anyone feels a defensive response is in order. The facilitator does not owe the team a response.

7. Thank the team members for their objective comments and their spirit of helpfulness. Thank the leader or facilitator for his or her willingness to accept feedback. Thank the timekeeper and scribe. Take down the flip charts and give them to the leader or facilitator.

COACH'S OBSERVATION
WORKSHEET: FORM J

Things the leader or facilitator did or said to help the team with its process:

Things the leader or facilitator might have done or said to help the team with its process:

One or two suggestions for the leader or facilitator:

30

DEMONSTRATING TEAM BRAINPOWER

Ed Rose

Overview
With rapid increases in computer power and similar advances in telecommunications, we have entered the Information Age, where horsepower has given way to brainpower. The traditional approach to leading employees has become archaic. New organizational structures filled with newly empowered teams are now the norm. Team members need to understand the dynamics of teamwork and its benefits to the organization. This exercise challenges team members with a task that requires input from everyone in order to complete the task in 20 minutes. It can be used in a variety of team situations to demonstrate various learning points concerning team behavior.

The team is tasked with transporting marbles from point A to point B without touching them. The exercise requires team members to solve this task with creative thinking and working together, processing all inputs, allowing them to put theories of team problem solving into action. It allows the participants to experience the satisfaction of self-discovery. They should return to their work environment with a new enthusiasm about the value of teamwork and the importance of team dynamics.

Suggested Time
40 minutes (20 minutes for the exercise, 20 minutes for debriefing)

Materials Needed
✔ 1 tube per participant (recommended ³/₄-inch PVC pipe cut into 12-inch lengths, with the ends cut at different angles to make it difficult to line the ends up—do not cut them straight!!!)

✔ 5 marbles per team

✔ Form A (The Operation Marbles Task) and an envelope

✔ Form B (Example of Success)

Contact Information: Ed Rose, AET, Inc., 1900 S. Harbor City Blvd., Melbourne, FL 32934, 321-223-9640, edrose@cfl.rr.com.

191

Procedure

1. Place Form A into an envelope so the team members can open it and plan their strategy without your direction or help. Your role is one of providing clarification only.

2. When ready to begin, place one tube on the floor for each participant. The participants will select their own tubes. You should not direct any of this activity. Lay the envelope containing the handout down and let the members read it (this duplicates the real experience of data coming to a team and their utilization of that data). Load the marbles when asked.

3. The main idea is for the team to process according to the instructions and complete the task. You should take notes during the exercise for use during the debriefing session. *Note:* Participants particularly enjoy it when a facilitator captures a point they made during the exercise. Of course, it should not be an embarrassing issue, just an observation. Allow the group to evaluate the significance of your observation, and be sure to allow them to agree or disagree with it.

4. Once the group has reviewed the instructions on Form A, tell them that successful marble transport companies complete similar tasks in under 20 minutes, and point out that if they fail, the entire company could be out of business in a short period of time (the objective here is to add additional pressure to succeed).

5. Identify points A and B only after being requested to do so. You will determine the distance and obstacles the team will have to deal with in order to successfully deliver the marbles.

6. Do not volunteer information; make team members ask questions in order to obtain the information they seek. *Note:* Various debriefing issues will arise concerning this approach, which will promote lively discussions.

7. Review the solutions. One example of how to complete the task is found on Form B.

8. Use these questions to stimulate the team's reflection and learning about the exercise.

   ✔ How successful were you?

   ✔ What problems did you experience as a team?

   ✔ Can you identify specific behaviors that helped your team?

   ✔ What behaviors had a negative effect on the team?

   ✔ Did you experience any "aha's"?

   ✔ Did your concept of the task change?

✔ How was leadership handled on your team?

✔ How did ideas get processed? (Explain.)

✔ Did team members support each other?

✔ What types of "out-of-the-box" thinking occurred?

✔ What would you do differently if you were faced with this challenge again?

✔ How would you relate this experience to the day-to-day operation of your company?

✔ What learning can you take from this exercise to make you a better team member?

THE OPERATION MARBLES TASK: FORM A

TASK:

Your team must transport five marbles from point A to point B. The facilitator will identify these points for your team.

RULES:

✔ Ask the facilitator to load one tube with all five marbles.

✔ No one can touch the marbles.

✔ If a marble is dropped, all members lose the ability to speak!!!!

✔ When you are holding the tube containing the marbles, you cannot move your feet.

You have 20 minutes to complete this task.

EXAMPLE OF SUCCESS: FORM B

There is no right or wrong way to complete this task However, many teams have been extremely successful using only three tubes—one containing the marbles and the other two securing the marbles inside the carrying tube, preventing them from falling out:

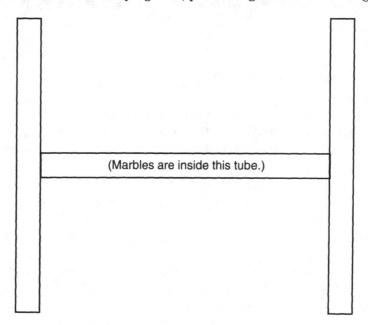

(Marbles are inside this tube.)

This allows the structure to be passed to each person rather than rolling the marbles down many tubes. Remember, it is only the person holding the tube(s) with the marbles who cannot move his or her feet. There are most likely other variations yet to be discovered, but this is the best one I know of. I've included this one as an example only.

31
BUILDING GROUND RULES FOR SUCCESSFUL TEAMWORK

Harriette Mishkin

Overview New groups, as they form and organize to define their purpose and explore their team norms, need to address two critical issues up front: 1) how to create guidelines for attendance and timeliness, decision making, managing conflict, and confidentiality; and 2) how to engage in meaningful discussions and reach consensus on critical issues.

This activity provides a team with an experience in both issues by combining the need to engage in group decision making in order to reach consensus on a set of 12 normative behaviors that are essential in building successful teamwork relationships. It can be used in the first meeting of a newly formed group or team prior to dealing with task items on the agenda, or it can stand alone as the first task of an ongoing group or team.

The rank order chosen by the participants becomes their set of "Ground Rules." When the activity is completed, this document can be displayed (reorganized according to the chosen rank) for all to see and follow during ongoing teamwork processes.

Suggested Time 50 to 60 minutes

Materials Needed ✔ Form A (Building Ground Rules)

✔ Twelve 5 × 8-inch index cards, one containing each of the 12 items on Form A, prepared prior to this activity, typed using at least a 16-point font

✔ Masking tape or drafting dots or tack pins

Procedure 1. Tell participants that this activity will give them the opportunity to build their team ground rules, while simultaneously giving them practice in meaningful discussions and reaching consensus.

Contact Information: Harriette Mishkin, Performance Concepts, 220 Locust, Street, Suite 21 B/C, Philadelphia, PA 19106-3946, 215-923-6925, harriette@society-hilltowers.com.

2. Hold a brief discussion on why it is important to establish team norms and guidelines for attendance, timeliness, decision making, managing conflict, and confidentiality; and on how teamwork outcomes improve when members engage in meaningful discussion and reach consensus.

3. Distribute copies of Form A and explain that members have 10 minutes, working on their own, to rank order the 12 items, using the column "Your Ranking" to indicate which item is the most important to them (use #1 to indicate what is most important and #12 to indicate what is least important). There are no right or wrong answers.

4. Call time and tell participants that they have 25 minutes for team discussion. Review ways to make decisions: majority rule (voting), the leader decides (unilateral), powerful minority decides, everyone agrees (unanimity), and consensus (general accord/agreement; though it might not be your preference, you can live with it because it was arrived at fairly).

   Tell them to strive for consensus; try not to compete or compromise, or argue for their own choices. Avoid voting, bargaining, or coin flips. Involve all team members in discussing, deciding, and managing the time allotted.

5. As a group, they are to use the column "Team Ranking" to identify what is most important to them (use #1 to indicate what is most important and #12 to indicate what is least important). Original rankings in the first column should not be erased.

6. Call time and discuss the team ranking results. Using the prepared index cards each containing one of the 12 items, post them in view of the participants in the order of the newly agreed-to guidelines. Explain how to reference them during discussions and teamwork processes.

7. Debrief the teamwork process: How did they decide, involve all participants, manage differences, deal with obstructive behaviors, reach agreements, and manage their time? How close did individual rankings come to the team ranking? Ask participants to look at their top three and bottom three rankings and compare them to the team ranking. This will give you a sense of how well they worked together, the degree of synergy that was produced.

8. Ask team members to identify three lessons learned that they can use immediately. Capture them on flip chart paper and display for reference.

BUILDING GROUND RULES: FORM A

Step 1: Each member of the team is to individually rank each of the 12 "Ground Rules for Successful Teamwork." (#1 is most important, #12 least). Place your responses in the first column under "Your Ranking." You will have 10 minutes to do so. Do not discuss the items until each member has finished the individual ranking.

Step 2: After everyone has finished the individual ranking, rank order the 12 items as a team. Use the second column—"Team Ranking"—to record your responses. Once discussion begins, do not change your individual rankings. You will have 25 minutes for the team discussion.

	Your Ranking	*Team Ranking*
1. If we must be late or absent, we will inform the team facilitator, liaison, or a team member at least a day in advance.		
2. We will always come to meetings prepared to work on the agenda that we will receive before the meeting. Our preparation and data collection will be complete, and we will be ready to discuss the issues on the agenda.		
3. We will always respect the opinions and feelings of all individuals. Each member has equal participation in our meetings. When discussing team business, members should expect to contribute to discussions and be listened to with respect.		
4. We will always avoid blaming people for the shortcomings of our team. If our team somehow fails to do its tasks properly, we will examine our team process and attempt to improve it. If individuals are having trouble meeting their commitments, the team will support them in every possible way.		
5. Members will support the decisions of the team after they are made. Undermining team decisions or second-guessing and bad-mouthing the team and its work outside the team setting to nonmembers is unacceptable behavior.		

BUILDING GROUND RULES: FORM A (*CONT.*)

	Your Ranking	*Team Ranking*
6. Members will live up to their team commitments, recognizing that failure to do so affects the whole team's progress. When in jeopardy of not meeting their obligations, members will notify the team in time for other members to take supportive actions.		
7. When faced with a decision, we will first decide how to make the decision. Our general rule is to (1) state the problem, (2) discuss different ideas, (3) examine the benefits and risks associated with different approaches, and (4) select an approach we can all support.		
8. We will deal with conflict in a productive way. Our general rule for conflict is to understand the problem as best we can from each side's perspective. To do that we will listen to all sides of the conflict, looking for facts and evidence. If there is still a conflict about facts, we will gather additional data. When the problem is understood, the team will help those in conflict create alternative approaches.		
9. We recognize that working on a team usually results in high-quality ideas and decisions. If we find we are not experiencing these benefits of teamwork, we will pause to assess how we are working together until we better understand our team and our work.		
10. We will not engage in sidebar conversations, whether or not they relate to the topic under discussion or other issues. Relevant conversations will be shared with all team members.		
11. Because of the time boundaries of this project and our desire to engage all participants in discussions and decisions, external interruptions will be kept to a minimum.		
12. The discussions and decisions of this team will be kept confidential and not shared with anyone outside of this group, until agreed to by all participants.		

PART **IV**

ORGANIZATION DEVELOPMENT

32
BUILDING ORGANIZATIONAL COMMITMENT

Cathleen Smith Hutchison

Overview In today's fast-changing business environment, many initiatives within an organization require demonstrated commitment from managers throughout the organization. However, there is often a lack of clarity about what demonstrates commitment. This is especially perplexing because commitment is an internal state of mind. What does a manager need to do or say to demonstrate commitment?

The goals of this exercise are to clarify and identify the observable behaviors that demonstrate the internal state of commitment. A second portion of the exercise may be used to identify specific actions that each manager will take to demonstrate his or her commitment to a specific initiative within the organization. The activity can often be used to advantage at the end of a program introducing a new corporate initiative. It also makes an effective transition from discussion of an initiative to taking action to support it.

Suggested Time 30 to 45 minutes (a very large group could run somewhat longer)

Materials Needed
- ✔ Flip chart pad and easel
- ✔ Markers
- ✔ Post-It pads (large size)
- ✔ Pens for participants
- ✔ Form A (Key Actions and Characteristics of Commitment)
- ✔ Form B (Key Concept Reading: Commitment)
- ✔ Form C (Individual Exercise: Personal Commitments)

Contact Information: Cathleen Smith Hutchison, Conifer Consulting Group, PO Box 1147, Cedar Crest, NH 87008, 505-281-4496.

Procedure *This training activity is in two parts. Although each can be conducted independently, there is greater impact when they are conducted together.*

Part I

1. Distribute copies of Form A to participants.

2. Ask participants to read the directions and complete the worksheet. Give them 5 minutes to do so. Distribute pens as needed.

3. Ask several participants to share their examples.

4. As they do so, write words that summarize their descriptive actions and characteristics on the flip chart. Prompt the group by asking questions such as "What did you see them do that showed you that they were committed?"

5. Chart several actions and/or characteristics that can be categorized into each of the four areas of "frequency," "energy level," "level of risk or personal sacrifice," and "level of accountability and personal responsibility," as described in Form B.

6. Lead a discussion on the similarities among what is observed in the variety of examples that have been shared (5 minutes). Help the group to reach categorizations of similarities that approximate the four areas listed in step 5.

7. Next, list the four areas on a flip chart. Distribute copies of Form B and ask participants to read it. Seek group consensus that these areas represent what they have described in their examples.

8. Ask if there are any other areas that should be listed and chart any additions.

9. Lead a group discussion on commitment and the implications for the participants in demonstrating their commitment to the specific corporate initiative. Ensure that all key points made in the concept reading (Form B) are made about the meaning of each of the four areas.

10. Ask the group for sample actions that might represent the individual's commitment to this specific corporate initiative.

Part II

11. Distribute copies of Form C to participants.

12. Distribute Post-It pads and pens as needed.

13. Give participants 5 minutes to read the directions and write out their commitments. Remind participants to sign them legibly.

14. Ask participants to come forward, read their commitments aloud to the group, and post them on the wall or a blank flip chart page. Continue until all participants have been heard from.

15. Charge all participants to hold themselves and their fellow participants accountable for the commitments that they have made to support this specific corporate initiative.

16. Collect all commitments and have them typed up with the names of the participants next to what they have committed to. Share the list of all commitments with all participants. (This can be done during the program or as a follow-up reminder a week or so after the program.)

Variation A large group may be divided into small groups to conduct steps 3 through 6. Then the large group reconvenes and the small groups debrief their discussions. The discussion in smaller teams tends to become more poignant and meaningful, particularly if they are conducted in small breakout rooms. Be aware, however, that the examples given may also become more emotional and personal in a small group.

KEY ACTIONS AND CHARACTERISTICS OF COMMITMENT: FORM A

PURPOSE

In this exercise, you will be discussing how to make the internal state of commitment an observable set of behaviors.

Step 1: Think of a time when someone you know was highly committed to accomplishing something. Examples can come from your friends and family and personal life or from your work experience. What did you see them do?

    a. Describe the situation.

    b. List the key actions and characteristics that you observed.

KEY ACTIONS AND CHARACTERISTICS OF COMMITMENT: FORM A (*CONT.*)

Step 2: Discuss with your group the actions and characteristics you wrote down in step 1.

✔ Are there consistent elements from all, or many of, the stories that the group tells?

✔ Are there other things that you can do to make your internal commitment observable to others?

List the key actions and characteristics that you observed.

KEY CONCEPT READING: COMMITMENT: FORM B

Commitment is an enigmatic concept. It is a state of being that exists inside the individual being observed. Many things can contribute to whether it is perceived by others, but it cannot be directly observed. It depends solely on the observance of secondary actions and characteristics.

An individual can, conceivably, be highly committed to making something happen, but feel very negative about the likelihood that it will happen. In some individuals, this negativism and cynicism may overshadow their commitment in the perceptions of others.

The key ways that people judge another individual's level of commitment to something are the following:

✔ *Frequency* of discussions and/or actions around the issue

✔ *Energy level* displayed when involved in discussion and/or actions around the issue

✔ *Level of risk and/or personal sacrifice* that the individual is willing to make because of the issue

✔ *Level of accountability and personal responsibility* that the individual takes for seeing that contributing steps are accomplished

FREQUENCY

People are generally drawn to those things to which they give high value. If they are committed to accomplishing something, it is usually something that they value for one reason or another. Therefore, they want to and/or do spend time involved with that issue or activity. A would-be athlete who is committed to making the team spends many hours practicing. Think of the movie *Rocky* and the amount of time spent in practice and preparation for the big fight. He made training for the fight his life's work.

ENERGY LEVEL

There is frequently a level of passion around a cause or issue to which an individual is committed. Individuals frequently display animated expressions and/or more energetic gestures when they are describing something to which they are passionately committed. Rightly or wrongly, we tend to expect to see a heightened level of energy as a signal of commitment.

Some individuals are very low-key. They may never display much animation or energy. The risk for our expectation of a high energy level as a signal of commitment is that it does not show up in every individual.

KEY CONCEPT READING: COMMITMENT: FORM B (*CONT.*)

LEVEL OF RISK AND/OR PERSONAL SACRIFICE

We also associate an individual's willingness to take risks or make some level of personal sacrifice with his or her level of commitment. The most common examples that we encounter involve dieting and quitting smoking. You can hear people say that they have to lose weight or they need to quit smoking almost every day. We recognize that those who are truly committed to accomplishing these goals must forego that piece of pie or must endure that craving for a cigarette. Without making such "small sacrifices," the weight will never be lost or the cigarettes given up.

The same is frequently true of accomplishing a business mission or vision. There may be late nights or weekends at work when you would rather be spending time with family or friends. There may be a trip out of town at an inopportune time. There may be a decision that must be made with incomplete information or an action that must be taken that could backfire or blow up if mishandled. Perhaps other priorities must be allowed to slip in order for you to achieve this one.

We expect that individuals who are committed will make these sacrifices and take these risks. We unconsciously tie personal sacrifice so closely to commitment that if sacrifice is not necessary, we may not recognize that commitment exists.

LEVEL OF ACCOUNTABILITY AND PERSONAL RESPONSIBILITY

Accountability has two components. One is the level of personal responsibility and accountability that the individual takes on for himself or herself. The other is the level of accountability that the individual expects from others. The two go hand in hand.

Being accountable and taking responsibility require believing that you are in charge of your own behavior. When you make decisions and take action, you must be willing to be accountable for what you have undertaken. This does not mean that you do not sometimes err or fail, for if you never fail you are not setting your targets very high. You are being accountable for your own actions when you are willing to take constructive risks and accept the consequences.

At the same time, someone who is committed to accomplishing something will not easily accept excuses from others for not completing their portions of the project. They hold others as accountable as they hold themselves. Committed individuals are willing to help others work through barriers to achieve their outcomes, but they are not willing to accept others' unwillingness to try and to make personal sacrifices also.

KEY CONCEPT READING: COMMITMENT: FORM B (*CONT.*)

When someone is committed to a group goal, she or he expects all members of the group to be equally committed. This translates to an expectation that all members will be accountable for and take personal responsibility for their own actions.

Personal responsibility and commitment by all employees are critical to an organization's ability to be competitive. Individuals in a position to be aware of an opportunity or need for improvement either take action and improve the organization's competitive position or they do not take action and they decrease the organization's competitive position. It is that simple and that complex.

If everyone in the organization steps up to the challenges, the organization's position improves. If just one individual ignores an identified opportunity or need, then the organization is not as competitive as it could be.

INDIVIDUAL EXERCISE: PERSONAL COMMITMENTS: FORM C

PURPOSE

In this exercise you will be making a personal commitment to action.

List 1 or 2 things that you personally can do and will commit to doing within the next 30 to 90 days to support [a specific corporate initiative].

Write them each on an individual Post-It note and sign your name legibly. Be prepared to read your commitment aloud to the large group.

NOTES

_____

_____

_____

_____

_____

_____

_____

_____

_____

_____

_____

33

FOSTERING CREATIVE PROBLEM-SOLVING SKILLS WITHIN THE ORGANIZATION

Tom Smith and David Price

Overview The I-Search Technique, first introduced by Ken Macrorie (1980), is adapted to enable participants to "search for answers to questions they've always wondered about." Beginning with the concept of the anomaly, participants scan their organizational environments to identify those naturally occurring irregularities that tend to impede progress. From this point participants begin to think critically within a collaborative environment and employ qualitative methodologies until emerging solutions are revealed. The technique encourages self-efficacy, the acquisition of new knowledge, and the development of collaborative problem-solving skills.

Suggested Time Two sessions of 2 hours each (for a group of 12)

Materials Needed
✔ Form A (Discovering Our Anomalies Small Group Exercise)
✔ Form B (Noting Form)
✔ Form C (Reference Sheet)

Procedure *Session I: Introduction of the Concept and I-Search Circle*

1. Introduce the concept of the anomaly using the following narrative as a guide:

   The I-Search Technique begins with the concept of the anomaly, those naturally occurring irregularities that tend to impede progress in organizational settings. They are "blips" in our routines

Contact Information: Tom Smith, 211-A Hodgin Hall, NC A&T State University, Greensboro, NC 27411, 910-334-7847, smithtg@athena.ncat.edu.
David Price, 111 Hodgin Hall, NC A&T State University, Greensboro, NC 27411, 910-334-7757, pricedw@aurora.ncat.edu.

that, when recognized, force us to pause and ask, "Why is this so?" and, "What is my response?" This may be as simple as recognizing a pattern of duplicated or contradictory communications to clientele, or it may be as personal as the realization that one's role and function within the organization, while secure, is no longer meaningful. Such anomalies erupt when one listens to one's "inner speech," that silent conversation one continually has with oneself Recognizing anomalies requires one to pay attention to oneself Devices such as keeping a daily reflective journal, guided imagery, or meditation are effective means of capturing anomalies in one's professional environment.

After explaining the concept of the anomaly, provide one or two examples from your own experience in the workplace and then invite participants to reflect on their own experiences through a small group exercise.

2. Ask participants to number off, depending on the size of group, in order to form small groups of 3 to 4 persons, and select a discussion leader. Distribute copies of Form A and allow 15 minutes of independent reflection followed by approximately 15 minutes of small group discussion following the format prescribed in Form A.

3. Explain that participants will now form an I-Search Circle. Arrange participants and yourself in a circle. Indicate that this is the time for each participant to share an I-Search Question. Further explain to the participants that their role is to help their peers to refine I-Search questions and to provide input into research sources and strategies for anomaly research (the I-Search Technique). Distribute copies of Forms B and C and invite participants to record the data on Form B.

   Then ask for a volunteer to report an I-Search Question. Model the process of critiquing and refining the question and invite other participants to provide further critique and to suggest resources and strategies to answer or resolve the stated question.

   From this point, ask each of the participants to report their I-Search Questions, which in turn are critiqued by the whole group.

4. Break into small groups and ask each group to develop I-Search plans by:

   ✔ Individually writing the final versions of their I-Search Questions.

   ✔ Identifying resources for the search (consult Form B and Form C, the Reference Sheet).

✔ Sharing the plans in small groups to further develop and refine, as needed, the search plans.

5. Summarize the session, inviting selected participants (based on observation of group work) to present their I-Search plans to the whole class. These typically are particularly unique or provide others with examples of unusual strategies or ideas. Provide advice on using primary sources for the search, interviewing techniques, and interpretation of data—paying attention to patterns and nonverbal clues.

6. Charge the participants to conduct their I-Searches following the plan developed and prepare a brief report of their I-Searches for presentation at Session II. Urge them to use this presentation format:

✔ What was your I-Search Question?

✔ What resources/strategies did you use?

✔ What are your findings?

Session II: Reporting of Completed I-Searches

1. Ask each participant to present his or her I-Search, followed by group debriefing (the "story of the hunt for data"). Allow approximately 10 minutes per participant.

2. Use the following debriefing questions:

✔ Did your research answer the anomaly?

✔ What worked?

✔ What didn't work?

✔ What other anomalies emerged during your search?

✔ Was the technique worthwhile?

✔ Will you apply the technique again?

Notes: The I-Search training plan, as presented here, may be expanded and developed into a regular quality circle program wherein participants meet periodically to present and discuss new I-Searches. Additionally, the process may be enhanced through the use of e-mail communications among participants throughout the search process.

References Macrorie, K. 1980. *Searching Writing*. Montclair, NJ: Boyton-Gook.
Spradley, J. 1979. *The Ethnographic Interview*. New York: Holt.

DISCOVERING OUR ANOMALIES SMALL GROUP EXERCISE: FORM A

Anomalies are those naturally occurring irregularities that tend to impede progress in organizational settings. They are "blips" in our routines that, when recognized, force us to pause and ask, "Why is this so?" and, "What is my response?" This may be as simple as recognizing a pattern of duplicated or contradictory communications to clientele, or it may be as personal as the realization that one's role and function within the organization, while secure, is no longer meaningful. Such anomalies erupt when one listens to one's "inner speech," that silent conversation one continually has with oneself.

Recognizing anomalies that lead to I-Search Questions requires one to pay attention to oneself. Often, I-Search questions are "Why" questions, e.g., "Why is my work no longer as personally satisfying as it was in the past?" or, "Why does it always take so long for purchase orders to be filled after they leave my desk?" or, "Why did this morning's staff meeting (or project team session) seem to go so much smoother (or rougher) than has been the case in the past?" The search question could also be a "What is," "How does," "What if," or "Should I" question, depending on the nature of the anomaly and how it is framed.

Within Your Group

1. Independently, reflect on your experiences of the past one to two weeks. Briefly inventory your day-to-day activities and prepare a short list, i.e., what did you do and with whom?

2. List three events or occurrences you might consider to be anomalies, for example:

   ✔ Did things happen that were puzzling or confusing to you?

   ✔ What things happened that were deviations from the norm?

   ✔ Were there oddities or aberrations?

   ✔ What has happened in the past two weeks that has surprised you?

3. Select one event and formulate your "anomaly" into a question.

4. When each participant in your group has had time to develop an I-Search Question, each of you should share and discuss your anomaly or question within the group. Consider:

   ✔ What resources and strategies might be employed to "answer" or "solve" the anomaly?

   ✔ Specifically, who might you talk to for relevant information?

   ✔ Who would you ask for "leads"?

   ✔ What other resources might you consult?

NOTING FORM: FORM B

RESEARCH IDEAS AND STRATEGIES	SOURCES	
	PRIMARY	SECONDARY

PLAN OF ACTION

Interviews:

1. _____

2. _____

3. _____

Other Data Sources:

1. _____

2. _____

3. _____

REFERENCE SHEET: FORM C

STEPS IN THE I-SEARCH TECHNIQUE

1. Scan Organizational Environment
2. Discover Anomaly
3. Develop the I-Search Question
4. Participate in I-Search Circle
5. Develop I-Search Research Plan of Action
6. Conduct Research
7. Present Results of Research
8. Debrief

DATA COLLECTION

Primary Sources: Firsthand information gained through interviews and available organization data or documents, such as:

Human interviews

Personnel information

Policy statements

Production data

Tax statements

World Wide Web

Organizational directories

Human Resource Office personnel

Memorandums

Phone logs

Professional associations

Secondary Sources: Secondhand data that has previously been interpreted, analyzed, and published, such as:

Published research reports

Newspaper articles

Book reviews

World Wide Web

INTERVIEW TIPS

✔ The person you interview is referred to as the informant.

✔ Know something about your anomaly before you conduct an interview.

✔ If you are worried that your informant may not have time to speak with you, ask him or her about other primary sources related to your topic. Also ask for names and telephone numbers of other individuals whom you could interview.

✔ Remember that your informant does not need an official title or to be a certain age. An expert simply knows a lot about something in particular.

✔ Begin your interviews with simple, descriptive questions before proceeding to structural and contrast questions.

✔ Limit your interviews to ten questions.

✔ Be sure to thank your informant for his or her participation.

REFERENCE SHEET: FORM C (*CONT.*)

TYPES OF INTERVIEW QUESTIONS

Descriptive Questions: These are the easiest questions to construct and to use. Descriptive questions such as, "Could you describe what you do in the plant?" or "Could you describe the conference you attended?" provide a broad overview of your informant's environment.

Structural Questions: These questions allow you to gain information about specific areas of interest. Structural questions may include: "What are the different divisions within your company?" or "What are the responsibilities of each staff member in this office?" Structural questions lead to more specific types of questions, such as "Can you think of any other responsibilities that this particular staff member might have?"

Contrast Questions: Contrast questions allow you to discover what an event, space, or object **means** to your informant. An example of a contrast question is, "Can you describe for me how an executive secretary's position differs from that of an office manager?"

34

MANAGING ROADBLOCKS TO GETTING THINGS DONE

Scott Simmerman

Overview   Perception plays a major role in people's tendencies to manage obstacles. Top performers by nature have fewer roadblocks, and poor performers generally have the most. By learning a better model of roadblock management, your clients can take action to remove the roadblocks that get in the way of their progress, a process I call *dis-un-empowerment*.

This exercise is focused on group dynamics and discussion about what gets in the way of getting things done. It is quite simple to deliver, participative and interactive in nature, and builds peer pressure to manage problems more effectively. Because it requires little preparation and few materials, it can be utilized as needed or delivered in a meeting when the situation warrants.

Suggested Time   30 to 90 minutes (depending on discussion time)

Materials Needed   ✔ Form A (Roadblock Analysis)
✔ Form B (Types of Roadblocks)
✔ Form C (Managing Roadblocks)

Procedure   1. Explain to participants that the session goals are multiple. You would like everyone to:

• Gain a better understanding of those things that are perceived to get in the way of getting things done.

• Gain employee involvement and participation in analyzing and solving these problems, and have them learn the thinking process involved.

Contact Information: Scott Simmerman, Performance Management Company, 3 Old Oak Drive, Taylors, SC 29687, 864-292-8700, Scott@SquareWheels.com, www.SquareWheels. com.

- Develop peer support for managing around these roadblocks.

Review with participants the general rules for the discussion:

- Everything gets written down.
- The goal is to generate as many roadblocks as possible.
- We'll come back and discuss them later.
- Everybody talks and participates.
- Limit negative comments.

2. Start by asking the group to take a few moments to list some of the roadblocks to improvement (some aspect of quality, productivity, etc.) in our organization. Try to keep the topic fairly tightly focused and relevant to what needs to be improved.

3. When they have processed a good bit of their thinking, stop and ask for their responses. Record the responses on newsprint. Write quickly and legibly. Pump ideas. Push for specifics. (For example, someone says, "Other departments" and you respond with, "Which departments? Which others are like that? Who else? What other people?") Hang each completed chart page on the wall with masking tape.

   Continue until the group has gotten a good number of roadblocks, and most of the main ones. Try not to generate them yourself, unless the process is really slow. In that case, mention one, such as "What about our systems and procedures?"

   Remember that your role is moderator. Be moderate. Encourage. Be very positive and *do not defend other people, departments, procedures, training, or anything.* Just write and prompt. Hang all the sheets on the walls.

4. Now share that you're going to talk about four types of roadblocks, and explain them in your own words. Distribute copies of Form A (Roadblock Analysis) and refer participants to the illustrations. Here's what you explain:

   "There are four types of roadblocks. The first [Draw a large rectangle as in the drawing.] *is a Type One. Picture this as four feet thick, twelve feet long, and ten feet high. It weighs forty thousand pounds.* [Draw large arrows like the ones in Form A and say:] *A large amount of pressure in this direction* [inside out] *results in only a little movement."* [Draw a tiny arrow.]

   "Do we have Type One roadblocks? Name a big one... [Get agreement that these really big roadblocks do exist. Then draw a thinner rectangle and call this one a Type Two.] *The Type Two is only six inches thick and weighs only four thousand pounds. Moderate force here* [Draw moderate arrows to one side.] *moves it a lot more*

easily. [Draw a larger arrow on the other side.] *But it is also diffi-cult. Do we have Type Two's?*

"The Type Three is also twelve feet wide and ten feet high but it is like this line and it is colored wallpaper, the color and texture of the concrete. You can't tell any of them apart by looking. You have got to push or move around to get a different perspective. And if you push, it moves easily. Do we have some roadblocks like this?

"Type Four [Draw dots.] *is like this. It is just like a Type One until you go to find it* [You can "sleepwalk" here to demo.] *... and then you can't. A Type Four is the one you have always heard is a roadblock, but you don't know for sure because you haven't seen it yourself.*

"When Scott Simmerman does this exercise [Use my name if the exercise is going well, but don't if it isn't!] *he normally finds that seventy to eighty percent of any list is made up of Type Threes and Fours.*

[Distribute copies of Form B (Types of Roadblocks) and give partic-ipants a chance to read it. Encourage any questions. Then proceed:]

"Let's go back over our list and try to rate these from Type One to Type Four." [Then "work" the list and get consensus. You might have to label the roadblocks 2/3 when the group gets stuck. Move on.]

5. Explain to the group that the different types of roadblocks all require different approaches to their management.

"Does it make sense for one person to push on a Type One? [Note: The answer is, only if the person is big and powerful and has lots of resources. Very senior managers can do this, on occasion.] *Type One Roadblocks are the kind that you delegate upward. Give those to me.*

"Teams can do a good job of managing Type Two roadblocks. [Consider allowing a team to take on the challenge of managing one or two from the list.]

"Type Three roadblocks can be managed by each individual, but that depends on your knowing that they are Type Threes and not Ones or Twos. That sometimes takes some discussion and perspective.

Type Fours? Just do it! Don't even think that these really exist. [At this point, you can revisit the list, make decisions about what the group may do, ask for commitments from individuals about which Threes and Fours they will work hard to manage this week, and so on.]

6. Distribute copies of Form C (Managing Roadblocks) as a summa-ry of the process.

ROADBLOCK ANALYSIS: FORM A

What are some of the things that might get in the way of improving teamwork and service quality in your organization?

_____
_____
_____
_____
_____
_____
_____
_____
_____
_____
_____
_____
_____
_____
_____
_____

Actions:

1.

2.

3.

4.

TYPES OF ROADBLOCKS: FORM B

Type 1—The Brick Wall

Some roadblocks are truly unalterable. In the real world, people face roadblocks that inhibit their performance and that they are not likely to change: the effectiveness of a foreign competitor's product, a slumping national economy, the international exchange rate, the organizational structure at the organization, the funding and paperwork processes for new product development, etc. These are all factors that affect employee performance but are well beyond individual or collective control. Characterize these as brick walls: immovable and real.

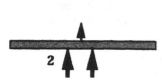

Type 2—The Partition

The second category of roadblocks includes those that can be managed with effort, time, money, additional personnel, or other resources. If that is the case, the individual employee might make some degree of progress in overcoming this particular inhibitor to performance. Often a small group of employees can make even more progress collectively. Most importantly, this type of roadblock can be managed, in large part or wholly, if supervision or management got involved. This type of roadblock is characterized as a partition. A partition, if pushed from the bottom, might move slightly; but if pushed from a higher level at the same time, it will often topple. These are real roadblocks that employees require assistance to remove.

Type 3—The Paper Wall

The third category of roadblocks is reminiscent of a football game in which the home team bursts through a paper barrier to the cheers of the crowd at the start. Until tested, this roadblock often looks impenetrable. Workplace examples are common, and include the belief that the boss will not approve; that it won't be supported by another department; that a process is "policy" or the way things have always been done; and so on. People discover that these roadblocks disappear when they test these perceptions. Others have done things differently and are doing things differently. Unless tested, this roadblock is just as effective in preventing performance as the first two. These roadblocks are manageable, but also real.

Type 4—The Mind-Set

This type of roadblock is the most troubling to management. It represents untested beliefs and perceptions. When people believe they can't do something, they are correct. These roadblocks are de-actualizing and restrictive, yet arbitrarily so because they really do not exist. Interestingly, these are the most common of all roadblocks and the ones that block below-average performers from improvement.

MANAGING ROADBLOCKS: FORM C

It is fascinating to observe how different employees manage the roadblocks they face. Top performers, as a group, are generally not impeded by many of the things that get in the way of average or poor performers. Their model of how things really work appears to be more proactive and behaviorally oriented. They are willing to test roadblocks to see which are which and are often quick to refer Type 1 and 2 roadblocks to management, whereas they push through the 3s and 4s themselves.

Average performers, on the other hand, are often observed to be stymied by roadblocks. Some may stubbornly push the 1s and try to get them to move, even though they do not have the power to do so. They may spend a lot of individual time on the 2s, trying to generate change and feeling good when they manage to get past them; this behavior, while well-intentioned, may not be time and energy effective!

Poor performers can generate long lists of roadblocks that get in the way of getting things done. They face innumerable hurdles in their everyday jobs and constantly point out the things that cause their performance levels to be low.

So, here's a dis-un-empowering exercise that you can do to help reshape the thinking of the poor performers and generate alternative behaviors among the average performers.

Use a flip chart and masking tape and start a meeting with the question, "What are some of the roadblocks to getting things done around here?" Allow the group to brainstorm and write down all their answers.

(Note: You might want to state the rules for brainstorming: "All comments are okay, everything gets written down, and we discuss the specifics of each idea when we complete the list. No negative comments or reactions are allowed in this part of the meeting.")

Write all the ideas down without reframing or rewording. Changing the wording might change the meaning or may be perceived as a put-down by an employee, who might then not participate any longer. Encourage the participation of everyone, but expect more roadblocks to come from the average and poor performers. You may also prompt, when the going gets slow, by saying something like, "How about interdepartmental issues?"

Post the sheets as they become filled and do not be surprised if you get ten or more pages. (My personal record is 22 pages!) The more the better.

When the list is essentially complete, share the model of Roadblock Management with the group, describing the categories and the general frameworks of each.

Now go back through the list and categorize, as best the group can, the nature of each of the roadblocks. Let *them* do this—that way it is their list and not yours!

What you will discover is that 80 percent of the roadblocks will be 3s and 4s, and that the top performers will often offer suggestions as to how to manage the 2s more effectively. The Type 1 roadblocks are those that you should volunteer to escalate; some of the 2s might be addressed by a team of your people, including some of the poorer performers.

Celebrate any ideas for improvement and attempts to address specific problems. Be sure to get out of the way as the group and individuals now engage in some dis-un-empowerment.

35

IMPROVING WORK DESIGN

Leigh Mundhenk

Overview Many organizations have downsized and are now operating with very lean workforces. That puts a high degree of pressure on employees, who often feel as if they are doing the work once done by several people. Yet much of this work is busywork that is not critical or even important to the performance of the organization. Because of competition in the marketplace, organizations cannot afford to have their employees doing work that is not directly related to enhancing productivity. One way to identify important work is for employees to determine the critical needs of their internal customers. Designing work around the needs of internal customers helps employees focus on essential work and leads to enhanced productivity.

This activity is designed to help people identify their top 20 internal customers and determine how they can best serve those customers. The activity can be used in several ways:

✔ as a tool for conducting a work redesign before or after a transition (downsizing, merger, etc.);

✔ as an exercise in a workshop to foster a culture oriented to internal customer service;

✔ as a team- or department-building activity;

✔ as part of a career development program that focuses on helping employees to market themselves;

✔ as part of an effort to improve interdepartmental communication or relationships.

Suggested Time 60 minutes (two 30-minute sessions)

Materials Needed
✔ Form A (Internal Customer List)
✔ Form B (Internal Customer Interview Form)

Contact Information: Leigh Mundhenk, University of Southern Maine, Lewiston-Auburn College, 51 Westminster St., Lewiston, ME 04240, 207-753-6581, mundhenk@usm.maine.edu.

Procedure

1. Go over the background information as presented in the Overview, customizing it to relate it to your needs.

2. Ask participants to give serious thought to who their top 20 internal customers are. If they don't have 20, ask them to pick a realistic number. Encourage them to consider people within and external to their departments or teams and to include such people as supervisors, direct reports, teammates, people in other departments who depend on them for work, subcontractors, and so on.

3. Ask participants to list their top 20 internal customers in forced rank order on Form A.

4. Ask participants to arrange for and conduct 15- to 20-minute interviews with their top 10 internal customers, using Form B to guide them in their questions. Ask them to include action steps that will ensure that appropriate action takes place

5. Reconvene the group at a later date. Process the experience and discuss progress and action steps.

6. Ask participants what they have learned about their internal customers that can help them to become more effective in their work.

7. Repeat the process for the next 10 internal customers.

8. Encourage participants to initiate follow-up interviews on an as-needed basis to enhance communication and identify new needs.

INTERNAL CUSTOMER LIST: FORM A

Name	Department Phone Number	Relationship and Importance	Interview Date and Time
1.			
2.			
3.			
4.			
5.			
6.			
7.			
8.			
9.			
10.			
11.			
12.			
13.			
14.			
15.			
16.			
17.			
18.			
19.			
20.			

INTERNAL CUSTOMER INTERVIEW FORM: FORM B

Use this form to guide you in asking questions during your interviews with your internal customers. Complete the action steps after each interview.

Open the interview by saying: "Because you are a top internal customer of mine, it is important that I provide you with the best service possible. The purpose of this interview is to find out how I can enhance the service I am currently providing." Change the wording to suit the manner in which you generally speak.

Interview Questions

What am I currently doing that is helpful to you and that you would like me to continue doing?

What would you like me to do more of?

What would you like me to do differently?

What should I do less of?

What else would it be helpful for me to know in order to provide you with the best service possible?

Action Plan

To better serve this customer, I plan to:

Continue:

_____

_____

Start:

_____

_____

Stop:

_____

_____

36

BALANCING ADVOCACY AND INQUIRY

Malcolm Burson

Overview Discussions and conversations of all sorts, whether in business or other parts of our lives, benefit when there's a good mixture of statements and assertions, on the one hand, and questions to explore the meaning of what's been said, on the other hand. From a reflective distance, this makes sense to most people. After all, unless you're in a formal debate and a third-party judge is going to decide who piled up the most points, we know that our ability to arrive at a decision or agreement benefits from a certain give and take. And many people admit that they'd like to improve the quality of conversations at work.

But in the urgency of business situations, where the need to get on with the work at hand makes us impatient, our natural desire is to make sure our point gets made. There's little incentive to listen, question, or explore the meaning of what's already been said. It's as if we came into the room, sat down, and stacked up our small pile of verbal hand grenades, to be pitched one at a time into the fray. Even if our team decides to change its behavior in this regard, in the hope of achieving better outcomes than the frustration we often experience in meetings, time pressure makes it nearly impossible to adjourn our work long enough to learn the skills we need.

As learning organization practitioners have repeatedly suggested, improving the quality of business discussions requires the intent to do so, agreed ways of behaving, and a common set of tools. Balancing inquiry and advocacy is a crucial part of this. If each participant in a meeting does little more than make a series of unconnected statements and unexplored assertions (advocacy), that does little to build the shared understanding needed for making good decisions. We can give more weight to the inquiry end of the teeter-totter by making room for questions that explore the implications of what has been said. In this

Contact Information: Malcolm Burson, Maine DEP, #17 State House Station, Augusta, ME 04333-0017, 207-287-7755, malcolm.c.burson@state.me.us.

way, we make sure that recognizing different perceptions of an idea or issue, for instance, allows the team to build a more complete picture and also increases the likelihood that the team will reach agreement as an outcome.

How to overcome our natural tendency toward assertion and advocacy, so we can step back toward reflection and inquiry? This activity provides a simple and slightly playful (if initially frustrating) way for team members to find a balance for themselves and the group. It works best in the real-time context of an existing team engaged in its usual work. It requires explicit agreement by all team members that improving the quality of discussion and conversation is a goal.

Suggested Time   45 to 60 minutes, in the context of a usual meeting

Materials Needed   ✔ Flip chart

✔ 3 × 5-inch cards, two for each participant, as follows: a card of one color (e.g., yellow) with **?** on one side; and a card of another color (e.g., blue) with **!** on one side of it. Note: Avoid red and green, as these colors convey a message that is at odds with the intent of the exercise.

✔ Form A (Template for Making **!** and **?** Cards)

Procedure   1. Give the team a brief overview of the usefulness of balancing inquiry and advocacy. Draw a picture of a scale or balance on the flip chart, with the "advocacy" side clearly weighed down. Explain that the team will be learning how to develop inquiry skills (or to move toward a better balance) while getting on with their usual tasks. Note that the purpose of inquiry is to ask questions that explore the implications of what has been said as well as to test assumptions, in order to build meaning that everyone shares.

2. Distribute the cards so that each team member has one of each color. Ask participants to place the cards on the table in front of them where everyone can see them.

3. Determine how the discussion or conversation will begin. It could pick up where the team left off the last time it met, or it could begin with a new topic. In either case, the topic should be written on the flip chart, in the form of either a statement or a question.

4. Explain the rules for discussion, as follows:

   Once the conversation begins, anyone may speak. If that person makes a statement or assertion, she or he turns the **!** card over. This person may not make another statement, even to answer a direct question, until she or he recovers the **!** card.

The only way to recover the **!** (advocacy) card is by asking a question that intends to move the group along; that is, by playing one's **?** (inquiry) card.

If the person making a statement is asked a direct question in response, someone else may seek to answer, thereby playing his or her advocacy card. Alternatively, someone could ask a question that probes more deeply into what has been said.

Note that the facilitator has the power to interpret the rules and to determine whether an inquiry or question is really a disguised assertion (against the rules!).

5. When all team members have had multiple opportunities to speak, call time and debrief the activity. Make sure to note on the flip chart the name of the last speaker, and the point to which the discussion has proceeded. This will allow you to provide continuity when the meeting resumes.

6. Close the intentional practice portion of the meeting by reopening the discussion at the point noted on the flip chart. Suggest that team members are no longer limited by the rules of the exercise, but may want to keep the cards in front of them as a reminder. In some teams known to me that meet regularly, I've observed people keeping the cards in the notebooks they bring to the meeting.

Debriefing Questions

*   Ask whether being forced to think of a question that would further the group's work meant that participants had to listen harder to what others were saying instead of planning their next assertion.
*   Ask how participants experienced the quality of the conversation: Did it seem more or less respectful, productive, or focused than usual?
*   Acknowledge that this approach may seem artificial at the beginning, but that the goal is to improve the quality of discussion over time. Point out that teams that find a good balance between inquiry and advocacy often observe that their effectiveness improves measurably.
*   If the team's task was problem solving or decision making, ask whether members think that progress was made.
*   In general, model inquiry in your own leadership of the debriefing, and see if anyone notices.

Variations

1. It may be useful to model the exercise briefly, using a fishbowl of 3 to 4 team members. With the others looking on, this group addresses the item from step 3. After 4 or 5 minutes and several interactions by all participants, the leader or facilitator invites the

rest of the team to join the discussion. In this case, it's best to give those in the fishbowl two advocacy cards each; otherwise the discussion may be too constrained, especially at the beginning. When the number of participants increases, the extra ! cards are no longer needed.

2. Allow the team to struggle with the limitations imposed by the rules. If and when the discussion lags, don't be in a hurry to break the resulting silence. On the other hand, a sense of humor helps defuse some of the frustration team members will experience when (as most will) they find themselves with something important to say, only to realize they must ask a question in order to earn the right to advocate.

TEMPLATE FOR MAKING ! AND ?
CARDS: FORM A

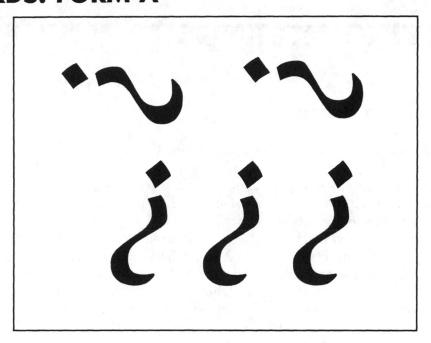

37

IMPROVING MEETINGS

Edwina Haring

Overview   This exercise serves several objectives. First, it allows team members to work with colleagues on the team other than those they interact with on a daily basis. Second, it levels the playing field; all parties are on equal footing in the exercise. Third, it provides practice in using a problem-solving model. Fourth, the exercise gives team members the opportunity to learn how to participate in team problem solving even though the problem may not be specific to their work duties. Fifth, at each round, each small group works with fresh content in another step in the problem-solving model, thereby reinforcing the skill of using the problem-solving model steps and stemming the tide of content saturation (whereby new learners may be tempted to skip steps). Last, it is fun, challenging, and active!

Suggested Time   3 to $3^{1}/_{2}$ hours

Materials Needed
- ✔ Forms A to D (Problem-Solving Relay) one copy of each form for each small group
- ✔ One copy of Form E (Problem-Solving Steps) for each learner, preferably printed on brightly colored paper
- ✔ 4 paper clips
- ✔ Pencils or pens
- ✔ Writing surface
- ✔ Sufficient room for learners to work in small groups without disturbing other small groups

Group Size   Ideal size is 16 to 20 participants in 4 small groups of 4 or 5 learners.

Preparation   Prepare three flip charts in advance with the following information:

Contact Information: Edwina Haring, Dynamic Performance Consultants, Newark, DE 19725, 302-455-1727, Eharing@magpage.com.

Flip Chart 1

Team Meeting Concerns

Making Team Decisions

Communication about Decisions

Professional Style Disagreements

Consistent Minutes and Distribution

Flip Chart 2

Problem-Solving Steps

1. Identify the Problem

2. Generate Solutions

3. Prioritize the Solutions

4. Create Implementation Plan

Flip Chart 3

Topic / Round	Round 1	Round 2	Round 3	Round 4
Making Team Decisions	A	D	C	B
Communication about Decisions	B	A	D	C
Professional Style Disagreements	C	B	A	D
Consistent Minutes and Distribution	D	C	B	A

Note: Insert team names in columns on your flip chart to replace A, B, C, and D where indicated. Reveal only one round at a time.

Procedure

1. Introduce the topic: "Today, we are going to learn an easy process for solving problems using the strengths of the team. Our target problem for this exercise will be our team meeting skills. We will work on four team meeting concerns while learning to use the problem-solving steps." (Use your own words.)

2. Show the prepared flip chart 1.

3. Divide learners into four small groups. Try to organize the small groups so that people are not working with the same people they work with every day. Ensure that learners have a pencil or pen, one paper clip per group, and a surface for writing. Separate the groups so they can work undisturbed by other small groups.

4. Ask the newly formed small groups to take one minute to introduce themselves (if necessary) and one minute to choose a team name.

5. At the end of 2 minutes, ask each small group for its team name and record the team names on a separate piece of flip chart paper.

Round One

1. Explain that the exercise begins with each group working on Step One in problem solving: Identify the Problem. Show flip chart 2. (Use the reveal method: Show only "Identify the Problem.")

2. Distribute a copy of Form A to each group, with the group's team name written at the top and its assigned topic circled or highlighted (see flip chart 3).

3. Review the instructions. Give the groups 30 seconds to choose a scribe and ask who the scribes are for this round.

4. Tell learners that you want them to discuss all the reasons why this is a concern and to list all their ideas about what may be causing the problem. Allow 8 to 10 minutes.

5. While small groups are working on Round 1, record the names on flip chart 3 in the appropriate places: Wherever there is a place for A, record the actual name the group has chosen instead. Do the same with the other group names for B, C, and D.

6. At the end of the time, ask each group to spend the next 5 minutes developing a clear, concise problem statement. Have the scribes record the statements at the bottom of the handouts. Collect each team's Form A.

Round Two

1. Reveal Step Two on flip chart 2, Generate Solutions.

2. Say, "The next step in problem solving is to generate solutions to the problem. How many of you have done brainstorming before? What are the rules for brainstorming?" Let them tell you how to conduct a brainstorming session; reinforce correct perceptions and correct or add rules where necessary.

3. Tell learners they will work with another group's problem identification (from Form A) and will have 10 minutes to brainstorm solutions and record them on Form B.

4. Redistribute the completed Forms A, along with a blank Form B, in the following sequence (see flip chart 3):

Distribute Team A's Form A to group B.

Distribute Team B's Form A to group C.

Distribute Team C's Form A to group D.

Distribute Team D's Form A to group A.

5. Resist the temptation to answer questions about why you are doing the exercise this way; that discussion is part of the debriefing.

6. Allow 10 minutes for brainstorming and recording, then call time and collect each team's Forms A and B.

Round Three

1. Reveal Step Three on flip chart 2, Prioritize the Solutions.

2. Say, "The next step in problem solving is to prioritize the solutions. We prioritize because we have to choose something to do first. Prioritization should consider the feasibility of each solution, the effort to implement the solutions, the time it may take, and its likelihood of success in correcting the problem."

3. Redistribute the completed Forms A and B, along with a blank Form C, in the following sequence (see flip chart 3):

Distribute Team A's forms to group B.

Distribute Team B's forms to group C.

Distribute Team C's forms to group D.

Distribute Team D's forms to group A.

4. Tell learners they will work with another group's solutions generated for another concern and that they will have 10 minutes to prioritize the solutions provided.

5. Call time.

Round Four

1. Reveal Step Four on flip chart 2, Create Implementation Plan.

2. Say, "The last step in problem solving deals with how we are going to implement the prioritized solution. You may not agree with the top solution selected by the previous group, but often we are called upon in the workplace to implement solutions that we did not choose.

"In this step, you will figure out how to make the solution a reality. List all the tasks that have to be done for this solution to be implemented. Name names or departments where possible. If you are unsure, suggest a name or position that may be responsible. Estimate how long you think it will take to complete each task and assign a tentative completion date. Don't hesitate to be precise—that's how solutions are implemented!"

3. Allow 20 minutes for teams to complete Form C, Prioritized Solutions. Then call time and collect each team's forms.

4. Redistribute the forms, along with a blank Form D, in the following sequence (see flip chart 3):

   Distribute Team A's forms to Team B.

   Distribute to Team B's forms to Team C.

   Distribute to Team C's forms to Team D.

   Distribute Team D's forms to Team A.

5. Tell learners they will have 20 minutes to create an implementation plan.

6. Call time after 20 minutes.

7. Distribute flip chart markers. Instruct teams to post their solutions and implementation plans on the flip chart paper provided and hang the flip charts on the wall.

Process Activity

1. Instruct the groups to choose a spokesperson to explain in 5 minutes the information the group received and the implementation plan they devised. Allow learners to ask a few questions about the group's plan.

2. Ask the group when they will make a final decision on what plans to implement and when. Look for commitments to the plans or commitments to the consideration of the plans.

Debriefing Activity

Ask the following questions:

- How did the exercise work for you?

- What did you learn?

- Why do you think the exercise was designed this way?

- Why didn't your small group keep working on the same concern throughout the afternoon?

Closing Activity   Distribute copies of Form E, Problem-Solving Steps, and review the steps one more time. Note that it is printed on bright paper so participants can find it easily when they need it!

Variations   1. Use any topics that surface in your analysis; adapt this exercise framework freely.
2. Reduce or expand the time allotted based on learner needs.
3. Allow small groups to work on the same content issue for all four problem-solving steps.

PROBLEM-SOLVING RELAY: FORM A

Round 1	Concern 1
	Concern 2
	Concern 3
	Concern 4

Identify the Problem:	Making Team Decisions
	Communication about Decisions
	Professional Style Disagreements
	Consistent Minutes and Distribution

Instructions: Your group has been assigned one of four concerns about how meetings are conducted within teams.

Your small group's assignment is:

1. Choose someone to be the group scribe.

2. Identify the exact nature of this problem using your personal, firsthand knowledge or what you have heard from others on the team. Think about the behaviors that cause this to be a concern. What doesn't work? What happens that prevents the team from being good at the concern noted above?

Note: Do not generate solutions!

Write a problem statement:

_____

_____

_____

_____

PROBLEM-SOLVING RELAY: FORM B

Round 2	Concern 1
	Concern 2
	Concern 3
	Concern 4

Identify the Problem:	Making Team Decisions
	Communication about Decisions
	Professional Style Disagreements
	Consistent Minutes and Distribution

Instructions:

1. Choose someone to be the group scribe.

2. Using the Problem Identification information from the previous group, generate solutions to the problem. Use brainstorming rules:

   - Be in a state of openness and focus.

   - All ideas are valid.

   - All ideas are heard and recorded.

   - Piggyback on each other's ideas.

   - Don't evaluate ideas during brainstorming.

Solutions:

_____

_____

_____

_____

PROBLEM-SOLVING RELAY: FORM C

Round 3   Concern 1

Concern 2

Concern 3

Concern 4

Identify the Problem: Making Team Decisions

Communication about Decisions

Professional Style Disagreements

Consistent Minutes and Distribution

Instructions:

1. Choose someone to be the group scribe.

2. Using the Solutions generated by the previous group, prioritize the solutions, considering the following attributes:

   - Feasibility

   - Likelihood of success

   - Ease of implementation

   - Time available to implement

   - Possible to do

Prioritized Solutions:

1. _____

2. _____

3. _____

4. _____

5. _____

PROBLEM-SOLVING RELAY: FORM D

Round 4   Concern 1

                     Concern 2

                     Concern 3

                     Concern 4

Identify the Problem: Making Team Decisions

                          Communication about Decisions

                          Professional Style Disagreements

                          Consistent Minutes and Distribution

Instructions:

1. Choose someone to be the group scribe.

2. Use Solution 1 from the previous group to craft an implementation plan. List the tasks necessary for this solution to be implemented. Assign responsibilities wherever possible. Provide estimated dates for completion of tasks. Post your plan on the flip chart.

Write Solution 1 here:

_____

_____

Implementation Plan

Tasks	Responsible person(s)	Estimated completion date

PROBLEM-SOLVING STEPS: FORM E

When your team is in trouble or just needs to resolve an issue, everyone is responsible for problem solving.

Here are the four steps to problem resolution:

1. Identify the problem...the real problem. Watch out for naming "symptoms" of the problem. Write a concise problem statement. This is necessary!

2. Generate all possible solutions to the problem. Go "outside the box" in your thinking. Use brainstorming rules. The most unlikely solutions are sometimes the best!

3. Prioritize the solutions generated in step 2. Let feasibility, time available, ease, and success factors influence your prioritization. (That's reality!)

4. Create an implementation plan that includes names, dates, and tasks that need to be accomplished. Think W3—Who does What by When.

38
RESOLVING CONFLICT EFFECTIVELY

Mel Silberman

Overview When a conflict completely overtakes a group and each side won't budge, you might try to move the process along by asking all parties to agree to engage in a four-step process.

Suggested Time 30 to 45 minutes

Materials Needed None

Procedure

1. Tell the group that, in your opinion, the conflict has deteriorated into an argument over who's right and who's wrong. Explain that you have a process to attempt to break the stalemate.

2. Ask each side to prepare a four-part presentation:

   The Conflict We're Having

   Discuss and agree on the positions being taken that oppose each other. Be objective and descriptive, and show that you have listened well to your opponents. Don't disparage their position. Be respectful of it.

   For example, consider a conflict over grade inflation between the academic dean of a college and the faculty. The faculty might state: It seems that we have opposite views about grade inflation. You want a greater distribution of grades so that we appear to have higher standards than are reflected in the current grade distribution. We think that the higher grades reflect well on us as a faculty. We must be doing something right.

   What Concerns Us

   Ask each party to share feelings, concerns, and needs about the issue in conflict.

Contact Information: Mel Silberman, Active Training, 303 Sayre Drive, Princeton, NJ 08540, 609-987-8157, mel@activetraining.com, www.activetraining.com.

The faculty might say: We are concerned that students will become obsessed with how they are graded rather than how they can be effective learners. We also worry that focusing on grade inflation emphasizes making things tougher for students...not rethinking what our basic teaching goals are and what we can do to facilitate them.

What We'd Like to Suggest

Each party shares a creative suggestion to get beyond the point where the group is stuck.

The faculty might now say: It would be ideal if we could agree to be more explicit about the performance criteria for different grading outcomes. If most students do well, there's no reason to have a grading curve.

What We're Willing to Do about It

Each party makes a statement about the actions it is prepared to take to create a better situation.

The faculty might conclude: We're willing to submit our current grading criteria to the Academic Dean and obtain recommendations on how they can be made clearer.

3. Invite each side to make its presentation.

4. Ask each side to comment on the presentations:

- How understanding was the other side?

- What suggestions hold promise?

- Is there a basis for moving to a win–win resolution of the problem?

Variation Sometimes, an issue is so explosive or the meeting is so tense that a full group discussion of a conflict seems unproductive. The best approach may be to adopt a small-group approach that minimizes open conflict and maximizes collaboration.

1. Devise three questions to ask participants about the conflict affecting the group. Here are three possibilities:

- How important is it that we resolve this conflict?

- What is the ideal resolution to this conflict?

- What practical ideas do you have to resolve this conflict?

Write the questions so that concrete answers are attainable. Avoid highly open-ended questions.

2. Inform participants that you would like the group to try a collaborative approach to conflict resolution that avoids extended discussion or public fighting.

3. Divide participants into trios. Give each participant one each of the three conflict assessment questions you have created. Ask each trio member to interview the other participants and obtain (and record) answers to his or her assigned question.

4. Convene in subgroups all the participants who have been assigned the same question. For example, if there are 18 participants, arranged in trios, 6 of them will have been assigned the same question.

5. Ask each subgroup to pool its data and summarize it. Then, ask each subgroup to report to the entire group what they have learned about the group's response to the question assigned to it.

6. Ask the group to reflect on the data that has emerged and assess what to do next.

39

COMMUNICATING WHAT YOU MEAN

Joan Cassidy

Overview   Everyone can relate to disasters that have occurred due to poor or mistaken communication. This simple activity quickly and effectively demonstrates why we have certain kinds of problems. It helps to drive home a number of points related to effective communication. One of these points is, "What you think you said is not what I heard." Participants have lots of fun while learning not to make assumptions. Their level of awareness is also raised relative to differences in thinking and communicating styles and the impact these differences have on effective communication.

Suggested Time   10 to 15 minutes, depending on the size of the group

Materials Needed   ✔ Overhead projector
✔ Flip chart
✔ Several colored markers
✔ Paper and pens or pencils for participants

Procedure   1. An overhead projector should be in plain view. It may be on or off, with or without a transparency on it. However, the activity is more interesting if the overhead is on and a transparency is on the projector.

2. Tell the participants that they will need some paper and pens or pencils for this exercise.

3. Next, tell them you are going to give them an instruction and when you do, they are to write down the first thing that comes into their heads.

4. Emphasize that they are not to look at what their neighbors have written down, nor are they to say anything out loud about the

Contact Information: Joan Cassidy, Integrated Leadership Concepts, Inc., 901 Naticoke Run Way, Odenton, MD 21113, 410-760-9192, DrJoanC@aol.com, www.drjoanCassidy.com.

exercise at this time. Also emphasize that it is important for them to write their responses (i.e., they should not just think of them).

5. Now, say the following sentence slowly:

   "Please take the overhead out of the room."

6. Repeat the sentence once, but do not respond to any questions or comments.

7. Allow about 30 to 60 seconds for them to write something down.

8. Check to see if everyone is ready. Don't allow too much time to elapse before continuing.

9. Now, go to the flip chart with a marker in your hand and ask each person in turn to tell you what he or she wrote down.

10. Record exactly what the participants say. It is okay to place check marks next to identically repeated items. Optional: Change the color of the marker for each response.

11. Within the first 3 to 5 responses, you will probably begin to hear other comments. However, continue to record the responses until you have everyone's on the flip chart.

12. Example responses include:

    • I would do it; Just do it; Do it.

    • Where do you want me to take it? Where?

    • Why?

    • When? Now? Later?

    • Do you mean me? Me?

    • Why don't you do it?

    • Do you mean the overhead projector or the transparency? (Variations are to ask whether you mean the ceiling, or overhead as it relates to financial matters.)

13. After you have recorded everyone's responses, lead the group in a discussion. Ask questions like these:

    • What happened here?

    • Why do you think we got so many different kinds of answers?

    • What can you tell me about these results?

    • What do we need to do in the future to keep a disaster from occurring?

14. During the debriefing, try to have some fun with the group. Take different examples and have a discussion around them. For example, if several people say they would do it, you might act surprised

and ask something like, "You mean all of you are going to do it? So who is going to end up being the one who does it? Are you going to have a knock-down, drag-out fight to decide?"

If someone gave a "Why?" response, ask, "Are you a trouble-maker?" or "Do you always question your boss when he asks you to do something?"

Often, participants will respond with, "I'm just trying to get more information so I'll know what to do" or "I need more information so I can be sure I do it correctly." If they respond in this manner, ask, "Does that sound like a good idea (i.e., to get more information)? Why?" If time allows, discuss several of the responses with the group.

15. End the exercise by having the group brainstorm lessons learned. Examples might include:

- There are a number of different ways to respond to a simple request.

- People with different thinking and communicating styles may respond differently to the same situation.

- You can't assume that people know what you mean.

- Depending on the situation (i.e., whether you have worked with someone for a long time, or the person is new to you or the situation), less or more instruction may be needed

40
UNDERSTANDING CULTURAL DIFFERENCES IN THE ORGANIZATION

Dianne Saphiere

Overview Cultural diversity can be an invaluable asset or a frustrating reality in any organization. The key is to foster understanding of cultural differences so that employees can use and work with the differences rather than inadvertently become tangled up in them. This tool uses a method for analyzing differing approaches and creating work practices that respect differences. Participants work in small groups to discuss a critical incident or case study and decipher it using a graphic framework. Each group's findings can easily and visually be shared with other groups.

Suggested Time 45 to 60 minutes

Materials Needed
✔ Form A (Lecture Notes)
✔ Overhead or flip chart of Form B (Basic Theory of Cross-Cultural Communication)
✔ A copy for each participant of Form B (Basic Theory of Cross-Cultural Communication)
✔ Overhead or flip chart of Form C (Story Debriefing)
✔ A copy for each participant of Form D (Critical Incidents)
✔ A copy for each participant of Form E (Cultural Detective Worksheet)
✔ One sheet of flip chart paper for each small group
✔ Two to three different colored markers for each small group
✔ Tape (to post the completed flip charts)

Contact Information: Dianne Saphiere, Nipporica Associates, 2516 West 90th Street, Leawood, KS 66206, 913-901-0243, dianne@nipporica.com, www.nipporica.com.

Procedure

1. Distribute copies of the handouts (Forms B, D, and E) to each participant.

2. Introduce the theory of cross-cultural communication using the Lecture Notes (Form A) or a few of your own organization's stories. Show participants the model on an overhead or flip chart (Form B).

3. As you tell the stories to explain the theory, ask participants what behaviors the two people in the story exhibited, and why (in other words, what were the cultural assumptions and values). Write participant responses in the appropriate box on the overhead or flip chart of Form C. Also fill in the Cultural Bridges box on Form C.

4. Explain that you'd like participants to gain fluency with the technique of understanding and working with cultural differences by using it to analyze some critical incidents.

5. Divide participants into groups of 3 to 5. Assign each group a critical incident (from Form D) to analyze.

6. Ask each group to take a few minutes to read and make sure all group members understand the critical incident (Form D).

7. Distribute a page of flip chart paper and markers to each group.

8. Ask each group to make a diagram identical to that on Form C (Story Debriefing) on the flip chart page.

9. Instruct participants to discuss their critical incidents in small groups and record their findings in the boxes on Form E (Cultural Detective Worksheet) and on the flip chart pages.

10. Ask participants to read each critical incident, one by one, and direct each group to present a summary of its learnings using its completed flip chart pages.

11. Assist participants to summarize and apply their learnings by asking them what aspects of this activity were most meaningful to them, and how they will use their learnings and this method in their jobs.

Variations

1. Use critical incidents specific to the participants' organization instead of those listed on Form D.

2. Use critical incidents involving the same culture to develop culture-specific knowledge (for example, when conducting a session on German Cultural Patterns).

3. Have all participants work on the same critical incident in order to gain more depth of learning and so that the small groups can compare their answers.

4. Instead of asking small groups to present their findings, have each group post its flip chart, then conduct a gallery walk or nonverbal review of participants' findings.

5. As follow-up, assign participants to complete the Cultural Detective Worksheet (Form E) for a real situation in which they have recently found themselves.

LECTURE NOTES: FORM A

1. Introduce the basic model described on Form B: two cultures, both with actions and behaviors that are motivated by cultural assumptions and values. People often do not think about these assumptions and values, but accept them as "correct" or "the only way." Between the two cultures is a culture gap (that could also be a gender, age, or work function gap) that causes behavior to be perceived differently from the way it is intended.

2. Tell two stories about cultural difference from your own experience. The stories should have two clearly different points of view.

   a. One story might be about two people meeting one another for the first time. One wants to stand close, shake hands vigorously, smile, and make direct eye contact. The other person wants to stand farther away, bow politely, use indirect eye contact, and maintain a serious facial expression. Assumptions and values involved for the first person include egalitarianism, informality, individualism, and directness; for the second person, they include hierarchy (high power distance), formality, and indirectness. Cultural bridges might include education for each person (so neither judges the other negatively) or an agreement between the two as to how they will greet one another.

   b. A second story might be about the use of space in an office. One person's cubicle has family photos, pictures drawn by young relatives, and a whiteboard with "To Do" notes displayed prominently. Another person's office has the company mission statement, interoffice phone list, and clearly labeled booklets of current projects; there are few personal objects in sight. This person has been known to use the first person's computer without asking permission, a practice that upsets the first person. Assumptions and values for the first person include personal space, the expectation of privacy, and verbal communication as a component of trust; for the second person, they include the idea of public or group space, expectation of teamwork, and implicit trust among members of a work team. Cultural bridges might include a dialogue between the two on their assumptions about office space, an agreement between them regarding the use of each other's computers, or a reconfiguration of the office space.

3. After you tell each story, ask participants to help you write in the behaviors and cultural assumptions of each person in the stories. Write them on an overhead transparency or flip chart of the graphic on Form C.

4. Take a few minutes to generate some solutions or cultural bridges with participants. These might include actions that members of each culture could take or systems that the organization could implement.

5. Summarize the key points of the theory of cross-cultural communication:

   a. No one culture or set of assumptions is better than another. All worldviews are valid.

   b. We need to learn about and be conscious of our own cultural assumptions in order to interact effectively across cultures.

   c. It is important not to try to change another's behavior, but to attempt to understand it, accept it, and work with it. Changing cultural assumptions takes years.

BASIC THEORY OF CROSS-CULTURAL COMMUNICATION: FORM B

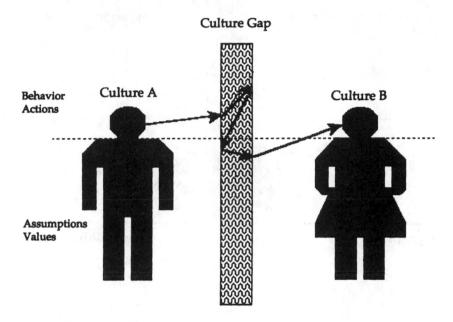

Assumptions and values support and motivate our behaviors and actions. We can easily observe behavior and actions, but often we must do some "sleuthing" to discover assumptions and values.

Early conceptualizations of the layers or depths of culture were developed by Edward T. Hall, Gary Weaver, and L. Robert Kohls.

STORY DEBRIEFING: FORM C

Behavior and Actions:	Behavior and Actions:

Assumptions and Values:	Assumptions and Values:

Cultural Bridges:

CRITICAL INCIDENTS: FORM D

1. A worldwide product management team

Five years ago, the American home office achieved a major technological breakthrough. The French subsidiary expressed interest in assessing the new technology, and the Americans agreed to provide it. The new product presented a wonderful opportunity for the French, and they invested a significant amount of money in preparing for its introduction.

The American organization encountered many problems with the production process, and because the technology did not have a wide market outside of France, they canceled further development. As a result, the French never received the new technology.

The American and French members of your team are quite upset with one another over this issue. The French are demanding that the Americans reimburse their expenses; the Americans are of the opinion that because the situation was unavoidable, they should not be held responsible for the expenses.

2. A U.S.–Korean joint venture management team

This joint venture has been in operation for five years; it required a major—but equal—investment by both partners.

Recently, the U.S. partner has been pushing for wider product distribution in order to achieve a 7 percent return on its investment. The Korean partner is resisting, preferring to limit distribution to selected dealers and thereby secure a longer-term market share. The Americans plead that their stockholders will bail out if there isn't a return soon. The Koreans emphasize that maximizing short-term profits will thwart long-term growth.

3. The financial management team of a Japanese subsidiary of a U.S. multinational

Last year, the U.S. home office audited the tax savings plan and, after talking with a Japanese tax expert, recommended an increase in the per capita meeting expense deduction of nearly 250 percent; they believed the Japanese tax law would permit that level of deduction.

The Japanese refuse to increase the deduction, arguing that the amount of the deduction depends on the purpose of the meeting and on whether alcohol is served, and that it would be too labor-intensive to check each and every meeting. They also contend that it is their civic duty to pay the taxes they owe; it is a contribution to the community and a legal responsibility.

The U.S. management team wants to follow the tax expert's advice, because saving the company and its shareholders money is their fiduciary responsibility.

4. A global management team for a European multinational

The Japanese developed a new technology a few years age that the Germans want to use; but the Japanese refuse to grant permission. They believe that while they have consistently invested in their R&D center over the years, other country organizations have not invested sufficiently. The Japanese seem to view the other country organizations as short-sighted; they do not want to share what they develop because they see nothing coming back to them in return. The Germans are angry; in their opinion, the Japanese look out only for themselves and are not team players.

CULTURAL DETECTIVE WORKSHEET: FORM E

Instructions:

1. Label the diagram below with the two cultures represented in your critical incident (for example, Culture A = French, Culture B = U.S. American).

2. Describe the behaviors of each of the cultures in the critical incident. Write your description in the appropriate Behavior and Actions box.

3. Fill in the cultural assumptions or values, the "hidden culture," for each culture.

4. In the Cultural Bridges box, list some steps that both cultures could take to improve communication, productivity, and teamwork.

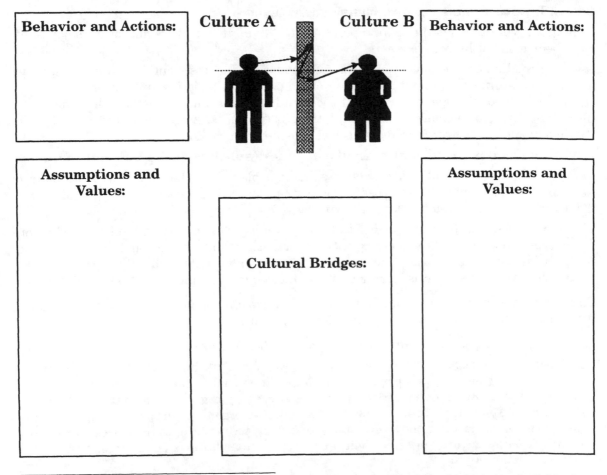

Behavior and Actions:

Culture A   Culture B

Behavior and Actions:

Assumptions and Values:

Cultural Bridges:

Assumptions and Values:

41

DEVELOPING ORGANIZATIONAL RESILIENCY

Mike Milstein and D. Annie Henry

Overview The old saying, "What you see is what you get," is quite true. Unfortunately, many organizational leaders see and focus on short-comings and issues rather than looking for possibilities and potentials. As a result, they tend to be preoccupied with problems rather than with strengths. This kind of thinking can lead to the development of policies and practices that emphasize difficulties and deficits rather than strengths and capabilities.

The pathological approach, based on a problem-focused, maladaptive, and "can't do" orientation, hinders the growth of an organization. What is needed for organizational growth and development is a resiliency approach based on a solution-development, adaptive, and "can do" orientation.

The approach that dominates—pathology or resiliency—can have a significant impact on your organization's effectiveness. Which is more representative of your organization? The intent of this exercise is to promote a dialogue that can lead to answers to this question. Your clients will then be encouraged to explore implications of the approach that dominates in their organization.

Suggested Time 60 minutes

Materials Needed
✔ A flip chart and a marking pen for each small group
✔ Facilitator's instructions to the group, taken from the Procedure
✔ A room large enough for subgroups to work without disturbing each other. The space should be flexible so that the format can shift from small groups to large group with ease.
✔ Tables that can accommodate the members in groups of 6 to 8.

Contact Information: Mike Milstein and D. Annie Henry, The Resiliency Group, 4520 Compound Ct. North NW, Albuquerque, NM 87107, 505-341-9450, adhenry@nmhu.edu.

Procedure　　1. Introduce and clarify the purpose of the exercise for the group: *"This discussion will provide an opportunity for you to explore how you think about challenges that confront the organization."* Expand upon the wording as needed.

2. Provide definitions for the two opposing ways of thinking about organizational challenges:

*"One way to think about organizational challenges is as **problems to be identified and solved.** Problem solvers see the world as a place with many pitfalls, shortcomings, and hazards; a place replete with risks, where it is likely that things do not, cannot, or will not work!*

*"Another way of thinking about organizational challenges is as opportunities to **promote resiliency.** Resiliency is the capacity to bounce back and grow stronger as a result of encountering challenges. We all have the potential to be resilient, but the extent to which this potential will be realized is highly dependent upon the explicit and implicit messages we receive from those around us. If those messages are problem- and deficit-oriented rather than strength- and resiliency-oriented, we are likely to become more sensitive about our shortcomings rather than confident about our capabilities.*

"Over time, if the messages we receive are mostly problem-oriented rather than resiliency-oriented, they can deter our growth and development and the well-being of the organization we work in.

"Problem solvers may be comfortable with identifying deficits, but they are probably not as likely to identify assets because they are predisposed to look for behavioral difficulties and work to correct them. Many organizational leaders may need to balance their thinking by becoming more aware of the strengths and capabilities that can be tapped for organizational improvement."

Respond to any questions that may arise after providing this information.

3. Ask the groups to think about situations in their organization that seem to be resistant to improvement. The situations should be important to group members. Examples might be as varied as low morale, poor role performance, or reduced productivity. Give members a moment to think about situations. Next, divide the group into smaller groups of 6 to 8. Provide each group with a flip chart, a marking pen, and a work area.

4. Ask the groups to listen to the situations their members have identified and select one that they are most interested in exploring. Then, provide the following directions:

"List all the reasons why things don't or won't work regarding the situation your group has selected. Be sure to list all the reasons given by group members on the flip chart, without censorship."

Move among the groups to be sure that the instructions are clear.

5. Ask the groups:

"Concerning the same situation, list all the reasons why things work as well as they do. In other words, things could be worse, but they aren't! Why not? What are the positive things that are going on? Be sure to record all the reasons given on the flip chart."

6. After the group completes the discussion give these instructions:

"Review the two lists your group has developed—the one that focuses on problems and the one that focuses on strengths. What practical things do you think might be done to improve the situation? Please record these suggestions on the flip charts."

7. Bring the groups back together. Lead a discussion based on the following questions:

- *How did the first activity, which focused on problems and shortcomings, feel to you?*

- *How did the second activity, which focused on strengths and capabilities, feel to you?*

- *How did the third activity, which focused on possibilities, feel to you?*

8. Finally, ask the group the following questions:

- *What is the organization's dominant way of thinking? Is it problem-focused or strength-focused?*

- *Is your individual approach to organizational issues deficit-oriented or resiliency-oriented?*

- *How comfortable are you with your organization's predominant thinking pattern?*

- *What are the implications of how we view our organization? How do we want it to function?*

Variations   1. Form small groups by departments or other appropriate job-related criteria. It may be important to look at how such ongoing groups view organizational situations, particularly if there are different subcultures among these groups.

2. Ask group members to share their responses to the following thoughts, paraphrased from Higgins (1994): Resilient people have three qualities in common. First, they have positive attitudes. Second, they confront issues and believe that they are in charge of their lives. Third, they believe that their lives have meaning and they have the courage to change their behaviors and habits.

Resources   Higgins, G.O. (1994). *Resilient Adults*. San Francisco, CA: JosseyBass.

Milstein, M.M. and Henry, D.A. (2000). *Spreading Resiliency*. Thousand Oaks, CA: Corwin Press.

V

STRATEGIC PLANNING AND CHANGE MANAGEMENT

42
EXPLORING ISSUES ABOUT MERGERS

Barbara Ferrarini

Overview   When organizations undergo mergers and acquisitions, major changes affect both the formal and informal cultures of the companies involved. This activity explores key issues that must be taken into consideration as the changes are planned and implemented. It provides the opportunity for participants to realistically test their knowledge, beliefs, and assumptions about the effect mergers have on employees and the subsequent impact on the company.

Suggested Time   2 hours

Materials Needed   ✔ Form A (Case Study)
✔ Form B (Character Scenarios)
✔ Name badges for facilitators and Kincade participants

Procedure   1.   Two facilitators are recommended (but not required) for this activity for the following reasons:

✔ To allow for facilitators' character roles to be introduced.

✔ To maximize opportunity for observations of group interactions to be discussed in the debriefing.

This activity was intentionally developed with built-in humor to enhance the learning experience. Although the goal is to discuss, experience, and reinforce the learning points, the facilitators should encourage a lighthearted approach to the activities.

2.   Begin the activity with a brief discussion of the process of change. Include key points such as:

✔ Planning change does not equal managing change.

Contact Information: Barbara Ferrarini, HR Manager, Lockheed Martin Corporation, Enterprise Information Systems, 12506 Lake Underhill Road, MP-143, Orlando, FL 32825-5002, 407-306-7066, barbara.ferrarini@lmco.com.

✔ The primary purpose of change management is to expedite the change process, moving the organization forward and minimizing the unproductive stages of change.

✔ Unproductive time associated with change can be costly. Pritchett & Associates, Inc. give the following example in *Business As Unusual*, 1991:

100 Employees

$22,000 Annual Salary

6 Months of Transition

3.6 Hours of Distraction per Day

$468,000 Impact

So Make It Quick!

At the same time, employees have to resolve their concerns about job security or retaining their benefits before they can effectively concentrate on changing work processes or other work-related business.

3. Brainstorm a list of key issues that the participants think they should be concerned with when planning for a merger or acquisition. List these on a flip chart and keep them in view during the role-playing activity that follows.

4. Give participants copies of Form A (Case Study) and ask them to read it.

5. Then explain the following:

The new company, KISS OFF, has decided to expand its product line with a new revolutionary toilet seat design. You and your teammates have just been assigned as a new team. The introduction of the team and kickoff of the task takes place at Kincade Headquarters Building. The team's task is to create the new product design and develop recommendations on where to manufacture the new product.

6. Now, divide participants into groups of five. *Note: Do not use groups smaller than five participants because each role adds necessary built-in conflict to the group's interaction.* If necessary, groups may be as large as seven, duplicating two of the roles to be used.

7. Explain that each group will be role playing as a work team and that each member of the team will have an individual role to play. Each group should include one of each of the roles. If the team is larger than five, duplicate the roles of Production Control and Planning Specialist and Manufacturing Worker. *Note: Emphasize*

that "staying in character" for the respective role is critical to the success of the activity.

8. Distribute the character scenarios by cutting Form B into five slips. Give participants time to read their individual roles.

9. Advise participants that each of the characters has "special instructions" that should not be shared with the other members of the team.

10. Begin the role playing activity in character. If there are two facilitators, one will portray the Vice President (VP) of *Kincade* and the other will become the General Manager (GM). If you are the only facilitator, combine the two roles. Wear a badge that says VP or GM.

    Vice President (VP) from Kincade personally distributes name badges to Kincade employees and shakes their hands while making introductions. Occupational employees do not receive badges or personal introductions from the VP. They are to be relatively ignored during this part of the activity. (Optional: You may distribute stickers to identify these people as non-Kincade employees—something that would convey that not much thought or importance was given to their presence.)

    General Manager (GM) welcomes the teams to the Kincade Headquarters facility and introduces himself or herself as GM (from Kincade). Announce that this is the kickoff of the first team meeting after the merger and that the teams will be designing a new company product. Urge them to be creative: The more revolutionary the toilet seat design, the better.

    GM announces that he or she and the VP are the management team available for assistance. *Note: During the activity, minimize their availability for assistance.* Tell teams to begin the activity (as outlined in the role-play scenarios) to design the new product and determine the location for its manufacture.

    During the role play, GM makes the following interruptions (timing and order are determined by facilitator):

    ✔ Advise participants that you forgot they need to determine product sale price, based on manufacturing costs. Since you are not clear on this action item from your management, you really can't give any additional information.

    ✔ Midway through the activity, advise that each team will be expected to draw a new product design on the flip chart paper before the end of the activity.

✔ Ask for the designs when you know the teams don't have them, and tell them they have only 2 minutes left.

11. After role play, lead the group in a discussion that allows you to debrief participants using the four phases of an experiential cycle. Each stage of the cycle is explored with structured questions that allow participants to gain additional insights.

Step One: Reporting

First, discuss participants' observations during the activity. Your intent is to encourage observations of events that allow participants to hear what went on in other groups. Encourage them to relay specific conversations that took place, nonverbal responses, comments, and content related to the activity.

What were your observations? What emotions did you experience about your role? When you were given badges (or not given badges)? What was the conversation that took place at the beginning of your task? How did the group approach the work? What dynamics did you see within the group as it formed?

Key Learning: Groups that take the time to introduce themselves and establish some type of relationship first often find the task less frustrating.

Step Two: Processing

Ask participants to discuss common themes in the observations they experienced. Discuss patterns and trends that are examples of typical reactions that would be experienced. Have them explore, "What do our observations mean?"

How were *your* reactions similar to or different from those you've heard expressed? How do these reactions relate to what it might be like when the organization is actually trying to merge? Is your experience realistic? Why or why not? What other patterns might you see during this time? How are these reactions and experiences like what really might happen during a merger or acquisition?

Key Learning: Most people experience similar reactions—negative feelings such as resentment, embarrassment, frustration, anger, feeling left out, etc. The group can extrapolate that most of the real problems are caused by a perception of favoritism and lack of communication. Most people feel out of control and like victims within the organization.

Step Three: Generalizing

Lead a discussion to raise awareness about the learning. Here is the opportunity to reflect on the discussions during the mini-lecture on change and the brainstorming.

If our experiences suggest real life, what do we know about how we should address issues during mergers and acquisitions? Do your experiences in this activity reflect the same issues that we addressed in our brainstorming prior to the role play? Which items on our list do we now think are most important to consider when managing changes like this? What important principles of change management should we give specific attention to?

Key Learning: Handle the "me" issues first and be sure that people have an opportunity to develop some relationships with each other before beginning the task (introductions, backgrounds, experiences and skills, etc.). Communicate frequently and at regular intervals. Pay attention to symbols and nonverbal ways in which favoritism may be perceived. Be sure all people have access to information (technology, proximity, structure, etc.).

Step Four: Applying

Have participants discuss how they will use this information and knowledge. This is the opportunity to transfer the experience from the activity to their own organizations.

How can you use this information in your organization? What are the most important issues as they relate to your company? What can you do differently from the activity that will ensure better change management? How will you plan to involve others in your actions? What ways are most effective in your organization to influence strategies that incorporate the learning here? What will your first step be? How will you follow up?

Key Learning: Apply the new ideas that you have discussed in a way that ensures you will take the learning in the activity into a usable strategy within your organization.

Variation If the participants are actually facing a merger or acquisition, you might proceed with real action planning to address the key issues that they experienced. If members of the workshop have gone through a real experience, ask them to relate personal examples that illustrate the key learnings.

At a micro level, all organizations experience similar reactions whenever divergent cultures are blended. For example, two departments are merged under a new manager or a new executive is inserted into the hierarchy with a cultural bias from the old organization. An effective facilitator should debrief the specific applications to the participants' current situation to allow maximum transfer of learning and impact.

CASE STUDY: FORM A

Kincade Industrial Sanitary Seating (KISS) has recently acquired *Occupational Fixtures and Fasteners* (OFF). *Kincade* is the leading manufacturer of toilet seats and other peripherals, including fully assembled toilets. *Occupational* is the leading manufacturer of the hardware that holds on the toilet seats. This acquisition was carefully planned and executed quickly with little information leaking to either company prior to the finalization of the purchase and subsequent merger of the two companies.

Kincade has three locations—Mississippi, New York, and California—and because it is the leader in the industry, all the facilities will most likely stay in operation. It has approximately 650 employees with an extremely strong management team. *Kincade*'s management team is very traditional, communicates through the chain of command, and believes that the primary reason they lead their industry is the fact that they cut costs whenever and wherever possible. They provide adequate medical benefits, have a nominal vacation policy, and very strict rules and regulations for work hours and overtime pay practices.

Occupational has only two locations, both within 60 miles of *Kincade*'s California location. *Occupational*'s workforce is primarily represented by the Factory Laborers United for Sanitary Hardware (F.L.U.S.H.) union. Most of their 300 employees have been with the company since its beginning 25 years ago. Although the workforce is significantly union represented, the relationship with management is extremely good and the two parties operate like a large family: lots of self-directed work teams, flexible work hours, an excellent medical benefits package, and an extremely liberal vacation policy. In general, the working environment is much more progressive than *Kincade*'s, and the employees are used to participative management, with decisions made at the lowest level and a continuous flow of communication from the top. *Occupational* was on the verge of expanding its manufacturing capability to include toilet seats resulting from an employees' idea of a revolutionary new design.

The new company's president is Mr. M.Y. Whey, who was the president of *Kincade*. Although the new organization structure has not yet been designed, nor has the management been selected, rumors are strong that *Kincade*'s management will be the "selected" management team for the new company, KISS OFF; that benefits are going to be slashed for the *Occupational* employees; and that there is the potential for at least one *Occupational* plant closing, even though their manufacturing facilities could be easily and cost-effectively transitioned to accommodate toilet seat manufacturing. Despite *Kincade*'s superiority in the industry, KISS OFF will not be able to survive without the cooperation of at least half of the manufacturing workforce currently at *Occupational*.

CHARACTER SCENARIOS: FORM B

SUPERVISOR

You are a *Kincade* manufacturing supervisor. You are used to giving direction to the workers and the work getting done efficiently and without questions. You have worked for the new company president from *Kincade*, Mr. M.Y. Whey, for ten years. He was your mentor during your career with *Kincade*. Mr. Whey has asked you to lend your expertise to this team, suggesting that you are a strong candidate for the new department manager's position and that your primary focus is to ensure that the *Kincade* culture remains after the merger.

SUPERVISOR

You are an *Occupational* manufacturing supervisor. You are used to leading teams and trying to allow each team member the opportunity to have input. Your 25 years of experience have proven that if people feel that they have been heard, they are more likely to be happy with the final team decision, even if it wasn't their idea. You are also committed to keeping employees informed and helping them with the concerns they have resulting from the acquisition. You have been told that you are the likely candidate for managing this department, due to the fact that KISS OFF will need the expertise of *Occupational* to maintain market share. Because the final organization has not yet been announced, you have been asked not to discuss your impending new role.

MANUFACTURING WORKER

You are an *Occupational* employee working in manufacturing as a union-represented production worker. You have worked at *Occupational* for 25 years, have always been extremely enthusiastic about offering new ideas, and are 18 months from retirement. Rumors about cutting benefits have consumed you and you are unable to concentrate on work. You are not sure who will be the new department manager, so you tend to agree with everyone, except on the issue of where to manufacture the product. You are emphatic that manufacturing be done at one of the *Occupational* facilities.

MANUFACTURING ENGINEER

You are a *Kincade* employee working on the manufacturing floor. You have been with *Kincade* for three years, straight out of college. The turmoil that you are experiencing is extremely frustrating, both personally and professionally, and since you don't believe that you have a lot to lose, you are inclined to voice your frustrations and opinions openly. You have been personally selected by the new company president, Mr. M.Y. Whey, to be the star participant in a rotational program that will give you lots of visibility with the new management team of KISS OFF. You are anxious for this team to be successful in its task accomplishment.

PRODUCTION PLANNING AND CONTROL
SPECIALIST

You are an *Occupational* employee supporting production as a planning and control specialist. You have extensive educational and work experience in the production environment. You have been with *Occupational* for the past eight years and have been instrumental in influencing and training production teams to recognize inefficiencies and change processes, resulting in cost savings and higher quality control. You are a single parent with three children and must keep your job, salary, and benefits to maintain an acceptable standard of living for you and your family. You frequently change conversations about work-related issues to try to substantiate rumors about layoffs.

43
UNDERSTANDING CHANGE THROUGH OTHER PEOPLE'S EYES

Vicki Schneider

Overview By the time leaders ask their organizations to change, they have already analyzed the situation, determined the best course of action to take, and are standing, banner in hand, wondering why their team isn't charging up the hill behind them.

The reason is rather simple. In the process of contemplating the change, the leaders came to grips with the personal losses they would incur and had identified, at least on a visceral level, the rewards that would replace them. To the leaders, who have already gone through the thought process, the need for the change is obvious and the sacrifices that have to be made are accepted as necessary and reasonable.

What leaders often fail to realize is that change, especially significant change, will force others to give up things they value greatly. Until the leader recognizes and understands what each person is being asked to give up, the change, no matter how essential, will likely be met with crippling resistance. The loss each team member anticipates may seem insignificant to an outsider; but it may be important enough to cause the individual to resist or even undermine the change.

This interactive exercise helps leaders and associates look at change and its related losses through other people's eyes; understand better why they and others resist change; and develop insights that will lead to a more sensitive and successful change climate.

Suggested Time 30 to 60 minutes

Materials Needed
  ✔ Three pennies
  ✔ Three stick-figure drawings or colorful scribbles
  ✔ Three $20 bills

Contact Information: Vicki Schneider, Vantage Solutions, 4434 Waveland Court, Hamburg, NY 14075-2003, 716-627-3345, VSTECNY@aol.com.

✔ Form A (Instructions for "Contestants")

✔ Form B (One set of cards for each member of the "audience")

Procedure
1. Select three members from the audience to be contestants in "The Great Giveaway."

2. Give each contestant one of the cards from Form A, one penny, one drawing, and one $20 bill. Tell the contestants to read their instructions to themselves and stay apart from the other contestants.

3. Divide the audience into thirds. Assign one-third of the audience (left, center, right) to each of the three contestants.

4. Distribute one set of cards from Form B to each member of the audience.

5. Tell the audience that each contestant will be asked to give up one of the three objects in order to move forward. The contestant will eventually give up two of the three objects. The audience members' job is to predict which object their contestant will have left at the end of the game—the penny, the drawing, or the $20 bill. (Show the audience the three objects.)

6. Ask the audience to make their predictions. Instruct them to keep the card that has that item written on it. Caution the audience not to show their cards to anyone until they are asked to.

7. Collect the rest of the cards from the audience members, taking care to keep the audience and the contestants from seeing what's on them.

8. Have the three contestants line up next to one another across the front of the room.

9. Ask the contestants to decide which of their three objects they want to give you. Take that object from the first contestant, announce the object, and have the contestant take one step forward. Repeat this process for the other two contestants.

10. Ask the contestants to decide which of the remaining two objects they want to give you. Take that object from the first contestant, announce the object, and have the contestant take one step forward. Repeat this process for the other two contestants.

The three contestants are now at the finish line. In all likelihood, they have kept different objects.

11. Ask the first one-third of the audience (right side) to hold up their cards, showing which object they thought their contestant would have kept.

12. In all likelihood, some of the audience will be correct and some will be wrong. Ask volunteers to explain why they chose what they chose.

13. Ask the first contestant why he or she kept that object.

14. Repeat steps 11 to 13 for the second contestant (middle section of audience), and again for the third contestant (left section of audience).

15. Debrief by asking

- What did the contestants know that you didn't? What effect did your differing perspectives have on the outcome? How could you have had a better chance of predicting the right object?

- As we ask people to change, we ask them to leave things behind—both tangibles and intangibles. Many times people resist change because we are asking them to leave behind something of value to them that we value differently. How can we use what we learned from this activity to better understand why people (or why you) resist change?

Select from among the following questions, depending on your learning objectives, and have participants share their experiences in groups of 2 to 5. After 20 minutes, ask for volunteers to provide insights into what they have learned about themselves and others.

- Think of a major change you are going through right now. What are you being asked to leave behind? If you embrace the change, what things of equal or greater value to you might replace that loss?

- Think of a change you've gone through in your life that you resisted. What were you being asked to leave behind? Why was that such a difficult loss for you? How did you overcome your resistance? If you successfully implemented that change, what replaced the thing(s) you lost?

- Think of someone who is resisting change. What do you think the person is being asked to leave behind? How can you find out? How can you help the person identify something to replace that loss?

Reinforcing Activity Conduct a "brain dump" at the end of the session: Ask participants to state the insights they gained from the session. You or a scribe should write them, without discussion, on a chart. Keep adding comments until all comments have been exhausted.

THE GREAT GIVEAWAY: FORM A

Instructions to Trainer: Cut these cards apart and give a different card to each of the contestants.

Instructions to Contestant A:

During this game you will be asked to give away two of the objects you start the game with.

In making your decisions, keep in mind that the penny is worth $.01, the drawing is a worthless scribble, and the $20 bill is worth twenty dollars.

None of the objects has any unusual significance or value.

Instructions to Contestant B:

During this game you will be asked to give away two of the objects you start the game with.

In making your decisions, keep in mind that the drawing is a worthless scribble and the $20 bill is worth twenty dollars.

The penny, however, is a very rare coin that completes your collection and is worth a lot of money.

Instructions to Contestant C:

During this game you will be asked to give away two of the objects you start the game with.

In making your decisions, keep in mind that the penny is worth $.01 and the $20 bill is worth twenty dollars.

The drawing was the first piece of artwork your autistic child ever drew, and it has a great deal of sentimental value for you.

THE GREAT GIVEAWAY: FORM B

Instructions to Trainer: Copy this entire form for each member of the audience. Cut the sections apart into three cards before distributing a full set to each audience member.

At the end of The Great Giveaway,
I believe my contestant will be left with

A Penny

At the end of The Great Giveaway,
I believe my contestant will be left with

A $20 Bill

At the end of The Great Giveaway,
I believe my contestant will be left with

A Drawing

44

MINIMIZING RESISTANCE TO CHANGE AND INNOVATION

Scott Simmerman

Overview   Managing and leading change requires both influence and involvement. It helps to know the desired direction of the initiative, it's important to have a sense of the process of change, and it's imperative that change masters involve and engage people in the transformation process as it occurs. People involved in the process understand the real expectations and are less surprised as things change.

This exercise includes one of my favorite organization development metaphors and is packaged to be quite flexible in delivery. It is easy to lead, engages people in a discussion of "The Answer," and lends itself to the discovery that teams create a far better set of possibilities than any one individual can. The exercise is meant to be done "with" people rather than "to" them, so that we minimize resistance to change and generate active participation within the metaphor and among participants.

Materials Needed   ✔ Form A (Square Wheels One)

✔ Form B (It is dangerous to know The Answer)

✔ Optional: A wide variety of butterfly stickers, pins, balloons, stuffed toys, calendars, and other colorful images

Suggested Time   20 minutes

Procedure   1. Distribute copies of Form A or present the image as an overhead transparency.

2. Explain that you heard a good joke. Say:

There were two caterpillars riding on a wagon and a beautiful butterfly floats by.

Contact Information: Scott Simmerman, Performance Management Company, 3 Old Oak Drive, Taylors, SC 29687, 864-292-8700, Scott@Square Wheels.com, www.SquareWheels.com.

One caterpillar looks up and says to the other,

"You'll never get me up in one of those things!"

3. Now, ask people if they "get the joke" and even ask for a show of hands. [This is a simple joke, but it is more than the punch line that is important here. I had been telling this joke for about two years when I told it in Hong Kong to a group of English-speaking Chinese people. The reaction was a bit mixed, so I simply asked them to discuss the joke among themselves so that they could tell me The Answer. They did this with an increasing amount of laughter and interaction between tables. When I asked them to share their thinking, they gave me 32 different answers to the joke. All this time, I had been telling the joke thinking that the answer was "Resistance to Change." I would never have realized that there are many answers to the joke if I had not been paying attention to the reactions of others.]

4. Now, share the following comments:

   In the U.S. Open Tennis Tournament, John McEnroe, the retired tennis star, once said in a press conference upon losing: "That taught me a lesson, but I am not sure what it is."

   There was a lesson in the telling of this joke. Take two minutes to discuss this with your associates and see if you can discover "The Lesson" in the joke.

5. Have participants discuss "The Lesson" in small groups. As the energy level dies down among the participants, call a halt and ask people for "The Lesson."

6. Invariably, they will share various lessons, such as:

   • Change is inevitable.

   • It's important to have a vision of the future.

   • It's better to ride on the wagon than crawl in the dirt.

   • Flying is frightening.

7. Respond that each of these lessons can be derived from the joke, but none of them is The Lesson.

8. Say:

   The lesson is simple:

   It is dangerous to know The Answer.

   [Present Form B as an overhead transparency.]

   Leadership, innovation, teamwork, and change all require us to realize that there are lots of possibilities and lots of perspectives, and just knowing The Answer tends to limit our thinking. In the initial telling of the joke, people invariably get The Answer and quit thinking about other possibilities, and thus limit their thinking and perspective. Different people see and understand things differently. Only by talking about these differing perspectives can we become more aware.

9. You can also link these points to a model of change management, using this script:

There are four components to teamwork and change. By increasing any one of them, we increase the likelihood that change may occur. The four components are:

- *The current level of discomfort with the way things are now.*
- *The attractiveness of the vision of the future.*
- *The individual's or group's previous success with change.*
- *The peer or workgroup support for the change.*

By increasing the understanding of the change process key factors, we can help people become less comfortable with maintaining the status quo and help them perceive a more attractive vision of what we can become. By allowing them to feel creative and come up with new ideas and work together to generate ideas for improvement in the workplace, we make them more likely to succeed.

One key is to recognize that there are different perspectives. People cannot consider what they do not contemplate. By working with others to generate different ideas in relation to the joke, we open them up to consider different ideas of what they can choose to do differently in the future.

For managers and talent alike, it is important to recognize that knowing The Answer is limiting one's discoveries.

See the article "Teaching the Caterpillar to Fly" at www. squarewheels.com/content/teaching.html for a more detailed description of the metaphor, delivery ideas, and the change model presentation.

SQUARE WHEELS ONE: FORM A

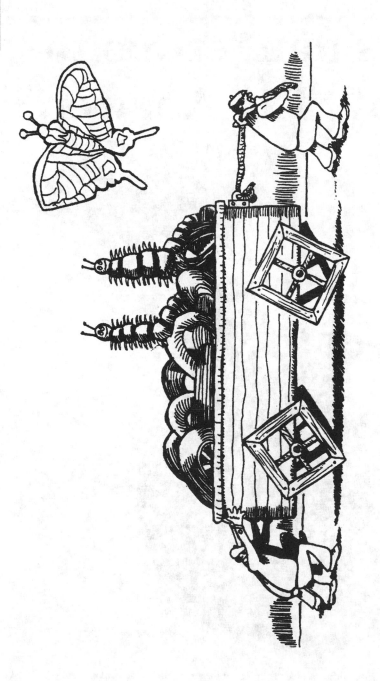

It is dangerous to know The Answer.

45
THINKING POSITIVELY

Jeanne Baer

Overview This activity encourages participants to examine their own "explanatory style" in reacting to events, and to replace pessimistic reactions and associations with more positive, optimistic ones. By developing better resilience in times of turbulence, participants can build their self-confidence and adapt more easily to change, benefiting themselves and their organizations.

Suggested Time $1^1/_2$

Materials Needed
- ✔ Form A (What's Your Explanation?)
- ✔ Form B (ABCDE Episodes)
- ✔ Form C (Your Own Alphabet!)
- ✔ Form D (Turbulent Times Checklist)

Procedure
1. Introduce the topic of change by observing that in turbulent times, some people seem less stressed by changes than others. Comment that some people seem to be "born optimists," while others feel pessimistic about changes and uncertainties.

2. Define "optimists" not as people who are "Good-Ship-Lollipop" naive, but rather as those who believe that they're ultimately responsible for their own success. It's not that optimists refuse to see the negative, but they refuse to dwell on it or to give up.

3. Distribute copies of Form A and ask participants to circle their appropriate responses.

4. Explain that the first two situations have to do with "personalization." These scenarios deal with whether you may tend to internalize or externalize credit or blame. Explain that people who blame themselves when they fail or when something goes wrong

Contact Information: Jeanne Baer, Creative Training Solutions, 1649 South 21st Street, Lincoln, NE 68502, 800-410-3178, jbaer@grex.cyberspace.org, www.cts-online.net.

usually have low self-esteem. People who blame external events don't lose self-esteem when bad events strike. Offer some anecdotes to support this theory.

5. Then explain that the second two situations have to do with how permanent you believe an event's outcome is. Explain that people who give up easily often believe the causes of the bad events that happen to them are permanent—the bad events will persist, and will always be there to affect their lives. They use words like "always" and "never" versus "sometimes" and "lately."

6. Explain that the last two situations have to do with how pervasive you believe an event's outcome is. People who make widespread explanations for their failures give up on everything, even when a failure strikes in one area. But people who make specific explanations may become helpless in that one part of their lives, yet march strongly on in other parts of their lives.

7. Explain the ABC's of our thinking process when something goes wrong:

   A = Adversity (Something goes wrong, and we react by thinking about it.)

   B = Beliefs (Often so habitual or ingrained that we hardly realize we have them.)

   C = Consequences (Our beliefs lead to what we feel and what we do next.)

8. Explain that before we do something based on pessimistic explanatory habits, we should engage in "D"—Disputation. (Argue with unhealthy beliefs that are causing continuing pessimism and preventing us from reaching our full potential.)

   Explain that there are four important ways to make disputations convincing:

   ✔ Helpfulness—Even if your belief is well-founded and you're correct, how *helpful* is it to be obsessed with it at the moment?

   ✔ Other causes—What else could have caused this problem you're blaming yourself for?

   ✔ Proof—What material proof do you have that this is personal (your fault), permanent (vs. temporary), or pervasive (coloring everything else you'll ever do)?

   ✔ So what?—Even if the negative belief about yourself is correct, is it truly that catastrophic, in the long run? Make a point to "decatastrophize" it.

(It is important that you develop examples or anecdotes to accompany each of the preceding.)

9. Explain to participants that when they take ownership for their own attitudes and maintain positive outlooks, the result will be "E"—Energization. Remind participants that when they believe in opportunities, they actually help them appear.

10. Invite participants to consider the two examples on Form B. (If you have time, white out the Disputation and Energization steps. Invite participants to consider individually or in small groups what the possible disputations and energizations might be. You may choose to consider both examples, or focus on the example most appropriate to participants. You may also wish to invite role plays, if you have time.)

11. Once you feel participants understand the steps, invite them to consider an example of their own, using Form C. Ask that they share their examples with a partner; each can check for the other's application of the five steps, and correct or confirm understanding.

12. Close by going quickly over the points on Form D, and adding any personal anecdotes that would be meaningful to the group. (This is a self-explanatory checklist, which can simply be distributed without elaboration if time is short.)

WHAT'S YOUR EXPLANATION? FORM A

Read the description of the following situations, and vividly imagine this situation happening to you. Even if you haven't experienced it, circle a or b, according to what you honestly think your explanation would be for this event.

1. You invite someone to join you on a team project, and he or she turns you down.

   a. It's me—I'm not very competent in this area.

   b. He or she was already overcommitted to other projects.

2. You get a bonus.

   a. I got lucky; the company had a great year and it can afford to toss a bonus my way.

   b. I deserve it; I've done the right things, and I've done things right.

3. You forget to attend a meeting.

   a. I'm just not good at remembering dates.

   b. I was preoccupied with an urgent project I was working on.

4. You make some great contributions to a brainstorming meeting.

   a. I was especially "up" that day.

   b. I'm a creative person.

5. The data you submitted on a report turns out to be inaccurate.

   a. I guess I'm just sloppy.

   b. This is an isolated incident; I should have proofread it more carefully.

6. Your team members are all upset about organizational changes, and you're able to calm them down and point them in a positive direction.

   a. I had heard about the changes earlier, so I had a chance to think through the issues and prepare for the team meeting.

   b. I'm good in tough situations.

ABCDE EPISODES: FORM B

ABCDE EPISODE IN SALES

Adversity: I made my 20th call and I've got just four appointments.

Beliefs: This is a waste of time. I don't have the energy to succeed. I'm so disorganized.

Consequences: I feel frustrated, tired, depressed, and overwhelmed.

Disputation: Four appointments in an hour isn't bad! It's only 3:00, and I can still do another hour and a half of calling. I can take 10 minutes now to get better organized so I can make more calls this hour than I did in the last hour.

Energization: I feel less overwhelmed and depressed, and I've got more energy, since I'm planning out a course of action.

ABCDE EPISODE IN MANAGEMENT

Adversity: My department is falling behind schedule and my boss is starting to complain about it.

Beliefs: Why can't these people do what they're supposed to do? I've shown them all they need to know, but why can't I get them to work better? That's why I was hired. Now my boss probably thinks it's all my fault—that I'm incompetent.

Consequences: I feel really mad at my people, and I want to call them all in and chew them out. I also feel bad about myself and nervous about my job. I want to avoid my boss until we get back on schedule.

Disputation: It is true that my department is behind. But I've got several new employees, and it takes time for them to get up to speed. I haven't done anything wrong. I've explained all this to my boss, and she knows it's true. But she's under pressure, too. I'll talk to her again and ask her directly if there's something she thinks I should be doing differently. Meanwhile, I'll keep encouraging the new people and see if I can get more help from the "vets."

Energization: I don't feel like chewing them out now—I feel like I can discuss the situation with them calmly. I'm not nervous about my job because I know I have a good record here. And instead of avoiding my boss, I'll meet with her to give her a progress report and answer any questions she may have.

YOUR OWN ALPHABET! FORM C

What are some examples of adversity, beliefs, and consequences in your own life? When you hit that negative self-talk "wall," can you counterpunch with effective disputations and then enjoy the resulting energization? Take time to write an example of your own, based on a past experience or on one that you anticipate will happen in the future.

Adversity:

Beliefs:

Consequences:

Disputation:

Energization:

TURBULENT TIMES CHECKLIST: FORM D

The following checklist is made up of tips and techniques to help you develop and maintain a more optimistic outlook. Place a check mark beside those that are the most meaningful to you. Then use the space to add specific reminder notes to yourself. Use the list to create your own action plan!

❑ 1. Ask yourself, Is it *helpful* to have this belief right now?

❑ 2. Ask yourself, Are there *other* causes for this situation?

❑ 3. Ask yourself, What is the actual *proof* that this bad situation is permanent, pervasive, or personally my own doing?

❑ 4. Ask yourself, So what? In the long run, is this *really* important?

❑ 5. Stop the rumination! Snap a rubber band on your wrist, carry an index card ... just say "No!" to circular worrying.

❑ 6. Jot down what's bothering you, and schedule a time to worry about it. (Then don't bother to keep that "appointment!")

❑ 7. Visualize doing well. Relax, and picture in great detail the success you deserve and *expect*.

❑ 8. Refuse to be a victim! Think of yourself as a problem solver, capable of overcoming the barriers that sometimes pop up. Don't waste time and energy being a finger-pointer.

❑ 9. Team up. Meet with a friend; keep each other on track and hold each other accountable for progress.

❑ 10. Do a kindness every day, to build self-confidence and a positive self-image.

❑ 11. End each day by reminding yourself of three positive things you've done today or three positive qualities you have.

❑ 12. Let it go! Anger and disappointment about the past poisons your present potential.

❑ 13. Sort out what you can and can't control, and then go with change rather than against it. In this world of high-velocity change, surrender serves us better than "fight" or "flight."

❑ 14. Act as if you feel good, as if you're positive and enthusiastic about the future. By acting so, you become so.

❑ 15. Start today! What's one positive thing you want to continue doing or start doing?

46

IMPROVING THE QUALITY OF STRATEGIC PLANNING

Tom Devane

Overview Strategic Squares is a useful exercise for improving the quality of strategic planning in an organization. It's ideal to use in a newly formed or existing team, but can also be utilized as a simulation exercise in a training session. Any fan of "systems thinking" who has read Peter Senge's *Fifth Discipline* understands that in a complex system, it's more important to focus on the *interrelationships* of various components than it is to focus on selected *components* within the system. Strategic Squares provides a simple, easy-to-learn framework in which to apply this important principle.

Suggested Time 30 to 60 minutes

Materials Needed ✔ Form A (Strategic Square), one copy per participant

Procedure 1. Explain that the purpose of this exercise is to create a relatively risk-free environment for team members to discuss and articulate ideas that will improve the organization.

2. Distribute copies of Form A. Indicate that major ideas for change, ideally, improve the quality of services or products, lower costs, and show respect for the individuals who are affected by the change. In an ideal world, all three criteria are met. In a less than ideal world, some go by the wayside or actually conflict. Explain that the strategic square is designed so that a team can generate or assess change ideas by considering the interrelationships between these factors.

3. Ask the team to generate up to six change ideas that meet the two criteria suggested by each open box. Point out that no one factor should supersede the other. For example, a change idea that both

Contact Information: Tom Devane, Premier Integration Enterprises, 317 Lookout View Court, Golden, CO 80401, 303-898-6172, tdevane@mindspring.com.

improves the quality of service or product and, at the same time, shows respect for the individuals affected by the change would be placed in the box found in the first row, second column or in the box found in the second row, first column.

4. A team that has already developed some change initiatives can use the square to assess those initiatives. Which interrelationships do they support? They can also ask themselves how the interrelationships between any two factors could be maximized in the future.

Variation When you want to use the strategic square in a training session in which intact teams do not exist, do the following:

1. Organize into subgroups. Each subgroup will represent a senior management team for an organization. Attempt to group people together who have similar industries, contexts, roles, and so forth.

2. Provide a copy of Form A to each subgroup. Explain that they are to assume the role of a senior management team that is charged with articulating a change strategy that maximizes the interrelationships suggested by the Strategic Square.

3. Ask each group to generate change ideas (appropriate to their common industry, context, or role) that meet the two criteria suggested by each open box.

4. Promote a sharing of ideas across groups and discuss their reactions to the exercise.

STRATEGIC SQUARE: FORM A

	Service/Product Quality	Respect for the Individual	Low Cost
Service/Product Quality			
Respect for the Individual			
Low Cost			

47

LEARNING PATIENCE

Karen Lawson

Overview This exercise has three objectives: 1) to demonstrate how a team moves too quickly and too impatiently at times; 2) to assess how a team develops or fails to develop a process or method of operation; and 3) to determine how a team wants to change its process. It is designed for teams of six or more members. (If you use this exercise with one team, adjust the procedure accordingly.)

Suggested Time 45 to 60 minutes

Materials Needed ✔ Copies of Form A (Observer Sheet) for observers

Procedure
1. Place each team at a table. Obtain two observers from each team. Use a random method of selection such as the team members with the two earliest birthdays in the year or with the two first initials that come earliest in the alphabet.

2. Give copies of Form A to the observers. Provide them with a few minutes to read their instructions and get ready for the activity.

3. In the meantime, give the team(s) the following instructions:

   Your task is to set goals for the next 12 months. What would you like to accomplish in the next 12 months? You will have 30 minutes to begin this process. You are to assume that you will have more meeting time in the future to accomplish this task.

   If you are a new team, you will be setting goals for the first time. If you are an existing team, you may consider goals that have already been established as well as new ones.

   Do not let anyone press you to clarify the task any further. It is purposely vague so that the observers can assess whether the team takes the time initially to clarify the task for itself. Also, do

Contact Information: Karen Lawson, Lawson Consulting Group, 1365 Gwynedale Way, Lansdale, PA 19446, 215-368-9465, klawson@lawsoncg.com, www.lawsoncg.com.

not tell them about the nature of the instructions given to the observers. Promise that they will be revealed at the end of the activity.

4. Begin the meeting. About 2 minutes before the time is up, give participants a 2-minute warning.

5. Stop the meeting and ask observers to give their feedback. Encourage them to give feedback that is descriptive and specific rather than judgmental and general.

6. Allow the participants to clarify the feedback and obtain their reactions. Do everything in your power to keep the climate open and nondefensive. Accept "excuses" that participants give such as, "We assumed that we had to get the job done soon."

7. Debrief the activity. Ask the following questions:

   ✔ Do you think that teams "jump the gun" sometimes by not patiently setting up their process? by not clarifying what their task is? by debating ideas before hearing and clarifying all of them? by making decisions even if time hasn't been taken to establish that everyone agrees to or can live with a decision even when they don't prefer it?

   ✔ How would you assess *your team's* "patience"?

   ✔ What would you like to do in the future to change the process of your team?

Variation Videotape the meeting. Play back samples of it and allow the participants to observe themselves.

OBSERVER SHEET: FORM A

To the Observers: Do not reveal to your teammates what you are assessing. Your team has been given the following task:

Your task is to set goals for the next 12 months. What would you like to accomplish in the next 12 months? You will have 30 minutes to begin this process. You are to assume that you will have more meeting time in the future to accomplish this task.

If you are a new team, you will be setting goals for the first time. If you are an existing team, you may consider goals that have already been established as well as new ones.

Often, when teams are given this task, they "jump the gun" by proceeding too quickly with discussing and perhaps deciding upon goals before establishing how they will go about the task. Your job is to assess how impatient your team is. Specifically, consider the following:

1. Does the team take time in the beginning to clarify the task before them or does it just plunge into it?

   Notes:

2. Does the team develop a process or method of operation as to how it will proceed in working on the task? If so, what is the process they discuss?

   Notes:

3. Do participants take positions early on about the goals they want the team to set? Does this create a competitive climate in the team? What happens to the quality of team communication?

   Notes:

4. Do participants act as if they have to make decisions by the end of the meeting? If they do make any decisions, are they made by active consensus or is there an assumption that everyone agrees?

   Notes:

48

INTRODUCING PLANNING

Becky Mills and Chris Saeger

Overview   What is it about planning? It seems to hold much promise. We all talk about it, and most people think it is important; yet when we sit down to do planning the mood of the group often shifts to one of resignation. The Planning Game is an excellent start to any strategic planning session. It provides an interesting and informative way to explore organizational issues of trust, shared commitment, and customer focus.

The game does this by placing the participants in a simulated organization with a stovepipe departmental structure and a lack of customer focus. Over several rounds, the participants attempt to coordinate action and produce products to serve the customer. From the simulation, participants can:

- Observe the effects of trust on planning.

- Observe the effects of planning on customer service, team performance, and use of resources.

- Observe the benefits of involving the customer in planning.

- Identify improvements in the planning process and workplace applications.

Suggested Time   60 to 90 minutes (depending on the depth of the debriefing)

Materials Needed   ✔ A table with six chairs for each set of players. Players must be within arm's reach of each other and the middle of the table.

✔ A deck of UNO cards, sorted to include only numbers 1 through 6 in green and yellow, and numbers 1 through 7 in blue and red.

✔ Instruction sheets, Forms A to F, for each of the six players. Cut apart and place the appropriate instruction sheet face down at each seat.

✔ A piece of flip chart paper and a marker.

Contact Information: Becky Mills and Chris Saeger, American Red Cross, 703-206-7312, millsr@usa.redcross. org.

Setup Shuffle the cards well and deal out three cards for each of the four places along the sides of the table. Seat players at the table so that the Department Heads are along the sides (where there are three cards set out for each); the Customer is at one end; and the Investor is at the other. Give each person an instruction sheet: four Department Heads, one Customer, and one Investor. Give the Investor the rest of the sorted UNO deck.

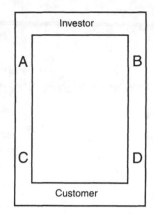

Procedure

1. Give these initial instructions:

   "Please read the instruction sheet in front of you. Do not discuss your instructions. Each of the four players with cards represents a Department Head of a service organization. This is the start of the fiscal year, and the cards you already hold represent the resources you already have. All of the department heads are new to your jobs, but you have some idea of what you are to do.

   "The player at this end of the table is the Investor. The Investor holds a lot more resources, and will be giving them to your organization during the course of the game. The player at the other end of the table is the Customer. The Customer desperately needs the services (represented by sets of cards) provided by your organization.

   "When the game begins, the Investor will start contributing resources to the Department Heads, who will assemble the resources into sets (or services) and then deliver them to the Customer.

   "For this first round of the game, no talking among you is allowed before we start. As in so many organizations, new employees are expected to 'roll up their sleeves,' 'hit the ground running,' and 'just get the job done.'

   "Investor, are you ready to deal? Department Heads, are you ready to assemble and deliver your sets of cards? Customer, are you ready to receive the services? Go!"

2. Conduct a discussion after the first round. During this and other discussions, participants will report the number of acceptable services produced and the waste rate for each table. Record these on the flip chart.

   Ask the Customers: *"Did you get what you needed? Are you satisfied with the service you received? How many usable services did you receive?"* (Count the acceptable card sets.)

Ask the Department Heads: *"You were certainly working hard. How do you feel about the work you've done? How many resources went unused?"* (Count any cards that were not passed on to the client and any cards the client could not use.)

Ask the Investors: *"What do you think about how the company used the resources you invested?"*

Tell all participants: *"I'm sure you have some ideas about how your organization could do better in using Investor resources to meet Customer needs. You have five minutes to discuss how you want to do things differently, and then we will play through the next fiscal year. Investors, please collect all the cards, shuffle them, and redeal three to each of the Department Heads. In five minutes, we will begin the game again."*

3. Conduct a discussion after the second round.

Ask the Customers: *"How do you feel about the services you received this time? How many usable services did you receive?"* (Count the card sets.)

Ask the Department Heads: *"How do you think it went this time?"* (Count the unused cards and cards that were unusable to the Customer. Compare this to the first round.)

Ask the Investors: *"How do you feel about the organization now?"*

Ask all participants: *"What differences did you see between the first and second rounds? Do you believe that you can further improve your services or improve relationships with customers and investors?"*

Note: The best possible score is four complete product sets and four waste cards. If the groups are close to this outcome, you may want to stop the simulation here. Otherwise, give the participants another 5 minutes to discuss process improvements, and then proceed with round three.

4. Conduct a discussion after the third round.

Ask the Customers: *"How do you feel about the services you received this time? How many usable services did you receive?"* (Count the cards.)

Ask the Department Heads: *"How do you think it went this time?"* (Count the unused and unusable resources. Compare with previous rounds.)

Ask the Investors: *"How do you feel about the organization now?"*

Ask all participants: *"What differences did you see between the second and third rounds?"*

Conduct a final debriefing by asking:

- How did you feel about the simulation play?
- How was the simulation play similar to or different from your experience at work?
- How did you improve service delivery during the simulation?
- Ask for discussion (and make a list on newsprint): What do you see are the benefits of planning? (E.g., makes better use of resources, helps to meet customer needs, encourages cooperation and communication.)

Debriefing Topics   *Effects of Trust on Planning:*

During the first round, participants will grab for resources without regard for the resource needs of the other departments. Players will sometimes hoard cards in the hope of meeting their departmental objectives. There is no focus on the customer. Players compete simply to meet their own departmental objectives. As the rounds progress, players begin to cooperate and have a sense of trust that the other players are engaged with them in meeting the customer needs, not simply meeting departmental objectives.

Effects of Planning on Customer Service,
Team Performance, and Use of Resources:

A dramatic aspect of the game occurs after the participants play a second and possibly third fiscal year. As they implement their strategy and engage in conversation and cooperation throughout the fiscal year, the number of useful products increases dramatically. Teams often go from producing no useful products to producing the maximum number of useful products. The teams are accomplishing more, yet they are using exactly the same deck of cards, and hence, exactly the same resources they used in the first fiscal year. The difference can be found in the waste rate. The waste rate is the number of cards left unused at the end of each fiscal year. Even the most efficient teams will still have four cards that are not in a completed product at the end of the year, since it is impossible to delete all waste from a system.

If the participants have input into the budget process for your organization, they may see parallels in resource use and allocation. During the first fiscal year, each department tries to grab as many resources as possible. The process becomes more orderly and productive once the team formulates a strategy for allocating resources. Rather than stockpiling, departments take only the resources they can effectively use. Perhaps more importantly, participants clearly demonstrate for themselves that meeting departmental goals is not enough to ensure the success of the organization. After developing a shared vision of success, they cooperate with one another to employ each particular resource so that it most effectively meets the goals of the organization.

The Benefits of Involving the Customer in Planning:

The key to improving organizational performance is to determine the customer's expectations. The team does not receive credit for products that fail to address the needs of the Customer, no matter how much energy or enthusiasm went into producing them. In a real competitive market, customers will switch to another organization's services or products if their current provider cannot meet their expectations, so it is important to determine current customer expectations.

Unfortunately, customer expectations aren't static. In fact, as quality improves, customer requirements often become more stringent. When an organization takes a product or service to a new level, customers expect future products to meet or exceed the new, higher standard. In the game, the initial customer requirements may simply be to receive the packs of cards in the necessary order. In later rounds, customers may demand that the cards in each pack be in numerical order or that the packs be delivered in a particular manner.

Improvements in the Planning Process:

Improvements in the planning process that past participants have identified include: taking a multidepartmental approach; tying objectives to the real results expected in the organization; building a shared vision; and implementing workflow improvements. Over the rounds, players have usually modified the workflow procedures in the game. We use the game workflow and the changes participants have made to begin to talk about the organization's workflow and coordination.

WELCOME TO THE PLANNING GAME!: FORM A

Your role in the game today is Head of Department A. Please do not show these instructions or your cards to the other players in the game.

The Planning Game is about a service organization. Other players in the game are:

Three other Department Heads.

A Customer, who depends on receiving services from you.

An Investor, who provides the resources you use to develop services.

You are new on the job at the organization. Your department's role has been to assemble sets of three cards—numbered 1, 2, and 3 (any colors)—and deliver the sets to your Customer.

On the table in front of you are three cards. These are the resources you start with at the beginning of the fiscal year. When the game begins, the Investor will start to issue new cards at a steady rate to the center of the table. Get the cards you need, assemble the sets, and deliver them to the Customer right away.

When the Investor has given away all the resources, the first round of the game is over.

WELCOME TO THE PLANNING GAME!: FORM B

Your role in the game today is Head of Department B. Please do not show these instructions or your cards to the other players in the game.

The Planning Game is about a service organization. Other players in the game are:

Three other Department Heads.

A Customer, who depends on receiving services from you.

An Investor, who provides the resources you use to develop services.

You are new on the job at the organization. Your department's role has been to assemble sets of three red cards (any numbers) and deliver the sets to your Customer.

On the table in front of you are three cards. These are the resources you start with at the beginning of the fiscal year. When the game begins, the Investor will start to issue new cards at a steady rate to the center of the table. Get the cards you need, assemble the sets, and deliver them to the Customer right away.

When the Investor has given away all the resources, the first round of the game is over.

WELCOME TO THE PLANNING GAME!: FORM C

Your role in the game today is Head of Department C. Please do not show these instructions or your cards to the other players in the game.

The Planning Game is about a service organization. Other players in the game are:

Three other Department Heads.

A Customer, who depends on receiving services from you.

An Investor, who provides the resources you use to develop services.

You are new on the job at the organization. Your department's role has been to assemble sets of three blue cards (any numbers) and deliver the sets to your Customer.

On the table in front of you are three cards. These are the resources you start with at the beginning of the fiscal year. When the game begins, the Investor will start to issue new cards at a steady rate to the center of the table. Get the cards you need, assemble the sets, and deliver them to the Customer right away.

When the Investor has given away all the resources, the first round of the game is over.

WELCOME TO THE PLANNING GAME!: FORM D

Your role in the game today is Head of Department D. Please do not show these instructions or your cards to the other players in the game.

The Planning Game is about a service organization. Other players in the game are:

Three other Department Heads.

A Customer, who depends on receiving services from you.

An Investor, who provides the resources you use to develop services.

You are new on the job at the organization. Your department's role has been to assemble sets of three cards—numbered 4, 5, and 6 (any colors)—and deliver the sets to your Customer.

On the table in front of you are three cards. These are the resources you start with at the beginning of the fiscal year. When the game begins, the Investor will start to issue new cards at a steady rate to the center of the table. Get the cards you need, assemble the sets, and deliver them to the Customer right away.

When the Investor has given away all the resources, the first round of the game is over.

WELCOME TO THE PLANNING GAME!: FORM E

Your role in the game today is the Customer. Please do not show these instructions to the other players in the game.

The Planning Game is about a service organization. Other players in the game are:

Four Department Heads from the organization (whom you depend on to provide the services you need); and

An Investor, who provides the resources they use to develop services.

As the Customer, you can use as many units of useful services as the group produces. A useful service consists of twelve cards (four sets of three cards each). To count as one useful service, sets must be received in the following order:

three cards numbered 1, 2, 3 (any color);

three cards numbered 4, 5, 6 (any color);

three blue cards with any number;

three red cards with any number.

When the game starts, the Department Heads will begin assembling sets of cards. When you receive the first set of 1, 2, and 3, place them in front of you. Then watch for a set of 4, 5, and 6. Place these in front of you. Do the same for the blue set and the red set. Any sets not received in order cannot be used. You should set these to the side.

You have a need for as many useful services as the company can provide. If you complete a group of four sets, start a new group of four, beginning with the set of 1, 2, and 3.

When the Investor has given away all the resources, the first round of the game is over.

WELCOME TO THE PLANNING GAME!: FORM F

Your role in the game today is the Investor. Please do not show these instructions or your cards to the other players in the game.

The Planning Game is about a service organization. Other players in the game are:

> Four Department Heads from the organization; their job is to turn the resources you invest into services for the Customer; and

> A Customer, who depends on receiving services from the organization.

On the table in front of you is a deck of cards. These are the resources you will invest in the organization. When the game begins, deal the cards, one at a time and face up, onto the center of the table at a steady rate (about one per second).

When you have given away all the resources (cards), the first round of the game is over.

49
CREATING A MISSION STATEMENT

Sivasailam "Thiagi" Thiagarajan

Overview   This is a multipurpose strategy that helps team members to focus on the big picture so they can identify key elements in their mission statement. This activity rewards participants' ability to identify, summarize, and prioritize essential elements associated with the team's mission. The activity works best with 4 to 16 participants.

Suggested Time   15 to 45 minutes

Materials Needed   ✔ Paper and pencils

Procedure   1. Brief the players. Explain that you are going to facilitate an activity that will require input from all team members toward the creation of a mission statement.

2. Get started. Ask each team member to work with a partner. Instruct each pair to come up with a mission statement for the team in exactly 32 words—no more, no less. Announce a 5-minute time limit.

3. Review the 32-word mission statements. Collect all mission statements from different pairs and read them aloud. Encourage everyone to listen carefully so they can borrow ideas from other people's statements for later use. Ask participants to identify the best statement by raising their hands as you read the statements again. No participant may raise his or her hand more than once nor choose his or her own statement.

4. Shrink to 16 words. Ask pairs to rewrite their mission statements in exactly 16 words. In this process, they may borrow ideas from other statements. Suggest that participants reduce the size of their statements by removing unimportant ideas, superfluous words, and redundant language. Announce a 3-minute time limit.

Contact Information: Sivasailam Thiagarajan, Workshops by Thiagi, Inc., 4423 East Trailridge Road, Bloomington, IN 47408, 800-996-7725, thiagi@thiagi.com, www.thiagi.com.

5. Reduce by 50 percent. Repeat the process of collecting and reading the 16-word mission statements. Select the best statement as before. Now ask pairs to reduce their statements to one-half the current size (to exactly 8 words) while retaining all essential concepts. Encourage pairs to leave out secondary ideas. Announce a 2-minute time limit.

6. Final four. Repeat the process of collecting, reading, and evaluating the mission statements as before. Then ask pairs to reduce the statements to exactly 4 words by dropping all but essential ideas and by tightening up the language. Announce a 2-minute time limit.

7. One more time. After reading and polling the 4-word mission statements, ask teams to reduce the statements to 2 words. Assign a 1-minute time limit for this round.

8. Synthesize the final mission statement. Work with the entire team for the last activity. Invite them to jointly create their final mission statement without any word limits. Encourage participants to recall and combine essential ideas and memorable phrases from the earlier activities.

Sample Statements

Recently we used this strategy with a team that was asked to develop and distribute Web-based learning materials for its organization. Here are the five mission statements each from two pairs of participants:

First Pair

32 words: To foster in each individual the spark of passion and the flash of creativity that will result in the knowledge, skills, and attitudes necessary to build continuous learning communities on the job.

16 words: To spark passion and ignite creativity resulting in the knowledge, skills, and attitudes for continuous learning.

8 words: Spark passion for learning knowledge, skills, and attitudes.

4 words: Spark passion for learning.

2 words: Spark learning!

Second Pair

32 words: To continuously deliver just-in-time on-line content and activities that enhance the feelings of safety, inspiration, and encouragement of individual learners so they can transform themselves, develop, grow, learn, and reach new heights.

16 words:	To provide safety, inspiration, nutrition, and encouragement resulting in transformation, growth, and the ability to fly.
8 words:	To provide elements for transforming slugs into butterflies.
4 words:	Turning slugs into butterflies.
2 words:	Nurturing flight.

50
DETERMINING WHAT CHANGES ARE NEEDED

Catherine Sees and Lewis Welzel Jr.

Overview The use of case studies is a well-integrated part of most educational plans for adult learners. "How do I apply this to real life?" is a common question among participants as they progress through new programs of instruction. After the content has been delivered and participants have had enough immersion in the new material to understand the basics, case studies provide an excellent way to review and to extend critical thinking skills, cementing the knowledge acquired in the learning process.

Historically, the case study method involves factual material delivered and analyzed from the perspective of the learning goals of the training program. While the case itself may or may not have actually transpired, the facilitator normally proposes a conclusive solution to the case study. This exercise takes that process one step further and provides a higher level of involvement for all the participants. In this unique reversal of standard case study procedures, the participants write the cases!

Suggested Time 60 minutes

Materials Needed ✔ Form A (Organization Needs Assessment)

✔ Form B (Example Case Studies)

Procedure 1. Form A is a handout explaining the different strategies, proactive and reactive, used in determining what change is needed in a work environment. This form contains the content on which the case studies will be based. Distribute copies of Form A to the participants and explain to them the different strategies involved in

Contact Information: Catherine Sees, McDATA Company, 310 Interlocken Parkway, Broomfield, CO 80021, 720-566-3521, csess@lamar.colostate.edu.

Lewis Weizel Jr., 1700 W. Plum #53F, Ft. Collins, CO 80521, 970-669-0114, lew @lamar.colostate.edu.

proactive and reactive needs assessments. Also explain that the assessment can be conducted at an organizational (macro) level or a workgroup (micro) level.

2. Hand out copies of Form B and share the example case studies with the participants. Discuss how these cases could be classified and analyzed using the different strategies provided on Form A. Ensure that adequate question and answer time is provided to allow the students to grasp the fundamentals of different needs assessments and of case studies.

3. Separate the participants into groups of 4 to 6.

4. Privately assign each group a strategy, proactive or reactive, for the case study they are to develop. Ask the groups not to share their strategy types with the other groups.

5. Allow 20 minutes working time for the groups to develop a case study similar to the examples with enough details to support the needs assessment strategy they have been assigned, either proactive or reactive. The members of the group should be able to articulate why their strategy would work best in the case they designed. Stress that the case studies developed must be brief and easily understood. After 20 minutes, they will be sharing their cases verbally with the rest of the class.

6. Bring the class back together as a whole but seated within the small groups. Randomly select individual groups to present their cases to the entire class.

7. Select one group to recite the details of its case without reference to the assigned strategy. Allow the rest of the class to ask questions. Encourage the presenting group to fabricate last-minute details as necessary to answer the questions and support the case strategy.

8. Have the groups not in the presenting group discuss the case and arrive at a consensus as to what case strategy should be used in the needs assessment of this situation. Verbally poll the groups to share their decisions. Then have the presenting group reveal its assigned strategy.

9. Conduct a short discussion about why the large group was or was not able to guess the assigned strategy. Allow participants to share their thoughts on the effectiveness of other strategies regarding this case study. This allows the participants an opportunity to examine the different strategies and how each might be applied effectively to the case study.

Important Points for the Facilitator

- Do not let the groups become overly concerned with providing excessive details.

- Make it clear that the case studies should be developed so that the strategy is evident. Presenters are generally surprised to find that even when they try to make their strategies evident, other groups are unable to discover the strategies easily.

- Assign at least one of the strategy types to more than one group. The options are:

  Proactive

  Reactive—solution at macro level

  Reactive—solution at micro level

  Reactive—postintervention at macro level

  Reactive—postintervention at micro level

- In discussion, encourage the groups to look at the present details from different perspectives prior to reaching a decision on the strategy.

- Do not require the groups to reach consensus on the strategy of the presented case. Allow them to reveal any dissenters in the final analysis. The exercise is not designed to teach consensus building, but to analyze the many options involved in the needs assessment process.

- In the concluding discussion on each presented case study, encourage suggestions as to how the case details could have been altered to make the strategy clearer.

- In the final discussion of the exercise, review how the role reversal of case analysis and case writing contributes to a higher level of understanding of the content.

ORGANIZATION NEEDS ASSESSMENT: FORM A

In the beginning of any needs assessment, preliminary information is obtained that helps frame exactly what, who, and where the focus or change is to be targeted. The needs assessment should then be classified according to the broad intent of its future design.

Proactive—Future-based needs assessment, conducted to:

- Prepare for an external or internal environmental change for an organization.
- Improve performance without regard to previously set standards.
- Examine existing performance standards to determine necessary changes.

Reactive—Present- or past-based needs assessment, which examines causes or backgrounds of problems or situations. Reactive strategies can focus on

- the macro level: the organization as a whole; or
- the micro level: an individual, work group, or department.

Solution-specific—Assessment that incorporates the assumptions about problem causes and solutions and focuses on determining the most cost-effective manner of applying the solution.

Postintervention—Assessment to determine how best to evaluate the results of a change program.

EXAMPLE CASE STUDIES: FORM B

CASE STUDY EXAMPLE 1

SSS Consulting, Inc. is a company that provides training on Internet products. It primarily offers courses to programmers and skilled technicians who already have an advanced technical background. The principals in the company have recently read that the number of new Internet users is increasing dramatically and that these users are in need of introductory Internet usage information. SSS would like to enter into this training arena, but the principals are not sure what types of courses are needed by new users of the Internet.

CASE STUDY EXAMPLE 2

Physical Therapy, Inc. is a small company that consists of 20 employees who share five offices. The firm specializes in orthopedic and sports rehabilitation, including back classes, sports assessments, massage, and orthotics. The company is privately owned and emphasizes personal treatment that involves both patient and doctor in all phases of care.

The owner has recently identified a problem with the paperwork flow. She claims that the doctors are not filling in the paperwork properly. Insurance companies deny claims for treatment if the therapists do not complete the accompanying paperwork accurately and quickly. Often this causes patients to have to pay for services that might otherwise be paid for by the insurance companies. This is becoming a major problem for patients and they are complaining loudly.